A SURVIVAL GUIDE
for the
JUNIOR HIGH/MIDDLE SCHOOL
MATHEMATICS TEACHER

Gregory R. Baur, Ed.D.

Indiana University at South Bend

and

Darleen Pigford, Ph.D.

Indiana University at South Bend

Parker Publishing Company, Inc.

West Nyack, New York 10994

© 1984 by

PARKER PUBLISHING COMPANY, INC.

West Nyack, NY

Library of Congress Cataloging in Publication Data

Baur, Gregory R.
     A survival guide for the junior high/middle school
mathematics teacher.

     Includes index.
       1. Mathematics—Study and teaching (Secondary)
1. Pigford, Darleen   II. Title
QA11.B36 1984   510'.7'12   83-17777
ISBN 0-13-879156-2

Printed in the United States of America

To
Our First Teachers—
Our Mothers
Ede and Elizabeth

About This Book

Much concern is being expressed today by mathematics educators and others about the junior high/middle school mathematics student, classroom, and curriculum. Many people feel that the students' needs are not being adequately met. Further evidence of this concern is demonstrated by the fact that many states now have specific certification requirements for teachers of junior high/middle school mathematics.

The purpose of *A Survival Guide for the Junior High/Middle School Mathematics Teacher* is to help classroom teachers provide a more effective instructional program for all of their students. As former junior high/middle school mathematics teachers ourselves, we have a good understanding of the day-to-day problems faced by teachers and students at this level. In this book we have tried to give teachers practical assistance in dealing with these problems through realistic classroom management, group diagnosis, and discipline techniques.

The book presents practical suggestions for mathematics teachers in grades 6 through 9. We view the teacher as a classroom *manager* and have detailed many useful "nitty-gritty" ideas and techniques to help the teacher be a successful manager with 30 students. Maximizing teacher effectiveness despite limited resources of time, energy, and money is the premise of the book. Although it is designed primarily for inservice teachers, the book may also be used in preservice classes.

In addition to a wealth of practical tips and guidelines, the *Guide* contains several other unique features. Specific competencies for the reader are listed in the introduction to each chapter, and review exercises to help the reader achieve the stated competencies are provided at the end of the chapter. Chapters include many diagrams, checklists, charts, and summaries for quick and easy reference. They also include dozens of ready-to-use instructional activities and procedures, including:

- step-by-step techniques for helping students improve computational skills with whole numbers, fractions, decimals, percent, integers, and exponents and roots

- sample metric measurement activities for teaching length, mass, and temperature
- activities for improving specific problem-solving skills
- examples of mathematics laboratory activities
- eight easy-to-use mathematics games for building specific skills
- a complete Computer Literacy Teaching Unit

Finally, chapters on discipline and the atypical learner highlight topics not usually found in other books of this nature.

The first five chapters of *A Survival Guide for the Junior High/Middle School Mathematics Teacher* focus on the student and management of the mathematics classroom. Chapter topics include the junior high/middle school student, management and discipline in the junior high/middle school classroom, diagnosis and correction, evaluation, and the atypical learner.

Chapters 6 through 11 feature curriculum considerations. Chapter topics include development of computational skills, development of problem-solving skills, the laboratory approach, the use of games, and the use of calculators and computers.

The junior high/middle school mathematics teacher as a professional is the subject of the last chapter. Survival and professional growth of the teacher are the main chapter topics. The Appendix provides a number of reproducible forms and assessment instruments as well as a "List of Commercial Sources of Instructional Materials," a useful "Glossary of Computer Terminology," and selected answers to the chapter review exercise.

We believe that teachers in the junior high/middle school mathematics classroom have a unique and important challenge to present the most effective instructional program possible. Our hope is that this book will serve you as a continuing and valuable help in meeting this challenge.

Good luck!

Gregory R. Baur
Darleen Pigford

Contents

12. SURVIVAL AND GROWTH AS A JUNIOR HIGH/MIDDLE SCHOOL MATHEMATICS TEACHER 253

APPENDICES 265

INDEX 319

1

The
Junior High/
Middle School Student

To begin this survival guide to teaching junior high/middle school mathematics, it seems appropriate to focus on the main object of our work—the learner. The following chapter looks at the distinct traits of our students and how they learn.

After reading and studying this chapter, you should be able to:

- Identify characteristics of the junior high/middle school students in each of these areas: psychological, physiological, and environmental.

- Describe how the junior high/middle school student learns in the cognitive and affective domains.

- Identify the learning style(s) of a given student.

- Assess the student's self-concept and attitude towards mathematics.

IDENTIFYING CHARACTERISTICS OF THE STUDENT

To successfully teach groups of junior high/middle school students, you must understand and accept them as preteens and teenagers. Thus, recognizing general characteristics of youth in their "middle years" is important. These characteristics may be organized into three major areas: physiological (physical); psychological (emotions); and environmental (setting).

Your students come to the classroom with distinctive physical, emotional, and environmental characteristics. You will not change these characteristics for your 100 to 150 students; you can only modify and emulate classroom activity to accommodate their adolescent personalities.

Physiological Characteristics

Physically, your students are undergoing drastic and rapid changes. They are changing from little girls and boys to physically mature young women and men. Puberty occurs for girls between the ages of 10 and 12, and for boys, between 10 and 14. Height and weight may drastically change. Since girls usually grow and mature faster than boys, you may find a wide range of physical developments in your classroom.

Since most childhood diseases are over, the adolescent is usually healthy. However, there are two major health concerns at this time—one, the complexion problem, and two, the nutrition (or lack of proper nutrition) problem. The complexion problem creates great anxiety for the youngster since it is always obvious and usually takes time to remedy. The adolescents, however, are not even aware of the nutrition problem. Few youngsters eat three balanced meals daily. The usual diet starts off with little or no breakfast and thrives on hamburgers, French fries, and soda or milk shakes.

Hence, as a classroom teacher, remember that your students are undergoing drastic physical change that make them awkward and ill at ease. Secondly, the complexion problems cause the adolescent much anguish, and the lack of balanced diets causes much frustration for the school dietitian and other concerned adults.

Psychological Characteristics

By age 10, a person's unique personality is, for most purposes, already developed. Since only strong emotional occurrences can alter this early personality formation, the adolescent comes to you with distinctive emotional tones and definite values.

Emotionally, adolescents want to be self-reliant and independent, particularly from the adult world. Peer approval is far more outwardly important than approval from parents or teachers. But despite this need for peer approval, adolescents respect discipline and order from both the home and school environments. Even though they outwardly complain about a strict classroom teacher, they inwardly respect and want consistency and security in their world. Hence, emotionally, the students need a classroom environment that is firm, fair, and consistent.

Fair play in the classroom is an "emotional" concern for adolescents. They are super-sensitive to their friends' feelings and how their friends are treated. If you mistreat one of them and break one of their "fair-play rules," you will find an entire classroom against you—even if you are right. Their sense of fair play extends only to themselves, however; they do not extend this fair play sanction to adults and teachers.

So, remember that the student is emotionally rebellious, resistant to the adult world, and sensitive to fair play and peer approval.

Environmental Characteristics

Each of our students is a reflection of his or her environment. Our American culture shapes the characteristics of our students. These major American influences center around family structure, role models, technological changes, and current national changes. Our purpose here is to note these changes, not to evaluate whether they are "good" or "bad."

As a classroom teacher, you must consider the great upheavals that are occurring in many American families. Divorces, separations, and other family stresses are causing traumatic changes for our youngsters. Of every five students in your classroom, two are probably involved in step-family or single parent homes. Emotional conflicts can easily arise from these new family situations.

Related to this are the corresponding changes in role models. The traditional idea that "daddy is the doctor" and "mommy is the nurse" are being replaced with different career implications for both sexes. Both the home and career worlds are being influenced by the changing roles of men and women. Since the national government supports programs to prevent sex discrimination in career training, employment, and sports/recreational activities, these new role models are easier for youngsters to accept than for their older parents and family relatives.

These role changes are related to the environmental characteristics caused by "our technological society." Forty years ago youngsters knew what their lifestyles would be. For most cases, the son would marry the girl down the street and live on daddy's farm or work in the same occupation. The lifestyle did not leave many major decisions to be made. Today with modern travel, automobiles, airplanes, television, and computer development, Americans travel more, see world events, and live in a highly technical society. Our youngsters have so many important career decisions to make and these careers usually involve costly training either through apprenticeships or college educations. Our technological environment has made today's world drastically different for parents and children.

Our current national environment is also shaping our classroom. With civil rights and desegregation, our American educational system is undergoing vast changes at all grade levels. Our youngsters are being exposed to many different racial and ethnic groups, and the problems that may occur are mainly between the parents and the children rather than between the youngsters from different racial or ethnic backgrounds.

Thus, our American environment has produced a youngster who is coping with changing family structures, role models, technologies, and new social orderings. The resulting conflicts between the youngster and the older generation are widened even more.

In summary, today's youngsters who come into your middle school or junior high classroom are physically mature, emotionally immature, and caught in a rapidly changing social environment. Faced with this description of the students, let's concentrate on how you maximize their learning potential both in the cognitive (mental) and affective (emotional) areas.

LEARNING IN THE COGNITIVE DOMAIN

During adolescence we know that the student has begun to develop the ability to reason and is more willing and better able to memorize specified information. But how does cognitive learning take place?

Two Approaches to Learning Mathematics

There are two basic approaches to the learning of mathematics. Most students probably use a combination of these approaches rather than only one or the other.

The first approach to the learning of mathematics is called the *process-oriented* approach, based on the thinking of people such as Piaget and Bruger. The essence of this approach is that there is a specified capability (mathematical concept or skill) to be learned. This capability is broken down into a series of prerequisites or such capabilities as pictured in Figure 1-1. As shown in the diagram, A and B are prerequisites to the capability to be learned while C and D are prerequisites to A and E is prerequisite to B. The student begins by examining the capability and decides which prerequisites are not a part of his or her knowledge. The student then proceeds to learn the necessary prerequisites that, when learned, will enable the student to achieve the desired capability. The process that the student uses to determine which prerequisites need to be learned is very important; some educators would claim that the process is of equal importance to the capability or product itself.

FIGURE 1-1

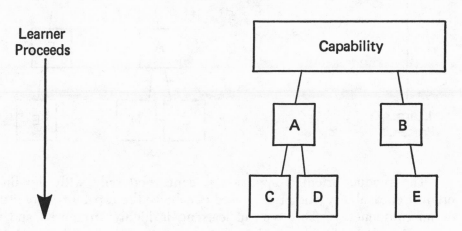

The process-oriented approach is a form of *discovery* learning. Discovery learning has, however, some inherent disadvantages. This approach is most appropriate for students who have good reasoning ability. Unfortunately, many students have not yet developed their reasoning abilities to the point where discovery is an effective mode of learning. Often, a teacher will offer guidance or assistance to the student so that this type of learning becomes meaningful. The use of the mathematics laboratory, for example, is a type of activity that may help the student develop the desired thinking skills. (Laboratory activities and their uses will be discussed more fully in Chapter 10.)

The second approach to the learning of mathematics is called the *product-oriented* approach. This approach is espoused by Gagné and may be pictured in the same basic fashion as the process-oriented as shown in Figure 1-2. The difference is that while the capability is still divided into prerequisites (A, B, C, D, and E), the student proceeds in the opposite direction from the process-oriented approach. The student begins by learning C, D, and E. When C, D and E have been learned, the student proceeds to A and B. When A and B have been learned, the student will have achieved the desired capability. You would probably recognize this approach if we called it *programmed* learning.

FIGURE 1–2

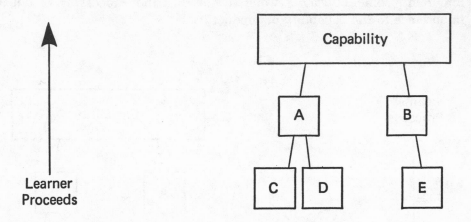

Learner
Proceeds

The product-oriented approach is concerned only with the final product of capability; the process used to achieve the capability is of little or no consequence. This type of learning is highly structured and is appropriate for students who have little reasoning ability. The product-oriented approach has not enjoyed widespread acceptance, perhaps because it is often boring to students. The boredom is caused by the fact that many students do not need the capability broken down into very small steps; they are often able to learn more than one prerequisite at the same time.

Mathematical learning activities presented by classroom teachers should be designed to develop thinking skills, since the student is beginning to develop the power to reason and think during the junior high/middle school years. Unfortunately, some teachers do little to stimulate students' thinking, with results that are less than desirable.

The Concrete-to-Abstract Continuum

Regardless of which approach (or combination thereof) the student uses, there is an underlying basis that is present. This basis is called the *concrete-to-abstract continuum* and is pictured in Figure 1–3.

The idea here is that, for any given concept to be learned, the student proceeds along a continuum through three stages (concrete, semi-concrete and abstract) toward the achievement of the desired concept or skill. In the concrete stage, the student uses manipulative materials. At the semi-concrete stage, the student is able to work with pictures of the concept or skill, while at the abstract stage, the student is able to work with numbers or other symbols.

FIGURE 1–3

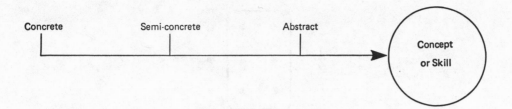

Let us pause and consider an example of the concrete-to-abstract continuum. Suppose that the concept of "1/2" is to be learned. At the concept level, the student may be given a set of objects, such as Popsicle sticks (an even number of sticks, of course) and asked to show 1/2 of the set (see Figure 1–4). Or the student may be given a circle of tagboard cut into sections and asked to show 1/2 by picking up the appropriate sections (see Figure 1–5).

FIGURE 1–4

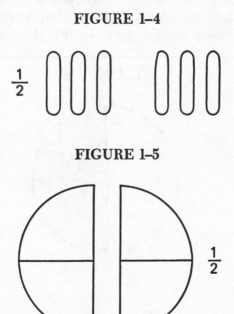

FIGURE 1–5

At the semi-concrete level, the student may be asked to indicate 1/2 of a group of dots by drawing a loop around 1/2 of them (Figure 1-6) or indicate 1/2 by shading in an area (Figure 1-7).

FIGURE 1–6

FIGURE 1–7

At the abstract level, the student may be asked to write the numeral representing the part of a circle that is shaded or the part of the areas (three boys and three girls) of students who are girls (Figure 1-8).

FIGURE 1–8

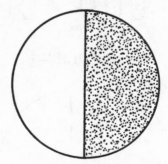

Q: What part of the circle is
   shaded?
A: 1/2

It is important to realize that when the student comes to you, he or she may be at any point on the continuum. Your responsibility is to provide experiences for the student that are (1) appropriate for his or her level, and

(2) going to help the student move to the abstract stage of learning for the concept or skill. The movement to the abstract stage by the student is often tedious and slow, but you must be patient and able to provide a variety of appropriate experiences.

The problem that you face as a classroom teacher is that students will be spaced all along the continuum when they come to class. You must determine the level of each and provide appropriate experiences.

The concrete-to-abstract continuum is based on several assumptions:

Learning is based on experience by the learner.

Sensory learning is the heart of learning.

Learning proceeds from the concrete to the abstract.

Learning must be active.

These four assumptions are self explanatory. What they say is that you as the classroom teacher must provide learning experiences for your students that are appropriate for that level (concrete, semi-concrete or abstract) and that require active student involvement. The learning experiences must be sequenced so that the student is given maximum opportunity to proceed along the continuum.

Learning Styles

There has been growing recognition among educators in recent years that learning is affected by several factors:

- immediate environmental (physical surroundings)
- emotional (motivation, perseverance, responsibility, structure)
- social (self concept, peers, adults, teams, groups)
- physical (time of day, body fluids, mobility perception)

Within the confines of these four factors, each student has a unique style of learning. Thus, learning style refers to the way(s) in which a student maximizes the four factors to his or her benefit. You as the classroom teacher must be sensitive to the four factors and to how the student internalizes these factors so that learning may be achieved in the most effective and efficient manner.

In order to maximize the students' opportunities to learn, let's examine various students' styles. We noted in the previous section that sensory learning is the basis of learning. Thus, we will be concerned with three types of sensory learning—audio, visual, and kinesthetic—and will discuss a technique for assessing a student's style.

If a student has an *audio* learning style, you will observe that he or she listens intently, possibly moving the lips or whispering as he or she tries to memorize. The *visual* learner will benefit from seeing the written word or other media, often closing his or her eyes or looking at the ceiling while trying to recall a visual picture. The *kinesthetic* learner relies on physical movement and needs a "write or do" activity. This type of student will often use fingers or other objects to count off items or write figures and symbols in the air.

There are several activities or methods you may use to maximize the learning styles of your students. For the audio learner, use lectures, tape recorders, explanations, or readings. Videotapes, charts, graphs, demonstrations, films, filmstrips, and the written word are useful for working with the visual learner. The kinesthetic learner's style is enhanced by the use of labs, projects, and simulation.

How can you assess the learning style of your students in the classroom? The easiest and perhaps the most effective way is through observation. By giving a group of your students a series of tasks and observing their behavior, you can determine the learning style of each of your class members. We suggest using a series of tasks such as those found in Appendix C.

Implications for the Classroom

As we review learning in the cognitive domain, it seems appropriate to examine how the concrete-to-abstract continuum and a student's style of learning are interrelated and how each may be used to aid you as you develop appropriate classroom activities for your students. To do this, let's consider a matrix in the format shown in Figure 1–9.

FIGURE 1-9

Learning Style

	Audio	Visual	Kinesthetic
Concrete			
Semi-concrete			
Abstract			

Level of Learning

Let's consider some examples of how this matrix can be used. A kinesthetic learner who is working at the concrete level will need to actively engage in learning activities that involve the manipulation of concrete materials. A visual learner at the semi-concrete level will learn best by seeing pictures of what is to be learned. An audio learner at the abstract level will be aided by listening to an explanation that uses the abstract symbols.

Not every student's learning style will fit exactly into one of the compartments in the matrix. However, if you use the matrix as a guideline, you will be able to successfully provide learning experiences that will maximize the student's style and level of learning.

LEARNING IN THE AFFECTIVE DOMAIN

Learning in the affective domain has received greater emphasis by educators in recent years. Basically, learning in the affective domain involves the development of self-concept, attitude, and values on the part of the student. Awareness of the need to develop self-concept, attitudes and values is especially important to the junior high/middle school mathematics teacher. Recall the discussion earlier in this chapter about the many changes which the student is undergoing in the junior high/middle school years.

Self-concept Development

Helping the student develop a positive self-concept is an extremely important task of the junior high/middle school mathematics teacher. A positive self-concept will enable the student to overcome many of the problems caused by adolescent changes. A poor self-concept will probably affect the student's achievement in mathematics and will certainly affect his or her motivation to learn it.

It is often possible to assess a student's self-concept by using the techniques of observation and interview.

In using observation, observe how the student is treated by his or her peers. From our earlier discussion, we know that the student is greatly affected by perceived thoughts of how he or she is viewed by peers. Where possible, you should attempt to help the student have good relationships with peers.

The technique of interview may be applied on either a formal or informal basis. Informally, talk with the student to try to help him or her solve some of the problems that are causing a poor self-concept. More formally, a scale to determine a quantitative measure of self-concept may be used. An example of such a scale can be found in Appendix C.

Attitude Development

Another important aspect of learning in the affective domain is the development of the student's positive attitude towards the learning of mathematics. Research has not conclusively shown that there is a high correlation between attitude and achievement in mathematics. However, it seems safe to assume that a poor attitude towards the learning of mathematics will likely cause poor achievement in mathematics.

As with self-concept, the techniques of observation and interview are very useful for the teacher to apply in assessing the student's attitude about the learning of mathematics. Observing the student at work or in class discussion will reveal a great deal about his or her attitude.

Talking with the student on a one-to-one basis may also be helpful. Sometimes, verbalization by the student about his or her attitude towards mathematics is sufficient for positive change to begin to take place. A poor attitude is often caused by a record of repeated low marks or failure in mathematics.

As before, a more formal assessment of attitude may be desirable. Few scales for this purpose are available, but an example of one scale is found in Appendix C.

Math Anxiety

A psychological phenomena known as math anxiety has been identified in recent years. Little research in this area has been conducted as to the nature and causes of math anxiety, but there are some obvious characteristics.

Math anxiety represents a fear of mathematics and may be manifested in the most severe of physical effects such as fainting or body shakes. It is often caused by one or more unpleasant learning experiences in mathematics. Math anxiety seems to be more prevalent in females than males, a conclusion that may be attributable to the traditional notion that females are not supposed to be good in or study mathematics. Fortunately, this idea is being dispelled to some extent, but the barrier has not yet been eliminated.

Implications for the Classroom Teacher

As the classroom teacher, you are responsible for not only the cognitive development of the student, but also the affective development. There are two basic axioms that will go a long way in helping the student develop a positive self-concept about him- or herself and a positive attitude towards the learning of mathematics.

1. Provide each of your students as many opportunities as possible for success in the learning of mathematics.

2. Be consistent and fair in your treatment of the students while they are in your classroom.

The first axiom will help break down barriers created by past experiences, many of which have been failure. It has been said that "a little success goes a long way," and no statement could be more correct. If you doubt the power of this statement, reflect for a moment on your own experiences, not only in mathematics learning, but in general life experiences as well.

The second axiom also has great importance for your classroom. The student in the junior high/middle school mathematics classroom is in the midst of adolescent development. The student desires and needs structure, but it must be structure that he or she feels is applied consistently and fairly to all members of the class.

QUICK REVIEW

1. Classify each of the following activities as concrete (C), semi-concrete (S), or abstract (A):

   _____ a.) Using pizza flats to represent fractional parts.
   _____ b.) Changing decimals to percents using paper and pencil.
   _____ c.) Constructing a model of a cube using straws and pipe cleaners.
   _____ d.) Determining what percentage of a given rectangle is shaded.
   _____ e.) Computing the area of a given circle.
   _____ f.) Reading data from a bar graph.

2. Classify each of the following activities as appropriate for learners who are visual-concrete (VC), visual semi-concrete (VS), visual abstract (VA), auditory concrete (AC), auditory semi-concrete (AS), auditory abstract (AA), kinesthetic concrete (KC), kinesthetic semi-concrete (KS), or kinesthetic abstract (KA).

   _____ a.) Listening to word problems on an audio recorder.
   _____ b.) Drawing a diagram to help solve a word problem.
   _____ c.) Using pieces of wood to make a specific fraction.
   _____ d.) Drawing a bar graph to represent given data.
   _____ e.) Watching a silent filmstrip about computing the perimeter of a geometric figure.

3. What are the basic differences between process-oriented and product-oriented learning?

4. What must the junior high/middle school mathematics teacher do to change student learning in the cognitive and affective domains?

5. Randomly choose four students (two female and two male) from your class.

   a.) Assess the physiological, psychological and environmental characteristics of each of the four students. How do their characteristics compare with the characteristics described in Chapter 1?

   b.) Make an informal assessment of each student's self-concept and attitude towards the learning of mathematics. Make an anecdotal record of your findings for each student.

   c.) Assess the self-concept and attitude of each student by using the scales provided in Appendix C. Do your informal findings agree or disagree with the scale results?

   d.) Recall the matrix shown in Figure 1–9. How would you classify each of your four students in the matrix?

6. Review the activities you use in conducting your mathematics class.

   a.) Do the activities that you use favor the audio, visual, or kinesthetic learner? How might you change your activities to provide for each of the different learning styles?

   b.) What provisions have you made for learning at the concrete and semi-concrete levels of learning?

2

Management of the Junior High/Middle School Mathematics Classroom

Good classroom management is essential to an effective program in junior high/middle school mathematics. As you plan your management strategies, there are many things to consider. This chapter provides many practical hints and suggestions you can incorporate in your management plan.

After reading and studying the chapter, you should be able to:

- Determine what you need to do before the school year, the first day and the first week of school start.
- Define procedures for handling day-to-day classroom routine.
- Describe various ways of physically arranging your classroom.
- Describe general guidelines for presenting a daily lesson, including techniques for using various teaching aids.
- Identify ways of dealing with selected classroom disturbances.

GETTING STARTED

Getting off to a good start is prerequisite to good classroom management. This means you must consider things to do before the school year starts, what to do the first day and what to do the first week or two.

Before the School Year Starts

There are several things to do before the school year starts. We remind you of these.

1. *Review your textbook and make a rough topical outline for the year.* Even if you have used the textbook for several years, it is a good idea to glance back over the topics to refresh your mind. Break out the units you are going to teach and roughly estimate the amount of time you are going to spend on each unit. Check also the local curriculum guide to be sure that your units are consistent with it.

2. *Formulate your general goals for the year.* As you look at each of your units, what are the general goals you want to accomplish this year? What is expected of your students after they finish the year with you? What have your students been exposed to prior to this point?

The statement of these goals is obviously very rough. You may find that you will need to adjust them depending on where your students are when they come to you.

3. *Decide on the rules for student behavior in your classroom.* Your rules of classroom conduct should be communicated to your students on the first day of class. This action will enable you to be prepared for situations before they occur. Be sure that the rules you decide upon are enforceable because your students will test you.

4. *Prepare an inventory test that you can give to your students during the first week.* It is important that you know as early as possible in the year what your students can and cannot do. An inventory test gives you a general diagnosis of your students' ability levels. After you have obtained the results from the test, you may want to alter your formulated goals.

5. *Inspect your classroom to view its physical arrangement.* If you have used the room before, you are already familiar with it. If it is a new room, you need to check student and teacher desk placement and the availability of storage area. (We will discuss physical room arrangements later in this chapter.) A clock in your classroom is essential for you and your students.

6. *Determine the need for any special instructional aids.* What instructional aids will you need besides the textbook? You may need things like an overhead projector, graph paper, or geometric models, to name just a few. Some of these aids may already be available while others may need to be purchased. Approach your department chairperson or principal about buying these materials for you. Inquire also how films and filmstrips may be obtained.

7. *Meet with your department chairperson and principal to discuss your plans for the coming year*. Keep your department chairperson and principal informed of your instructional plans for the year, including any special plans for projects. Let them also know how you plan to improve your own teaching performance during the upcoming year. Invite them to visit your classroom regularly during the year to see what you are doing and to offer constructive criticism.

8. *Review the school's rules of student conduct*. As you formulate your rules for student behavior in your classroom, be sure that your rules are consistent with school rules. Decide ahead of time how you will handle certain situations in your classroom so that you will be prepared to act when they occur.

The First Day of School

Someone has said that first impressions are lasting. The impression you make the first day of school with your students will go a long way towards successful classroom management. Remember that there must be order in the classroom before any learning can take place.

During that first day, your students must understand that you mean business—you can always loosen up later. It is almost impossible to tighten up after a loose beginning. This does not mean you should come across as an ogre or a tyrant, but it does mean that you need to clearly establish your role and the students' role in your classroom.

Here are some tasks to be completed during the first day.

- Introduce yourself and write your name on the chalkboard.
- Give each student an index card and ask the students to print their names on the cards.
- Collect the cards and read the students' names to check pronunciation. This also helps you associate names and faces.
- Indicate to the students what you expect in terms of classroom behavior and ask them if they have any questions. If possible, have your rules written on a piece of paper so that each student can be given a copy.

If there is time remaining, have an activity or game ready for your students. This will help demonstrate to them that you are prepared and organized. Avoid the temptation to let your students sit and visit with each other until the period ends.

The First Week of School

The first week of school is important because you will begin to learn a great deal about your students' current mathematical ability levels. You will also be busy developing the rapport with your students regarding their classroom behavior.

During the second day of class, establish your seating chart for the class, and check the class roll by again calling out each student's name. Go through the textbook, pointing out important features. (The textbook will be discussed in greater detail later in the chapter.)

You will probably administer your inventory test during the second or third class day. Keep the initial test reasonably short (about an hour) so that students do not become discouraged. Remind them that the test is not for a grade but to help you plan their instruction during the year.

HANDLING DAY-TO-DAY CLASSROOM ROUTINES

It is extremely important that you establish routine procedures with your students. Students want and need structure in the classroom and clearly defined routine procedures help stabilize the classroom atmosphere. As long as the procedures you establish are reasonable and you are consistent and fair in their application, there are not likely to be discipline problems. But, remember that you will be tested early and often until the students are satisfied that you mean what you say.

Establishing Ground Rules

The importance of establishing ground rules for classroom behavior was discussed earlier in the chapter. Here are some examples of ground rules that have been successful. There may be others you want to use and some you may want to delete.

1. Students should be in their seats when the bell rings to start class.
2. Textbook, paper, and pencil should be brought to class each day.
3. Pencils should be sharpened before class starts.
4. Students should raise their hands and be recognized by the teacher before speaking out in class.
5. Students should not talk with each other while another student or the teacher is talking.

6. Students should not leave their seats at the end of the class period until dismissed by the teacher.

7. Students should proceed in the preassigned manner during fire drills.

8. Students should not talk among themselves when the public address system is in operation.

9. Students should use the restroom during class break and not during class.

A few sensible rules will be much easier to maintain and enforce than a long list. Don't keep your students guessing what is expected of them!

Managing Student Papers

Good management of student papers, both in collection and distribution, will help your classroom run smoothly. Here are some ideas to help you manage the collection of papers.

1. Have students fold the papers lengthwise and write their name, date, and class period on the back of the outside page to the right of the fold.

2. Have papers passed from back to front of each row.

3. Ask one student to collect the papers from each row and give them to you or place in a designated box or basket.

Here are some ideas when returning papers.

1. Put grades on the inside of the paper so that a student's score or grade is not known by the other students.

2. Separate the papers by rows before class.

3. Give papers to the first student in each row and have them returned by passing front to back.

Changing Classes

Setting a routine for changing classes will eliminate confusion and make the change run much more smoothly. Here are some guidelines.

1. Anticipate the ending of class and dismiss your students immediately.

2. Proceed to the door and stand at the entrance to the room so that you can observe both your room and the hallway.

3. Greet incoming students by name.

4. Require tardy students to obtain a late pass from their teacher of the previous period or from the office.

5. Be visible to out-going and in-coming students at all times. Avoid the temptation to visit with fellow teachers during the class break.

Dealing with Classroom Disturbances by Students

Dealing effectively with classroom disturbances is not an easy task. Here are some guidelines to help you.

1. *Act quickly and decisively.* Don't hesitate to deal with a problem situation. When you hesitate, it appears to students that you are unsure of what to do and this may only worsen the situation.

2. *Don't overreact.* As long as you remain cool, the situation has a good chance of staying under control. Overreaction on your part could cause a situation to blow with potentially dangerous consequences.

3. *Never threaten action that cannot be enforced.* The other students in the class will watch your actions very carefully. If your actions are inappropriate or you threaten action that is not possible, you will lose credibility with the other students. The result is usually loss of control of the situation and the classroom.

4. *Never embarrass a student in front of classmates.* When you back a student into a corner, you have created a "no win" situation. The results will usually be worse than you anticipate.

5. *Avoid sarcasm as a means of classroom control.* The use of sarcasm will cause students to lose respect for you, and loss of respect means loss of classroom control.

6. *Use good common sense in your handling of student disturbances.* Good common sense will get you through any problem situation. Let it prevail.

7. *Try to anticipate potential disturbance situations and determine how you will handle the situation if it occurs.* Many times your anticipation will keep a situation from becoming a problem. For example, moving a student to a new seat, either in front or away from another troublesome student, may keep a problem from occurring. Deciding ahead of time how you will resolve a problem situation will enable you to react to the situation in a desirable manner and help eliminate the possibility of ill-advised action.

ARRANGING THE CLASSROOM

The physical arrangement of the classroom must be considered an important factor in good classroom management and control. There are a wide variety of desk arrangements, so you will probably be able to arrange the room any way you want.

The doorway, electrical outlets and location of chalkboards are factors to consider when arranging the classroom. The most critical is probably the chalkboard, so students should sit where they can easily view the chalkboard without a glare. Electrical outlets should be easily accessible for your overhead projector or movie projector, and be sure you have access to an extension cord if necessary. The screen for the overhead or movie projector will probably cause you no problem in terms of its location since it is usually portable or mounted above the chalkboard. If possible, arrange the desks so that the students do not look directly at the doorway; hallway distractions will cause some students to be inattentive.

Figures 2–1 to 2–8 show some possible room arrangements. Note that each arrangement makes it possible for you to move easily around the room, a good classroom control technique. The arrows in the diagram indicate the direction(s) that students face.

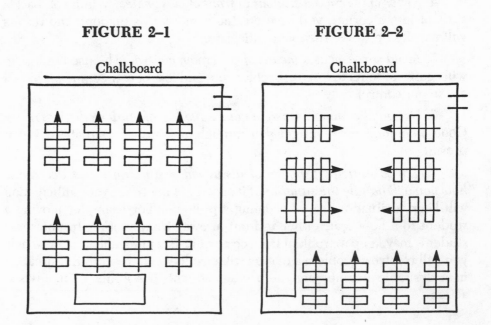

FIGURE 2–1   **FIGURE 2–2**

FIGURE 2–3

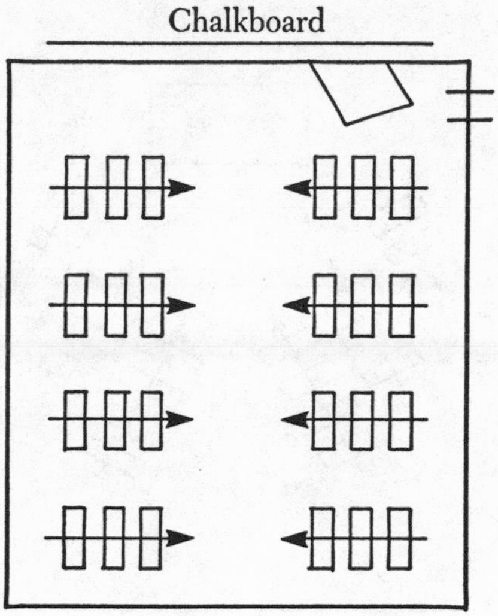

Chalkboard

FIGURE 2–4

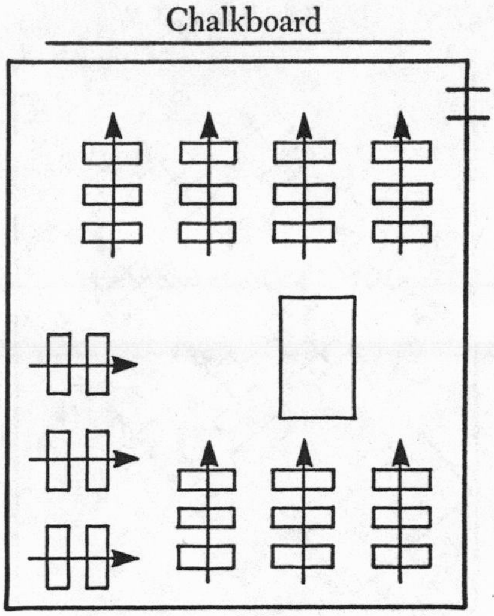

Chalkboard

FIGURE 2–5

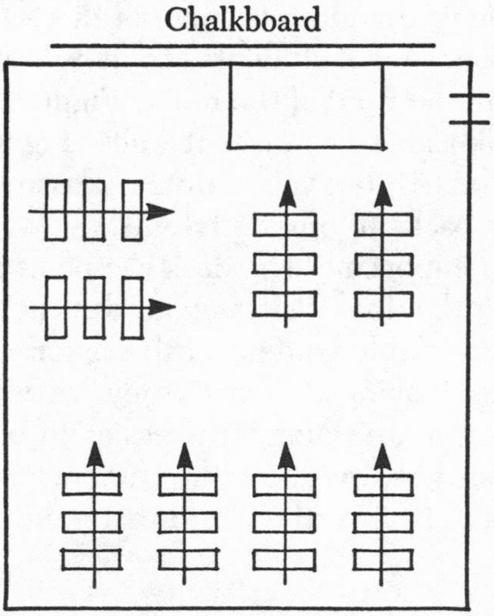

Chalkboard

FIGURE 2–6

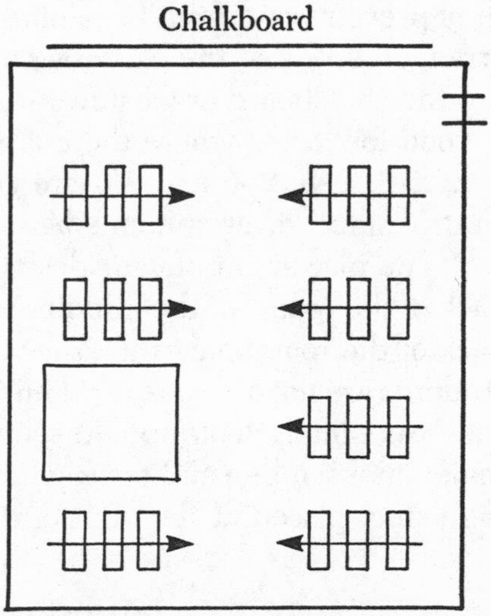

Chalkboard

As you look at the diagrams, notice that there is an emphasis on shorter rows, which enable you to move around the room easily. These room arrangements lead to good classroom management and lend themselves to small group work.

FIGURE 2–7   **FIGURE 2–8**

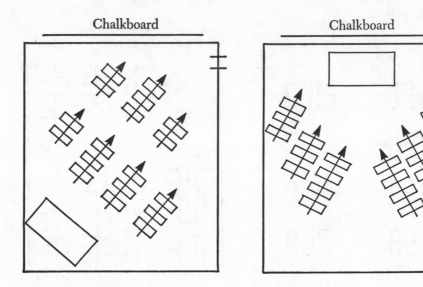

There are some special features associated with some of the diagrams. Figures 2–1 and 2–4 are good for rooms that are long and narrow because they prevent rows from becoming too long. In addition, note in these two arrangements that the back rows are offset so that students can more easily see the chalkboard or whatever else is in the front of the room. Figure 2–7 is good for rooms where there are chalkboards on adjacent walls. Figures 2–2, 2–3, 2–5, 2–6 and 2–7 are good for helping you maintain classroom control since fewer students have their backs to other students.

The placement of *your* desk is also important. The desk can be at the back of the room, in the middle, or near the door. Placing your desk at the back of the room makes it easier to see possible student misbehavior, and students are not as aware of when you are looking at them as they are when they can simply look up and see what you are doing. It is easier to both maintain discipline and teach when "your head" is above the students, so a high stool placed at the front of the room is a worthwhile investment.

PRESENTING A LESSON

A key to the effectiveness of your instructional program is the way you present your unit and its component lessons. Of course, you must have your goals, objectives and strategies in mind. Strategies will be discussed in later chapters; for now, let's focus on the presentation of the lesson and how various instructional aids can be used to foster good classroom management.

Presenting the Daily Lesson

Here are some general guidelines for presenting the lesson.

1. *Review before the presentation what you plan to accomplish and how you are going to do it*. Many teachers teach "off the top of their heads." With considerable experience, they may be able to do this and feel that they have done a good job. If, in fact, they have done an acceptable job using their "head," how much better could they have done if they had spent more time in preparation?

2. *Review examples to be used in the presentation beforehand*. The examples you use may make the difference between a student fully understanding your presentation or only partially understanding. If you rely on your "head," you may choose an inappropriate example that will only confuse the student.

3. *Use a variety of techniques and media in your presentation*. Your choice of a single approach or a piece of media may not be appropriate for all your students. Using a variety of things will help insure that as many students as possible will benefit from your presentation.

4. *Move about the room during your presentation*. Standing in one spot or sitting at your desk soon causes students to lose interest in what you are doing. Instead, move about the room to observe your students' attention and to keep class distraction under control.

5. *Tell your students before the presentation what you want to accomplish*. Let your students know what your presentation is about and what you want them to be able to accomplish at the conclusion of your presentation. This will help avoid student misunderstanding about your presentation.

6. *Summarize your presentation upon completion*. Repeating the key points that you made is very helpful to students. It enables them to understand the whole of your presentation.

Using the Chalkboard

The chalkboard can be one of your most valuable teaching aids. It can be found in almost any classroom and can be easily used by your students. There are, however, some points to consider in using the chalkboard.

1. *Write legibly.* Writing legibly on the chalkboard is not as easy as it sounds. It is something you need to practice so that students can easily read what you have written.

2. *Write on the upper half of the chalkboard as much as possible.* It is often difficult for some of your students to see writing on the chalkboard if it is positioned too low. You may want to move students who are shorter in height to seats in the front of the area nearest the chalkboard.

3. *Stand to the side of what you are writing.* Students cannot see what you are writing if you stand between them and what you have written. Blocking their view is distracting to students and may result in management problems.

4. *Do whatever is necessary to keep glare off the chalkboard.* It is impossible to read anything on the chalkboard when there is glare from a window or a light fixture. If the glare cannot be eliminated by shades or window blinds, avoid using that section of the chalkboard.

5. *Never turn your back on the students when reading from or writing on the chalkboard.* Maintain eye contact with your students as much as possible. This will greatly reduce the chances of "monkey business" while you are using the chalkboard.

6. *Use colored chalk.* Many diagrams that you put on the chalkboard will have much more clarity if different colors of chalk are used. This technique is especially helpful when drawing two- and three-dimensional geometric figures.

7. *Write class assignments on the chalkboard.* Use a corner of the chalkboard to write the next day's assignment so that students will always know where to look. Assignments given orally tend to be misunderstood by several students.

8. *Repeat orally what you are writing on the chalkboard.* By doing so, you are using two forms of learning styles: visual and auditory. The result will be that more students will probably be able to understand your point.

9. *Permit students to use the chalkboard for drill and practice.* When your students are working at the chalkboard, you will be able to easily see what they are doing. Thus, you can use the chalkboard as a diagnostic tool. (The importance of diagnosis will be discussed in Chapter 3.)

10. *Be sure you have an adequate supply of chalk and clean erasers.* There is nothing worse than trying to write with a piece of chalk that is one cm. long. And, there is nothing messier than using an eraser that has not been cleaned in a fortnight.

Using the Textbook

The textbook is likely to be your main source of teaching ideas, materials for students to read, and problems for student drill and practice. Since you will not always find the approach used in the textbook to be the one that works best for your students, you must use the textbook as a supplement—and not the "gospel"—to your teaching.

In using the textbook, keep the following strategies in mind.

1. *Point out textbook features to your students.* Show your students how to use the index and glossary as well as how to identify chapter key points. Don't assume that your students can simply pick up the textbook and use it appropriately and efficiently.

2. *Review problems before giving them as homework assignments.* Many teachers simply assign problems in a systematic fashion, such as "do the odd-numbered problems on page 79." But the odds may not be the problems that are appropriate for your students' needs. Although it is more work, consider giving differentiated assignments according to student needs. Remember, also, that textbook exercises are not always given in order of difficulty.

3. *Review textbook reading and examples before presenting them in class.* Sometimes there may be an inadequate explanation or a mistake in the textbook. Be aware of these problems ahead of time and you will find that your lesson will go much more smoothly.

4. *Use textbook materials that are appropriate for your students.* Materials that are not appropriate for your students' reading and/or math ability levels will not be useful. Such materials are likely to cause student frustration with no learning taking place.

Using Duplicated Materials

Many times you will want to use duplicated materials as worksheets for drill and practice. Commercially prepared spirit masters are available, but you may want to make your own so that the materials more closely fit the needs of your students. If you are preparing the master or duplicated materials, there are several things to keep in mind.

1. A typed master is preferable to a handwritten master because it is easier for your students to read. The school secretary might type the master for you, but advance notice *must* be provided. If you are like most other teachers, however, there will not be enough time so you will probably make the master yourself.

2. If you type the master, first type it on a sheet of paper and then make a photocopy. Next, use a thermofax process and make a thermohectograph master. The master can then be used to make the copies. It is less desirable but sometimes necessary to type directly on a spirit master. If mistakes are made, a razor blade is needed to correct the errors. If you type on the master directly, use an electric typewriter; a manual portable typewriter will not cut a good master.

3. For a handwritten master (the most common procedure) place the master on something soft, such as a few sheets of newspaper or a desk blotter. Press firmly with a ballpoint pen—pencils or marking pens will not work.

4. When you make a spirit master, be sure to remove the tissue between the top sheet and the carbon sheet. If you forget, you can use the tissue sheet to make a limited number of copies, but the copies will not be very good.

5. When you remove the tissue, don't throw it away. Staple the tissue to the back of the master when you are finished running the materials to keep the master from smearing on other masters when stored.

Using Other Teaching Aids

In addition to the chalkboard, textbook, and duplicating masters, there are many other teaching aids you may want to use. These are:

overhead projector
films and filmstrips
audio and videotape recorders
coordinate aids
geometry aids
other aids

Overhead Projectors. Although most classroom teachers have access to an overhead projector, many seem reluctant to use them. The overhead is especially useful in two ways:

1. You can quickly show students a diagram or written material that would normally take a great deal of time to put on the chalkboard.

2. You can always face your students while making a presentation.

Materials to use on the overhead can be prepared well ahead of class time and then reused in the future, a definite time-saver. Of special note is the transparent grid for coordinate graphing that can be used over and over again.

Using the overhead is quite easy. Simply lay your transparency on the projector just as you would look at a piece of paper. Stand to one side so that the glare does not bother your eyes. If you want to write on transparencies, be sure to have an extra marking pencil or two. You can also stand by the screen and use a pointer to emphasize particular points.

Making overhead transparencies is also fairly easy. You can write or draw directly on a blank sheet using a water-soluble pen. Many teachers prefer to put their material on a piece of paper first (it's easier to correct mistakes), make a photocopy, and then use a thermofax process to make the actual transparency. In the latter, the transparency is permanent; in the former, the transparency can be easily marred or erased.

If you have a choice, use an overhead projector that has a continuous sheet of writing surface. The sheet is attached to rollers on either side of the base so that when you have finished with one diagram or picture, the roll can be advanced to give a new, clean surface. At the end of the day, the entire roll can be easily cleaned with a cloth and some soap and water.

Films and Filmstrips. When you find a film or filmstrip that you think can be of use in your instructional program, first review it to be sure it offers what you want. Also, while films and filmstrips provide good variety in presentation of material to your students, never use one simply because it's available. The film's use must be of benefit to your students.

Many films that will be shown only once can be rented to avoid a high purchase price. However, if you find a good film that would be used often, it may be cheaper to purchase it. University or regional film libraries are good rental sources. Filmstrips, on the other hand, must usually be purchased outright but are generally not as expensive as films.

Audio and Videotape Recorders. If you have access in your school to audio and videotape recorders, it might be beneficial to purchase both audio and videotape instructional programs. You might also want to make your own tapes if you have the facilities. The advantages are that you can tailor the tapes to the needs of your students and yours is a familiar voice and/or face to those using the tapes. The disadvantages are that tapes take time to make and you may feel uncomfortable making them. An alternative might be to have one of your students make the tape presentation, a very motivating activity for some student(s). Giving oral tests with tapes is a good way to test and to emphasize listening skills. If you use a tape to make short answer tests or drill, make the questions short and play the drill tape twice.

Coordinate Grid. If you are teaching coordinate graphing, it may be helpful to have a large physical model of the coordinate plane as a demonstration device. A good way to make such a grid is to purchase a piece of dark pegboard one meter by one meter. Paint a vertical and horizontal line as in Figure 2–9, representing the x and y axes. Golf tees can then be used to mark points. A meter stick can be used to draw lines with chalk. The board is then easy to erase and clean.

FIGURE 2–9

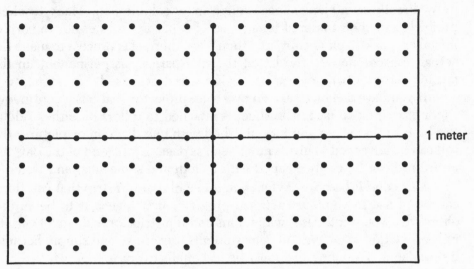

1 meter

1 meter

Geometry Aids. There are many aids for teaching geometric and measurement concepts. Probably one of the most useful sets is the compass, protractor and straight edge that can be used on the chalkboard for demonstration purposes at the same time that the students are using their own compass, protractor and straight edge at their seats. You may want to put a hook on the end of your chalkboard to hang your tools on so that they are easily accessible.

Burns Teaching Boards are another set of geometry aids that have been around for many years. Basically, they are large two-dimensional models of geometric figures that can be used to show various concepts. For example, in changing the median and altitudes of a triangle, the board might look like Figure 2–10. On the sides and verticals of the triangle are holes. A piece of elastic with pegs attached to either end can be stretched across the triangle to demonstrate the various medians and altitudes. Check a large school supply house catalog regarding availability and price.

Many other geometry aids are also available, some of which are described in Chapter 8.

FIGURE 2–10

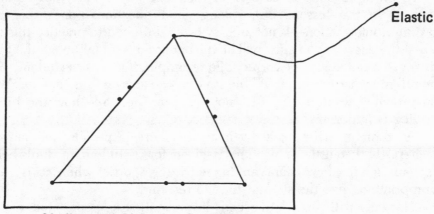

Median and Altitude of a Triangle

Other Aids. A wide variety of other teaching aids are available when presenting your lessons to the students. A number of these are listed in Chapters 7 through 12. In addition, Appendix B includes a list of commercial suppliers of instructional aids and the general areas in which each company has aids available. You might want to write for up-to-date catalogs and price lists.

Remember, however, that teaching aids are designed to *supplement* your presentation. Never use an aid just because it is available. Properly and judiciously used, teaching aids can be a valuable addition to any lesson, but they cannot make a poorly planned lesson a good one.

Using Questioning

A useful technique in presenting a lesson is questioning. Asking your students good questions can provide an excellent stimulus to their thinking and help them discover mathematical concepts for themselves.

Traditionally, questions asked of students in math class have been the kind that simply require a recall or single answer from the student.

"How much is 9 times 9?"

"What is 939 minus 3?"

Some questions have a very definite place, but are not the only kinds to ask. Questions that require higher level thinking skills or questions that have more than one right answer are also appropriate.

"How many different ways can you divide a square in half?"

"Which way of dividing fractions do you like best? Why?"

Asking questions in class is an excellent way to get your students involved in the lesson. But, asking good questions—ones that gain maximum information—is not an easy task. You need to practice this skill so that the answers you elicit will be the ones you want (although the given answer may not always be correct). For example, if you ask a student, "Can you tell me what is 9 times 9?" the student can answer "yes" or "no." What you probably wanted was "81," not "yes" or "no." See how the proper wording is important?

A common error made by many teachers, especially mathematics teachers, is that little or no time is given for a student to think before responding. Teachers want an immediate response when it is really appropriate to give the student time to respond.

Not only will you ask questions in presenting a lesson, students will ask questions of you. The manner in which you answer students' questions will determine whether or not questions will be asked in the future. Students' questions will give you a lot of insight into how well your presentation is coming across to the class and will indicate areas that may need clarification. The quickest way to eliminate students' questions is to downgrade or embarrass students because of a question they have asked!

It is true that students will sometimes ask "dumb" questions. But, treat each question as an important one even though—in your opinion—it may be trivial. Praise your students for asking good questions. If a student asks a question that is trivial or obvious, simply answer the question and go on. If a student asks a question that is not relevant to the point under discussion, simply indicate to the student that you will discuss the question at the end of the class period or at some other time.

Making Use of Class Time

No matter how well you plan your class period, you may find yourself with five or six (or even more) minutes of class time left until the end of the period. There is no time to engage in another major activity, so what do you do?

There are at least two techniques you can use. Whatever you do, however, avoid the temptation to let your students sit and visit with each other.

1. Allow the students to begin work on the next day's homework assignment.

2. Use a very short activity to help review some previous learning or the material in that day's lesson.

Some oral drill on multiplication facts or on equivalent fractions are two examples of these short activities. A short game designed for review could also be used.

For example, put a picture of the football in Figure 2–11 on the chalkboard or overhead projector, with numbers written inside. Tell your students to draw the football on a piece of paper.

FIGURE 2–11

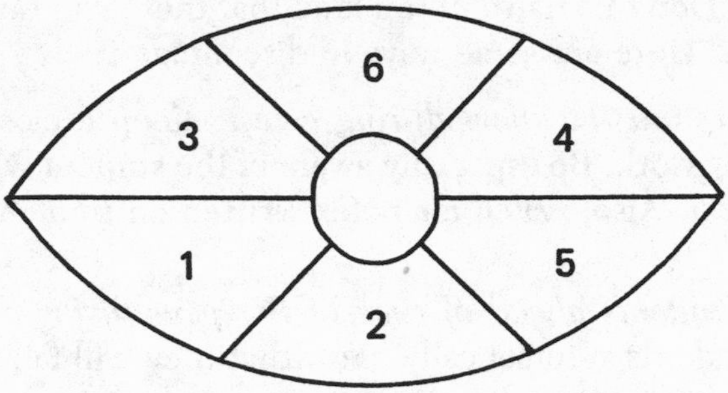

Put a number in the circle in the middle of the ball, and have students write the various equivalent fractions next to the numbers on the inside, as in Figure 2–12.

FIGURE 2–12

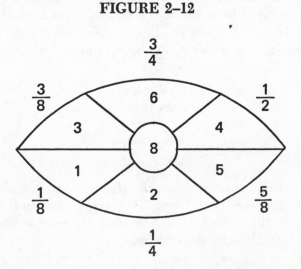

DEALING WITH COMMON CLASSROOM INCIDENTS

There are many common classroom incidents with which you must deal. How well you deal with these incidents will go a long way in determining whether or not you have good classroom control, a prerequisite to effective student learning. Your first axiom is to always let good common sense dictate your actions. Here are some ways to handle such common incidents as cheating, gum chewing, and being late for class. As you read this next section, keep in mind the general guidelines discussed on page 33.

Cheating. Don't be naive in thinking that there will be no cheating in your classroom. Here are some ways to discourage it.

1. *Walk around the room during a test.* Keep a close eye on your students as they work. Be especially aware of the student who is keeping a close eye on you. Also, watch for notes written on scratch paper, hands, arms, or cuffs.

2. *Warn students ahead of time of the penalty for cheating.* Don't assume that students automatically know that they will fail the test if they are caught cheating. Be sure that you can *definitely* document that a student has cheated before you accuse him or her.

3. *Use different forms of a test if it is given to more than one class.* There is more work in making up different forms, but, if you don't, the later classes will do better than they should have on the test.

4. *When grading the test, put a mark through an incorrect answer.* Students may change answers and tell you that there was a mistake in grading, especially if they are only a point or two from the next higher letter grade. Hence, be sure to place an "X" through the wrong answer instead of through the problem number as in the following example.

X) 324
(poor marking)

5) 3X4
(better marking)

5. *Pass out the test only when the students have cleared their desks.* This will help eliminate crib sheets. But, keep an eye on the floor where a crib sheet may still be visible. If your students need scratch paper, have them write on the back of the test page.

6. *Guard your grade book*. Never leave your grade book where students have access to it, either legally or illegally. The book should be kept locked in your desk or office.

Classroom noise. Insist on complete student attention when you are talking, and follow this rule from the very beginning of the school year. If students begin talking, stop and ask if one of them has a question. This will usually quell the talkers. You may also find that you will have to separate students who continuously talk with each other; do this early before the situation gets out of hand.

Crush on the Teacher. Almost every student at some point during his or her school experience gets a crush on a teacher. Since this may well happen to you, be on the lookout for it to occur. If a student develops a crush on you, do your best to extinguish the fire as quickly as possible; but, be gentle with the student's feelings as they will be very tender. Saying nice things about your husband or wife or having a framed photo of your spouse or children may be helpful.

Drugs and Alcohol. Unfortunately, the use of drugs and alcohol by junior high/middle school students has become much more prevalent in recent years. You might suspect a student in your class, but be very careful of accusing the student of drug or alcohol use. A rule of thumb is "don't accuse" because a student's actions could easily be caused by something else.

If the student's behavior is especially erratic, suggest that he or she go to the nurse's office. Ask one of your trustworthy students to go with the student in question to be sure that the nurse's office is indeed the final destination. If there is no nurse in the building or the student refuses to go, send a message to the principal or vice-principal and let that person handle the situation.

Fighting. Fighting between students usually occurs when students are coming into the room before class or while they are leaving after class. Be aware of potential incidents and do what you can to keep them from breaking into a full-scale fight.

If a fight does occur, have the other students move away from the combatants. Send an urgent call to the office for help; use the intercom system if one is available. If not, send a student for help while you remain in the room. It is dangerous to try to break up a fight yourself so wait until help arrives. If there is too much commotion, a fellow teacher may come to help. But, be careful, as some junior high/middle school students have tremendous strength when angry. Let discretion be the better part of valor.

Forgotten Materials. Students commonly will tell you that they have forgotten their book and/or paper and pencil. Sometimes the reason for forgetting the material is uncorrectable (it was left at home), but most often it is in a locker. Have materials available for students to borrow, but be sure you get them back at the end of class. Keep a supply of pencils and paper, and several sheets of used typewriter paper from typing class for emergency use. Sending a student back to a locker to get materials may be disruptive to the class, so use this technique with judicious care.

Whatever you do, don't permit the student to sit in class without materials. This makes it very easy for them to do nothing.!

Gum Chewing. For some reason or another, students of all ages love to chew gum. You will have your own feelings about gum chewing in class. Regardless of these feelings, if the school has a rule against gum chewing, you should enforce the rule. If no such rule exists, then it's up to you.

Let your students know the first day of school how you feel about chewing gum in class. If the school and you are against gum chewing, then simply watch for it. If you see a student chewing, simply walk over to the student quietly, hand him or her a small piece of paper, ask the student to deposit the gum on it and put it in the trash can.

Late to Class. You always see students who will come running into the classroom as the bell rings. Early on, stand at the door and watch the hallway. As the bell prepares to ring, you will be able to see students who are potentially late. If they are late, ask them why at the doorway. If another teacher has kept them late, ask the student to obtain a slip from that teacher. If there is some other reason, ask the student to get a slip from the office. Firmly dealing with this problem early in the school year will greatly decrease the number of tardy students.

Passing Notes. Ordinarily, it is probably best to ignore the passing of notes. However, if it becomes disturbing to other students or to you, then you need to put a stop to it. Simply moving around the room will discourage this behavior. Probably the most effective way is to intercept the note, put it in your pocket, return it unread at the end of class, and say nothing whatsoever. Never read the note out loud or have the sender (or receiver) read it out loud; the results could be very embarrassing.

Restroom Use. Students will ask you during class to go to the restroom. Sometimes the request is legitimate and you should permit them to go. You can usually tell by watching a student whether or not there is an emergency. If there is any question, let the student go. If the request becomes habitual for a student, you may need to talk with him or her individually about the problem. If the problem is medically related, ask the school nurse for help.

Vandalism. If you catch a student defacing school property (books, desks or whatever), confront the student immediately. Report the incident to the principal and make arrangements to have the student clean up whatever has been defaced.

Suppose you notice that something in your classroom has been defaced, but you did not see who did it. Since the chances are good that the student will return to the scene of the crime and perhaps repeat the action, be observant. If a desk is defaced, you can narrow down your suspects and watch them carefully during class.

Vulgar Language. Vulgar language is usually used by students seeking status from peers. If you have vulgar language directed towards you, don't ignore it. Ask the student to not repeat the vulgar language again. If it persists, quietly ask the student to go to the office and wait for you there. Inform the office by intercom or send a note via a student to the office indicating that Joe Smith or Mary Jones is being sent there to meet you. No reason need be given initially.

If the student refuses to go, send for assistance from the office. If the student is loud enough, you may have teachers from adjoining classrooms coming to your aid.

QUICK REVIEW

1. In managing your classroom, what must you do:

   a.) before the school year starts?
   b.) the first day of school?
   c.) the first week of school?

2. In planning your instructional program, what must you do:

   a.) before the school year starts?
   b.) the first day of school?
   c.) the first week of school?

3. Draw diagrams showing different ways you can arrange your classroom. What are the advantages and disadvantages of each? What arrangement would you choose for your classroom? Why?

4. What general guidelines must you keep in mind when presenting your daily lesson?

5. What teaching aids do you plan to use in your instructional program? How will you use each of them?

6. Several procedures for handling day-to-day classroom routine were described in Chapter 2. Are there other routines you need to consider? If so, what are they? Of the procedures described in this chapter, what, if anything, would you do differently?

7. Procedures for dealing with common classroom incidents were described in Chapter 2. What, if anything, would you do differently? Are there other incidents with which you have been confronted? If so, how did you deal with them? Would you do the same thing if the same incident occurred again? Why?

8. Investigate to see what policies your school board has regarding student conduct. Has your handling of problem situations been consistent with those policies? If not, why?

9. Your textbook is probably one of the best sources of material that you will use in your instructional program. What criteria would you use in selecting a textbook for your class? How does your list compare with the evaluation form found in Appendix A?

3

Diagnosis and Correction in the Junior High/Middle School Mathematics Classroom

The use of diagnosis and correction as integral tools to improve learning in the junior high/middle school classroom has received much attention from mathematics educators and teachers in recent years. Diagnostic and resulting corrective (prescriptive) techniques are viewed as ways of improving mathematics instructional programs at all levels of learning from kindergarten to adult. This chapter examines the nature of diagnosis and correction and how these techniques may be used by the classroom teacher. Some common error patterns in arithmetic often made by learners are also discussed.

After reading and studying this chapter, you should be able to:

- Define diagnosis and correction.
- State guidelines for successfully completing the diagnostic and corrective processes.
- Identify error patterns in computational skills which exist in a given case study.

- Identify common sources of errors in computation made by junior high/middle school students.
- List various diagnostic and corrective techniques and cite advantages and disadvantages of each.
- Describe an instructional model appropriate for classroom use which emphasizes diagnosis and correction.

DEFINING DIAGNOSIS AND CORRECTION

You are certainly familiar with the term "diagnosis." Its use has probably been in the context of what your medical doctor does when you go to his or her office because you are ill. By using your description of your symptoms and possibly some tests, your doctor tries to diagnose your illness and prescribe corrective treatment which will cure your illness. If your doctor makes an accurate diagnosis and prescribes the proper treatment, you will soon be well. Obviously, an accurate diagnosis is likely to mean a quick cure.

In a sense, you, as a teacher, are faced with the same problem as your medical doctor. A student may come to you with one or more "mathematical ills." To help the student cure the "mathematical ills," you must first decide the nature of the ill(s), and then plan and apply an instructional program designed to correct the diagnosed mathematical illness. The measure of your ability to diagnose and plan corrective procedures is the extent to which the student is able to progress towards a "cure." Of course, since you are only exposed to the student for a relatively short period of time, you are not expected to cure all of the student's mathematical illnesses. But, you can at least start the student along a path of recovery so that additional corrections can be performed by other teachers in the future.

Diagnosis, then, is a process that you use to determine what students *are* and *are not* able to do mathematically. Correction is what you do to help students progress towards mathematical levels that are appropriate for their chronological and intellectual ages.

The diagnostic-corrective process may be summarized as a series of steps in the form of questions:

1. What is the exact nature of the error?
2. What appears to be the cause or source of the error?
3. At what level (concrete, semiconcrete or abstract) is the student capable of working?

4. Given answers to questions one through three, what is the appropriate instructional strategy that may be used to correct the error?

Application of these four steps will give you a systematic way for implementing the diagnostic-corrective process.

To illustrate the above technique, suppose that you have received the following sample of a student's work.

A. 1.3	B. 1.01	C. .71	D. 2.2	E. 2.5
×7	×3	×5	×3	×4
9.1	30.3	35.5	66.	1.00

It is clear that problems B through E are incorrect. Your first impulse may be to say that the student cannot multiply decimals; however, problem A is correctly done. Closer inspection will tell you that the student is quite capable of doing the multiplication part of the problem, but is not able, for some reason, to correctly place the decimal point in the answer.

Possible sources of the error may be in the student's lack of understanding of the multiplication algorithm for decimals or of the concept of decimals in general. An oral interview with the student or examination of other work involving decimals may be needed to help you identify the exact source of the error.

After you have identified the nature and source of the error, consider alternatives for correcting the error. For example, if the student is working at the abstract level, a brief re-explanation of the procedure for placing the decimal point in the answer may be all that is needed. As your experience as a classroom teacher grows, you will be able to draw from a variety of instructional strategies that may be used in this situation.

GUIDELINES FOR DIAGNOSIS

There are several general guidelines to follow when you are diagnosing learning difficulties in mathematics. These guidelines will help you do a better job in obtaining desirable results.

1. *Use oral interviews*. Whenever possible, conduct an oral interview with the student and, listen to the learner. This one-to-one situation gives you an opportunity to have the student verbalize the thinking that caused the error(s) found.

2. *Be a data collector and not a teacher*. It is important to gather all of the factors that have caused the error(s); at this point, do not correct. There will be time later to be a teacher when correction is implemented.

3. *Look for patterns of errors*. Errors are often made consistently. Determining a pattern will help you make a more accurate and complete diagnosis.

4. *Be aware of affective variables*. Such variables as attitude and self-concept, as well as cognitive variables, may be responsible for the student's errors.

5. *Provide a comfortable atmosphere for the student during diagnosis*. The learner must feel confident that he or she will not be penalized for the fact that difficulties exist. The student must be made to feel that you are offering understanding and help—not criticism. Patience is a virtue at this point.

6. *Be as thorough and complete as possible in your diagnosis*. Your diagnostic plan should be carefully considered so that a maximum amount of information can be gained in a minimum amount of time.

7. *Determine the type of activities with which the learner seems comfortable*. A matrix for determining the appropriate level was described in Chapter 1.

8. *Be observant as the student talks and works*. Much can be learned about a student's difficulties as you watch his or her reactions and physical movement when problem situations are presented.

9. *Make your diagnosis from the "evidence" rather than from idle assumptions*. Many student difficulties turn out to be ones other than what you thought at first. Thoroughness and completeness in your diagnostic process will greatly minimize the chance of an incorrect diagnosis.

GUIDELINES FOR CORRECTION

As with diagnosis, there are guidelines for correction. Following these guidelines will enable you to provide effective and efficient correction for found mathematical learning difficulties.

1. *Provide maximum opportunity for success by the learner*. Many students who have had learning difficulties in mathematics have usually had a great number of failure experiences. These failures may well have caused the student to say, "Why try? I can't get it anyway." This feeling usually prevents any corrective action from being effective. A little success goes a long way towards helping the learner overcome this defeatist feeling.

2. *Share the objectives of the correction plan with the student*. The student should be made aware of what you expect. This awareness often gives the learner a sense of responsibility in seeing that the objectives are

achieved; such a sense may motivate the student to work as hard as possible.

3. *Provide corrective activities at the student's level.* Chapter 1 showed how learning levels may be designated relative to learning style. Accurate assessment of the types of appropriate corrective activities will make correction more enjoyable and efficient for both you and the learner.

4. *Use different approaches when presenting concepts and skills other than those already confronted by the student.* Using the same approach over and over again may frustrate the student, since it obviously did not work the first time. You need to have several different approaches at your disposal so that they may be used in case the initial approach does not work.

5. *Give frequent and immediate feedback to the learner about progress being made.* The student is less likely to proceed unless there is some feeling that the effort is being considered important. Immediate feedback helps reduce anxiety, and frequent feedback enhances your opportunities to provide plenty of success experiences.

6. *Use a variety of instructional materials.* By doing so, you can take advantage of the student's learning style and also give a "different look"— which just might be enough to correct the difficulty. Teachers often tend to use only paper-and-pencil drill sheets in corrective action, so the learner often becomes bored. A variety of instructional materials makes corrective activity more enjoyable and beneficial for both you and the student.

IDENTIFYING COMMON ERROR PATTERNS

It is generally accepted among mathematics educators that students tend to make errors systemically, especially in computation. In other words, errors are often consistent as they appear. To help you identify the consistent errors, let's see how skills are analyzed and examine some common errors made by students.

Analyzing a Skill to Be Learned

Mathematics is a highly structured subject. Learning from the very beginning (concept of number, spatial relationships, etc.) is used as a basis for building additional mathematical concepts and skills. This means that a student may have gaps in mathematical background, gaps which may have occurred in the early primary grades.

To assess these gaps accurately, you must have a thorough understanding of the development of mathematical concepts and skills in the elementary school. If you feel that you need some help in this area, consult an elementary textbook series, the state or school corporation curriculum guide or several elementary teachers.

Before you begin to identify errors, however, you need to analyze the skill to be learned. This analysis is done by breaking down the skill into its component parts (subskills or prerequisites).

To illustrate this, let's consider the problem of $1/2 \times 1/3 = 1/6$. What are the concepts and skills that must be learned before the problem can be solved correctly? Let's name them:

Concept of fractions

Concept of multiplication

Concept of basic facts of multiplication

Concept of algorithm for multiplying two fractions

If one or more of these concepts or skills has not been learned by the student, the end result will probably be an incorrect solution. If you are not able to, or do not break down the overall skill (multiplying two fractions) into its component parts, you will have no idea where the error(s) are being made. And, if you don't know what error is being made, how can you correct it?

You, as the classroom teacher, must be able to analyze each concept or skill found in your curriculum. Your ability to analyze the skill or concept will determine how effective you are likely to be in correcting student errors, let alone presenting the concept or skill initially to a class of thirty.

Being able to analyze a concept or skill will go a long way towards determining patterns of errors, a fundamental skill in diagnosis. Since errors tend to occur systematically, accurate diagnosis will enable you to correct error patterns more quickly and efficiently than if you used no analysis at all.

Finding Error Patterns

Let's see how this concept or skill analysis can be used to search for error patterns. Consider the following samples of Ginny's work on division problems:

$$
\begin{array}{llll}
\text{A.} \quad 3\overline{)66} \quad & \text{B.} \quad 3\overline{)117} \quad & \text{C.} \quad 3\overline{)75} \quad & \text{D.} \quad 5\overline{)155} \\
\end{array}
$$

	22		93		52		13
A.	3)66	B.	3)117	C.	3)75	D.	5)155
	60		90		60		150
	6		27		15		5
	6		27		15		5

Do you see the pattern? Ginny records her first partial quotient above the last number in the dividend. Then she multiplies her partial quotient by the divisor and then by 10 and places the number below the dividend. After subtracting, she divides the divisor into the difference and records the answer in the quotient to the *left* of the first partial quotient. *Hence, her digits in the quotient are always in reverse order.*

To help you develop this valuable skill, here are more examples of error patterns, done by a student named Tom. See if you can find the patterns.

A. $1/2 + 1/3 = 2/5$
B. $2/3 + 1/3 = 3/6$
C. $1/4 + 4/5 = 5/9$
D. $1/2 + 3/4 = 4/6$

Tom's error pattern is that he is adding the numerators together to get the numerator in the answer. He then adds the denominators together to get the denominator in the answer. Next, look at Brenda's work. What is her pattern?

$$
\begin{array}{lll}
\quad\ \ \overset{1.37\ \text{r}2}{5\overline{)6.87}} &
\quad\ \ \overset{1.4\ \text{r}6}{2.2\overline{)3.14}} &
\quad\ \ \overset{57\ \text{r}3}{4\overline{)2.31}}
\end{array}
$$

A.
$$
\begin{array}{r}
1.37\ \text{r}2 \\
5\overline{)6.87} \\
\underline{5} \\
18 \\
\underline{15} \\
37 \\
\underline{35} \\
2
\end{array}
$$
B.
$$
\begin{array}{r}
1.4\ \text{r}6 \\
2.2\overline{)3.14} \\
\underline{22} \\
94 \\
\underline{88} \\
6
\end{array}
$$
C.
$$
\begin{array}{r}
57\ \text{r}3 \\
4\overline{)2.31} \\
\underline{20} \\
31 \\
\underline{28} \\
3
\end{array}
$$

In Brenda's case, division is performed exactly as it is done with whole numbers, including the use of the remainder. The decimal point is placed correctly in problems A and B, but is omitted from the quotient in problem C. In problems A and B, the divisor is less than the first digit(s) of the dividend, but this is not true in problem C. Apparently, Brenda has some confusion over the placement of the decimal point in the quotient in situations such as problem C.

Did you correctly identify Brenda's error pattern? It takes a little time to become proficient at finding these patterns. Further practice in finding error patterns are found in the Quick Review at the end of this chapter.

Some Common Patterns of Computation Errors

To aid you in the diagnostic process, let's list some common patterns of errors that students make in division and multiplication of whole numbers, fractions, decimals, percent and exponents. These lists are obviously not exhaustive, but will give you a place to start.

Multiplication of whole numbers.

Error	Examples	

1. Algorithm is performed like addition (by columns).

$$\begin{array}{r} 23 \\ \times 17 \\ \hline 2321 \end{array} \qquad \begin{array}{r} 14 \\ \times 15 \\ \hline 120 \end{array}$$

2. Number "carried" is added before multiplying.

$$\begin{array}{r} {}^235 \\ \times 14 \\ \hline 200 \\ 35 \\ \hline 550 \end{array} \qquad \begin{array}{r} {}^426 \\ \times 7 \\ \hline 422 \end{array}$$

3. Multiplication is performed from left to right.

$$\begin{array}{r} 23 \\ \times 4 \\ \hline 812 \end{array} \qquad \begin{array}{r} 16 \\ \times 8 \\ \hline 848 \end{array}$$

4. Number "carried" the first time is also used when multiplying by the tens digit.

$$\begin{array}{r} {}^598 \\ \times 56 \\ \hline 588 \\ 500 \\ \hline 5588 \end{array} \qquad \begin{array}{r} {}^719 \\ \times 78 \\ \hline 152 \\ 143 \\ \hline 1582 \end{array}$$

5. Number "carried" is ignored.

$$\begin{array}{r} {}^114 \\ \times 3 \\ \hline 32 \end{array} \qquad \begin{array}{r} {}^529 \\ \times 6 \\ \hline 124 \end{array}$$

6. Multiplication by tens digit is not recorded correctly.

$$\begin{array}{r} 25 \\ \times 13 \\ \hline 75 \\ 25 \\ \hline 100 \end{array} \qquad \begin{array}{r} 13 \\ \times 12 \\ \hline 26 \\ 13 \\ \hline 39 \end{array}$$

7. Basic facts of addition and multiplication are incorrect.

$$\begin{array}{r} 27 \\ \times 9 \\ \hline 252 \end{array} \qquad \begin{array}{r} 19 \\ \times 17 \\ \hline 133 \\ 19 \\ \hline 333 \end{array}$$

Division of whole numbers.

Error	Examples	

1. When divisor is less than digit in dividend, division is performed normally with remainders dropped. When divisor is greater than digit in dividend, digit in dividend is divided into divisor.

$$\begin{array}{r} 213 \\ 3\overline{)639} \end{array} \qquad \begin{array}{r} 142 \\ 4\overline{)518} \end{array}$$

Division of whole numbers.

Error	*Examples*	

2. Division is performed in normal fashion, but entire dividend is used for product of divisor and partial quotient. Quotient is recorded from right to left.

$$
\begin{array}{r}
52 \\
3\overline{)75} \\
60 \\
\hline
15 \\
15 \\
\hline
\end{array}
\qquad
\begin{array}{r}
68 \\
6\overline{)516} \\
480 \\
\hline
36 \\
36 \\
\hline
\end{array}
$$

3. After dividing initially, next two numbers are used as dividend.

$$
\begin{array}{r}
32 \ \ r3 \\
9\overline{)2721} \\
27 \\
\hline
21 \\
18 \\
\hline
3 \\
\end{array}
\qquad
\begin{array}{r}
78 \ \ r2 \\
6\overline{)4250} \\
42 \\
\hline
50 \\
48 \\
\hline
2 \\
\end{array}
$$

4. Basic facts of multiplication are incorrect.

$$
\begin{array}{r}
66 \ r13 \\
15\overline{)903} \\
80 \\
\hline
103 \\
90 \\
\hline
13 \\
\end{array}
\qquad
\begin{array}{r}
48 \ r5 \\
7\overline{)348} \\
28 \\
\hline
68 \\
63 \\
\hline
5 \\
\end{array}
$$

5. Basic facts of subtraction and subtraction algorithm are incorrect.

$$
\begin{array}{r}
27 \ r2 \\
12\overline{)336} \\
24 \\
\hline
86 \\
84 \\
\hline
2 \\
\end{array}
\qquad
\begin{array}{r}
62r7 \\
8\overline{)547} \\
48 \\
\hline
16 \\
16 \\
\hline
7 \\
\end{array}
$$

Fractions.

Error	*Examples*	

1. Lesser number is divided into greater, with quotient used as numerator. Greater number is used as denominator.

$$\frac{4}{6}=\frac{1}{6} \qquad \frac{3}{9}=\frac{9}{3}$$

2. Numerators are added together. Denominators are added together.

$$\frac{1}{3}+\frac{1}{4}=\frac{2}{7} \qquad \frac{2}{3}+\frac{3}{5}=\frac{5}{8}$$

3. Whole numbers in problem are ignored.

$$
\begin{array}{r}
3\frac{1}{4}=\frac{2}{8} \\
+1\frac{1}{8}=\frac{1}{8} \\
\hline
\frac{3}{8}
\end{array}
\qquad
\begin{array}{r}
7\frac{1}{2}=\frac{2}{4} \\
+5\frac{3}{4}=\frac{3}{4} \\
\hline
\frac{5}{4}=1\frac{1}{4}
\end{array}
$$

Fractions. (cont.)

Error	*Examples*

4. Regrouping process involves ten rather than fraction name.

$$^5 6\frac{1}{8} \qquad ^3 4\frac{1}{4}$$
$$- \ 3\frac{3}{8} \qquad - \ 1\frac{3}{4}$$
$$2\frac{8}{8}=1 \qquad 2\frac{8}{4}=2$$

5. Subtraction process is applied incorrectly.

$$3 \qquad 8$$
$$-2\frac{1}{4} \qquad -2\frac{5}{6}$$
$$1\frac{1}{4} \qquad 6\frac{5}{6}$$

6. One of the two numbers is inverted before multiplying.

$$\frac{1}{4}\times\frac{2}{3}=\frac{1}{4}\times\frac{3}{2}=\frac{3}{8}$$

$$\frac{1}{6}\times\frac{1}{2}=\frac{1}{6}\times\frac{2}{1}=\frac{2}{6}$$

7. Whole numbers are multiplied together and fractions are multiplied together.

$$2\frac{1}{2}\times3\frac{1}{5}=6\frac{1}{10}$$

$$1\frac{1}{4}\times2\frac{1}{2}=2\frac{1}{8}$$

8. Fractions are changed to common denominators and then numerators are multiplied.

$$\frac{1}{2}\times\frac{3}{2}=\frac{3}{2}$$

$$\frac{1}{3}\times\frac{3}{4}=\frac{4}{12}\times\frac{9}{12}=\frac{36}{12}=3$$

9. Dividend is inverted instead of divisor.

$$\frac{1}{4}\div\frac{2}{3}=\frac{4}{1}\times\frac{2}{3}=\frac{8}{3}$$

$$\frac{2}{3}\div\frac{1}{2}=\frac{3}{2}\times\frac{1}{2}=\frac{3}{4}$$

10. Numerator is divided by numerator and denominator is divided by denominator. Remainders are ignored.

$$\frac{13}{20}\div\frac{5}{6}=\frac{2}{3}$$

$$\frac{3}{4}\div\frac{2}{2}=\frac{1}{2}$$

Decimals.

Error	*Examples*

1. Decimal places are marked off in answer.

$$.3 \qquad\qquad .7$$
$$+ \ .9 \qquad\quad +1.4$$
$$.12 \qquad\qquad .21$$

Decimals. (cont.)

Error	*Examples*	

2. Subtraction process is incorrectly applied.

$$\begin{array}{r} 4 \\ -2.3 \\ \hline 2.3 \end{array} \qquad \begin{array}{r} 5 \\ -1.49 \\ \hline 4.49 \end{array}$$

3. Numbers are added like whole numbers. Decimal point is placed in answer according to greater number of decimal places found in a single number in the problem.

$$1.1 + .4 + 1.3 = 2.8$$
$$2.36 + .7 = 2.43$$

4. Decimal points are kept in line.

$$\begin{array}{r} 3.2 \\ \times\ .3 \\ \hline 9.6 \end{array} \qquad \begin{array}{r} 1.2 \\ \times\ .3 \\ \hline 3.6 \end{array}$$

5. Decimal point in the answer is placed from the left.

$$\begin{array}{r} 1.4 \\ .12 \\ \hline 28 \\ 14 \\ \hline 168. \end{array} \qquad \begin{array}{r} 14 \\ 1.3 \\ \hline 42 \\ 14 \\ \hline 1.82 \end{array}$$

6. Decimal point in divisor is ignored.

$$\begin{array}{r} .5 \\ .7\overline{)3.5} \\ 35 \end{array} \qquad \begin{array}{r} .4 \\ 1.2\overline{)4.8} \\ 48 \end{array}$$

7. Problem is written so that divisor and dividend are interchanged.

For .7 ÷ 1.4,
student writes
$.7\overline{)1.4}$

8. Remainder is recorded using a decimal point.

$$\begin{array}{r} 38.3 \\ 4\overline{)155} \\ 12 \\ \hline 35 \\ 32 \\ \hline 3 \end{array} \qquad \begin{array}{r} 36.1 \\ 3\overline{)109} \\ 9 \\ \hline 19 \\ 18 \\ \hline 1 \end{array}$$

Percent.

Error	*Examples*

1. Percent sign is ignored.

14% of 60 = 84
10% of 30 = 300

2. Percents are incorrectly converted to decimals and vice versa.

.01% = .01
.5% = .5
.3 = 3%

Exponents.

Error	*Examples*

1. Exponents are added in an addition problem.

$$2^2 + 2^2 = 2^4$$
$$3^2 + 3^4 = 3^6$$

Exponents. (cont.)

Error	*Examples*

2. Exponents are multiplied in a multiplication problem.

$2^2 \times 2^3 = 2^6$
$4^2 \times 4^2 = 4^4$

3. Base number and exponent are multiplied.

$2^3 = 6$
$3^2 = 6$

4. Base numbers and exponents are added respectively.

$2^2 + 2^2 = 4^4$
$3^2 + 4^2 = 7^4$

5. Base numbers and exponents are multiplied respectively.

$2^3 \times 3^2 = 6^6$
$4^2 \times 3^2 = 12^4$

6. Square root is found by dividing by 2.

$\sqrt{16} = 8$
$\sqrt{8} = 4$

7. Square root of the sum is found by taking the sum of the square roots.

$\sqrt{4+4} = 2+2 = 4$
$\sqrt{25+36} = 5+6 = 11$
$\sqrt{9+16} = 3+4 = 7$

USING DIAGNOSTIC AND CORRECTIVE TECHNIQUES IN THE CLASSROOM

Thus far in this chapter, diagnosis and correction have been defined, guidelines for the use of diagnosis and correction have been discussed, and error patterns have been identified. Now let's examine some diagnostic and corrective techniques and how you might use them in the junior high/middle school mathematics classroom.

Diagnostic Techniques

There are a wide variety of diagnostic techniques you may use to assess learning difficulties in mathematics. On a formal basis, diagnosis may be done with the use of standardized or teacher-made paper-and-pencil tests.

Standardized tests have the advantage that they are usually valid and reliable. Scores are often reported as normed grade equivalents that make interpretation of test results relatively easy. They may also include a profile for different skill and concept areas that have been tested. Both group and individual tests are available.

Standardized tests do have some limitations, however. Their results tend to be more of a general nature, so you may need or want to do more detailed diagnosis. They are also relatively expensive to purchase, which could be a potential problem for your school budget.

Teacher-made tests have the advantage of being able to pinpoint much more precisely the errors made by your students. Construction is relatively easy and the test does not require special testing conditions such as time limits. In many instances, you will probably find that your own test will more adequately meet your needs as a diagnostician.

There are several cautions, however, to the construction and use of a teacher-made test. For one thing, you must have a thorough knowledge of the hierarchical nature of mathematics as it is taught in the elementary and junior high/middle school curriculum. This knowledge is necessary so that you can develop a sequence of test items that adequately isolate the component parts of the concept or skill to be tested. Second, constructing your own test is time consuming at best.

There are also a variety of informal techniques you may want to use for diagnostic purposes. These techniques can give you a great deal of useful information and are easily applied.

1. *Observation*. You should always be a continual observer in your classroom. Watching your students while they are doing seat work or working at the chalkboard may give you valuable clues as to why they are having difficulty. Observation will also be of great benefit to you in classroom management and discipline, as was discussed in Chapters 2 and 3.

2. *Interview*. Sometimes, the very best way to gather information about what is causing a student's difficulty is to sit down on a one-to-one basis with the student so that his or her thinking about a problem or process can be verbalized. This sort of session is difficult to do with every learner who is having difficulty because of your time constraints, but it will be well worth the effort.

3. *Homework*. A review of homework by a student who is having difficulty may give you the information you need to make an accurate diagnosis. You must remember, however, that homework assignments should be carefully screened before assigning so that they will accomplish what you want.

Regardless of which diagnostic technique(s) you decide to use, remember that an accurate diagnosis is the key to helping students correct their difficulties. Also, the technique(s) you use should be in tandem with the guidelines presented on page 53.

Corrective Techniques

When you have completed your diagnosis, the next obvious step is to correct the found difficulty(ies). Correction, however, must be done in a systematic fashion to be effective.

Begin by outlining your objectives to be achieved by the corrective process. These objectives should be stated in terms of observable behaviors that will be exhibited by the learner. These objectives should be shared with the student so that desired end result(s) will be clear to both of you.

There must also be continuous evaluation and feedback to the student during the corrective process. Keep the student continually apprised of progress being made.

In addition to the guidelines discussed on page 54, you will no doubt use many different kinds of activities to give the student ample opportunity to drill on the troublesome concept or skill. Games are often an excellent medium to help make drill more enjoyable. Guidelines for the choice and use of games will be discussed in Chapter 11.

Some general remarks about the use of drill seem appropriate here. Drill is a very useful tool not only in the corrective process but also in the regular classroom instructional setting. However, the word "drill" has always had a bad reputation because it was associated with an unpleasant task, such as doing 100 fraction problems. The problem was that many teachers felt that anything could be learned mathematically if you drilled long enough on it. Drill was the only way to learn mathematics.

A more reasonable view of drill is that its purpose is to reinforce a concept or skill to be learned. Not all students, therefore, need the same amount of drill to master a concept or skill, so drill activities should be assigned with this in mind. Drill will be effective when there is understanding by the student of the concept or skill to be learned. Drill should also be enjoyable to the student so that motivation to learn will be enhanced. This does not mean that drill should be "all fun and games," but it means that drill must have a purpose that is understood by the learner.

Whichever corrective techniques you decide to use, remember that you must address the needs of the learner and provide for these needs in the corrective process. If you do so and have a well-planned corrective process, the end result will be that the student can overcome the mathematical difficulty which will bolster his or her attitude and self-concept.

An Instructional Model

It is appropriate at this point to examine a model of instruction that you can use in your classroom. This model incorporates the principles of diagnosis and correction discussed in this chapter. The model is shown in Figure 3–1.

FIGURE 3–1

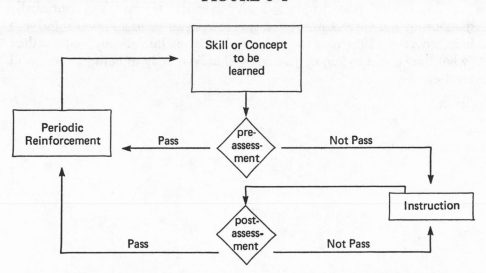

This instructional model may be used either with your entire class or with individual students. The pre- and post-assessment phases may be either formal or informal in nature, with specific diagnosis used in either phase. The instruction phase is used to either give initial or corrective instruction. After the student has demonstrated learning of the concept or skill in the post-assessment phase, you must provide periodic reinforcement of the concept or skill to assure retention by the learner.

A special advantage for including the pre-assessment phase is that its results will enable your precious classroom instruction time to be used more efficiently. For example, if you find that your students have already learned the concept or skill, then no instructional time is needed, and you can use several activities for reinforcement. The pre-assessment will also help you determine which students are having difficulties so that you can begin to correct their difficulties more quickly.

Use of this model also enables you to group your students in the classroom for instructional purposes. The groups are determined by the found needs of the students. An advantage here is that the groupings are dynamic in nature, which will be better for the students and also remove some of the stigma associated with inflexible or static groupings. The number and size of groups that you use in the classroom depends on your wishes and style; you must be comfortable with your scheme for grouping.

Remember, real diagnosis and correction is ongoing, continually diagnosing and correct in the classroom. As you keep an open mind and increase your willingness to accept "what is mathematically" rather than "what they ought to know," you are well on your way to being a successful teacher.

QUICK REVIEW

1. Define diagnosis and correction as they each relate to the junior high/ middle school mathematics classroom.

2. Give a breakdown of the prerequisites needed for each of the following:

   a.) fraction addition
   b.) mixed number multiplication
   c.) decimal division
   d.) fraction-to-decimal conversion
   e.) fraction-to-percent conversion
   f.) fraction multiplication

3. "If a student hasn't mastered whole number arithmetic by the seventh grade, forget it and just give the student a calculator to use." What is your reaction to this statement?

4. Identify the error pattern for each student.

a.) *Mary:* $\dfrac{^13}{2}+\dfrac{1}{3^1}=\dfrac{2}{3}$ $\dfrac{^24}{5}+\dfrac{4}{2^1}=\dfrac{6}{6}=1$

   $\dfrac{7}{^210}+\dfrac{^15}{6}=\dfrac{8}{8}=1$ $\dfrac{2}{3}+\dfrac{6}{7}=\dfrac{8}{10}=\dfrac{4}{5}$

b.) *Frank:* $\dfrac{2}{3}\div\dfrac{1}{2}=\dfrac{4}{6}\div\dfrac{3}{6}=1\dfrac{1}{6}$ $\dfrac{3}{4}\div\dfrac{3}{8}=\dfrac{6}{8}\div\dfrac{3}{8}=2$

c.) *Billy:* $10^3\times10^4=10^{12}$ $2^5\times2^3=2^{15}$

d.) *Judy:* $\sqrt{9+25}=3+5=8$ $\sqrt{8^2=5^2}=13$ $\sqrt{10^4-10^2}=90$

e.) *Wilson:* $3^2=6$ $2^4=8$ $5^3=15$

f.) *Meredith:*

$$3\dfrac{1}{3}$$
$$-1\dfrac{1}{2}$$
$$\overline{2\dfrac{1}{6}}$$

$$5\dfrac{1}{4}$$
$$-2\dfrac{3}{4}$$
$$\overline{3\dfrac{2}{4}=3\dfrac{1}{2}}$$

$$1\dfrac{3}{8}$$
$$-\dfrac{7}{8}$$
$$\overline{1\dfrac{4}{8}=1\dfrac{1}{2}}$$

g.) *Tony:*

```
      2 3
  13)2639
     26
      39
      39
```

```
      2 4
   7)1428
     14
      28
      28
```

```
      2 3 r3
  12)2439
     24
      39
      36
       3
```

h.) *Beth:*

113	148	245
×103	×207	×304
339	1036	980
000	000	000
113	296	735
1439	3996	8330

i.) *Albert:*

17	23	27
×18	×13	×28
156	29	456

j.) *Alice:*

```
  1000 r8        1221 r4        1121 r2
5)7231         3)4783         2)3243
  2              1              1
  2              1              0
  3              2              0
  1              0              1
```

5. In addition to the error patterns shown in exercise 4 and in the chapter text, what other patterns have you noticed the students make?

6. What do you see as advantages and disadvantages of the instructional model discussed in this chapter?

7. You may find it desirable to ask a student to help diagnose his or her own problem. What can be gained by doing this even though you may be quite sure of what the error is?

8. Much of the discussion in this chapter has centered on diagnosis of an individual student. A short pretest may also be used to diagnose your class prior to instruction on a topic(s). What experience have you had with the use of a pretest? How might you use the information from a chapter or unit test after instruction to diagnose?

9. Carelessness is often cited as a reason why students have made mistakes. Some possible causes for this carelessness might be:

a.) assignment is too long
b.) student is in a hurry to finish
c.) student is sloppy

Can you think of other possible causes? What might you do to help avoid these causes?

4

Evaluation in the
Junior High/Middle School
Mathematics Classroom

The need for and importance of evaluation in the junior high/middle school mathematics classroom has increased tremendously in the past decade, a trend that is likely to continue in the future. Two things have happened which are probably responsible for the increased importance. First, classroom teachers are being held much more accountable for what happens in the classroom, and, second, there is a move among state legislatures to establish a minimum set of competencies in mathematics (among other subjects) for high school graduation.

To adequately meet these demands by the lay public, you must be able to accurately evaluate all aspects of your instructional program in mathematics. When you stop to think about it, doing a good job of evaluation is of great benefit both to your students and to you as a classroom teacher. You should be able to demonstrate your performance in the classroom, and the end result will probably be an instructional program in mathematics which is much more effective and efficient, a desirable situation for all concerned.

After reading and studying this chapter, you should be able to:

- Identify different methods for assessing student performance, including both informal and formal techniques.

- State guidelines for using commercial and teacher-made tests.
- Outline procedures and guidelines for testing with teacher-made tests, including planning, writing, scoring, giving, and returning the test.
- Describe a different system for assigning letter grades.
- Describe how your own performance may be assessed.

EVALUATION AS AN ONGOING PROCESS

Traditionally, evaluation in the junior high/middle school mathematics classroom was used only to obtain a mark for a student's performance in mathematics. But it is also appropriate to evaluate student attitude towards mathematics, your effectiveness as a mathematics teacher, and the effectiveness of your instructional program.

To be effective, evaluation must be continuous on an ongoing basis. It must be concerned with all aspects of your instructional program in mathematics, and be systematically applied so that its results provide a comprehensive view of what you have done in your mathematics classes.

Remember that evaluation must be based on a set of goals and objectives. The purpose of evaluation is to determine to what extent you have attained your stated goals and objectives.

Moreover, evaluation in this chapter will discuss assessing student performance (using commercial and teacher-made tests), preparing tests, testing different levels of knowledge, and assigning test grades and term grades. Although helpful hints on improving your evaluation techniques will be the focus of this chapter's discussions, you may find several suggestions that you disagree with. This is fine. Just remember to let the reality of your classroom shape your final evaluation of the hint!

ASSESSING STUDENT PERFORMANCE

In this section, both informal and formal techniques of evaluating student performance will be discussed. The focus will be on student learning in the cognitive domain, a topic introduced in Chapter 1.

Evaluating Informally

Most of the time you spend on evaluation in your classroom is devoted to the use of informal techniques. These techniques are informal because they are based, in most cases, on your subjective perceptions of student behavior.

There are four basic techniques you will find useful in evaluating student performance in your mathematics classroom.

1. *Be a keen and continuous observer.* So much can be learned about students and their performance in mathematics by observation. Watching students at work will often tell you where they are having difficulty and whether or not they need help. A puzzled or a frustrated look on a student's face will tell you a great deal. Sending students to the chalkboard to work through problems, an old-fashioned technique often neglected today, is an excellent way to observe how they do the problems.

2. *Use oral interviews.* Many times a student will say to you, "I don't understand..." By talking to the student on a one-to-one basis, you can often evaluate what is causing the student to have difficulty. Once you determine the cause, move to correct it. Sometimes a student will be able to correct the difficulty simply by verbalizing the process of thinking used. This technique is highly effective, but at the same time, you will probably not have sufficient time to use it in every situation.

3. *Inspect homework.* Valuable information can be gained about a student's performance by inspecting homework papers. Inspection of homework papers is very useful as a substitute for an oral interview as you assess a student's progress. This inspection can be done at your leisure and gives you an opportunity to study the thought process insofar as it is recorded on paper. Encourage your students to show their work so that you will have as complete a picture as possible of their thinking and progress.

4. *Make anecdotal records.* Don't trust your memory to recall all of the things you have noted by using the first three techniques. Make frequent notations about students and their progress so that you have a complete picture when you sit down to review a particular student's work. Be as thorough as possible in your record keeping. In reality, you will probably keep anecdotal records on "problem students."

Evaluating Formally

Along with informal techniques of evaluation, you will want to use formal techniques. There are several formal evaluation techniques you may find useful in evaluating your students:

Graded homework

Paper-and-pencil tests

Oral tests

Homework has the advantage that it can be collected and evaluated on a regular basis, and gives students an opportunity to make mistakes without a great fear of penalty. Homework also offers you the opportunity to reflect on the work and to diagnose errors that may occur, as discussed in Chapter 3. The disadvantage of homework is that the checking of it is very time consuming and that you cannot always be sure the paper you received represents actual student work.

The paper-and-pencil test, whether commercial or teacher-made, has traditionally been the most commonly used form of evaluation in the classroom. It gives the students an opportunity to perform under controlled circumstances. A disadvantage is that it may produce student anxiety, resulting in an inaccurate evaluation. Paper-and-pencil tests might be either short quizzes of only a few questions or a written exam covering the entire semester's work. Other advantages and disadvantages of paper-and-pencil tests will be discussed later in the chapter.

Oral tests are not used as much by classroom teachers as they might be, although they probably give you a better evaluation of a student's thinking as though processes are verbalized. Oral tests are time consuming to administer, however. When students consistently do poorly on written tests, an oral test is recommended.

USING COMMERCIAL AND TEACHER-MADE TESTS

As mentioned earlier, commercial and teacher-made paper-and-pencil tests are the most common formal evaluation technique used in the junior high/middle school mathematics classroom. In this section, guidelines for the use of each type of test and a detailed outline for preparing a teacher-made test are discussed.

Using Commercial Tests

Standardized achievement tests have become very popular in the last thirty or so years. This popularity is reflected by the fact that school corporations spend a great deal of time and money annually in the administration of such tests.

Standardized tests have the basic advantage that they are written by professional test writers who conduct validity and reliability studies to improve the tests. Test results are expressed as norms and grade equivalents, which make interpretation of results relatively easy for you as the classroom teacher. The tests are relatively easy to administer and score.

While there are some real advantages to using standardized tests, there are also some definite problems that you may or may not have ever thought about.

1. *The test may not cover the content of your curriculum*. The result is that your students may not perform at the level at which they are capable.

And, if a school administrator places a great deal of importance on test results, you may end up altering your curriculum to fit the test, a sad situation at best.

2. *The reading level of the test may not be appropriate for your students*. This problem is especially critical when you have students who are not good readers and when another form of assessment may be much more indicative of students' performances.

3. *Test items are usually of only a single variety*. Test scoring, especially by machine, dictates that the items be of the multiple-choice variety. This is not to say the use of multiple-choice items is bad but, because you see no student work, you really know very little about the student's thought process.

4. *The test is usually timed*. This fact is a great disadvantage for the student who works more slowly but is capable of answering the question. The result is that the basic criteria for success (high score) is speed and not knowledge of concepts and skills.

5. *Test results are often misused by teachers and administrators*. It is not the fault of the test that its results are misused, but the misuse can be a real problem. The misuse usually occurs in two ways:

   a) Decisions about placement of a student are often made on the basis of a single test score without regard for or review of other variables that might have affected the test score.

   b) There is the danger that a single test score may shape a teacher's expectation of student performance, a shaping that may be quite inaccurate and unfair to the student.

In spite of the above problems, standardized tests may be a way of life in your school corporation. As long as you recognize the problems along with advantages and keep the results in perspective, you will properly use the test and its results.

Another form of commercial tests are the *Chapter and Unit Tests* that often accompany the text you are using. These tests are usually prepared by the authors of the text and relate very specifically to the content of the text. You may want to use all or some of these items in your evaluation process. As long as the items used meet the purposes or objectives of your instruction, they will prove very useful. But, *don't* use the items just because they are available.

Using Teacher-made Tests

In most instances when you want to use a paper-and-pencil test in your classroom, you will probably design and construct your own test. By so doing, you are able to fit your evaluation process to the needs of your students so that assessment of performance will be as accurate as possible.

The teacher-made test has the distinct advantage that it is usually constructed by the person who has selected the objectives of instruction. Hence, there should be a high correlation between the objectives of instruction and the items on the test.

However, preparing a well designed and constructed test is not as easy as it sounds. It is time-consuming, and you must have the objectives of your instructional program clearly in mind. Guidelines for preparing your own is discussed in the next section.

TESTING WITH TEACHER-MADE TESTS

There are two important stages to preparing a teacher-made test. First, the test must be planned carefully and then written with good judgment. Let's examine some guidelines that when followed, will enable you to design and construct a test that will accomplish its purpose. To make the discussion more concrete, let's suppose you have taught the Pythagorean Theorem to the seventh grade class and you now want to design a cumulative test for a 50-minute class period.

Planning the Test

The first step in preparing a test is to plan its scope and format. To do so, you must have clearly in mind the kind of information you want to get from the test. Planning the test involves two basic steps:

1. Reviewing the objectives of instructions—what skills at what levels.

2. Determining the layout of the test—kinds of questions, number of questions, and scoring.

The first basic step is knowing what skills you want to test for and at what level—knowledge, understanding, or problem solving.

Testing for knowledge of the Pythagorean Theorem involves the testing of facts and ideas that can be recalled by the student. This level is the easiest one to evaluate; if students are to learn a process or skill, you simply give them an example for them to complete.

Some examples of knowledge-level test items on the Pythagorean Theorem follow:

1. Find c if $c = \sqrt{25 + 16}$
2. Find c if $c = \sqrt{5^2 + 3^2}$
3. State the Pythagorean Theorem.
4. What is the longest side of a right triangle called?

At the second level, the student is asked to apply or use knowledge in order to demonstrate understanding. Questions are posed that do not have memorized answers.

Some examples of items that test understanding of the Pythagorean Theorem follow:

1. The three sides of a right triangle total 24 cm. One of the legs is 6 cm long and the hypotenuse is 10 cm. What is the length of the other leg?

2. If two sides of a right triangle are 4 cm each, what is the length in centimeters of the third side?

The problem-solving level is the highest level and is, therefore, the most difficult to evaluate. At this level, students are asked to use knowledge and understanding in order to solve problems. Working problems, writing proofs, and discussing ideas are the most common forms of items used to evaluate problem solving.

Some test items that evaluate problem-solving skills on the Pythagorean Theorem follow:

1. In a right triangle, if you double the length of the two legs, do you double the length of the hypotenuse? Why or why not?

2. Does $\sqrt{a^2+b^2}=\sqrt{a^2}+\sqrt{b^2}$? Why or why not?

3. If the hypotenuse of a right triangle is 5 cm, what can you conclude about the lengths of the other two sides?

In reality, the skills and levels should be decided *before* the unit is taught. These objectives are modified, however, as you teach the material. Returning to the example, let's suppose that from the original objectives and analysis of your teaching, you decide to test for the following skills:

1. Identify hypotenuse, leg, square, square root.

2. Explain the Pythagorean Theorem in words, in symbols, and in a geometric diagram.

3. Given two legs of a right triangle, compute the length of the third side. Leave the answer under the square root sign unless it is a perfect square.

4. Estimate to the nearest positive whole number the square root of a given number.

In determining objectives, observe the following guidelines:

1. Emphasize vocabulary (hypotenuse).

2. Convey the meaning of symbolism ($\sqrt{\quad}$).

3. Isolate skills (computing $c = \sqrt{5^2 + 4^2}$ is a different skill from computing $a = \sqrt{41}$ correct to two decimal places).

4. Identify prerequisites (a student cannot deal successfully with the Pythagorean Theorem without understanding square root and the order of operations in $\sqrt{a^2 + b^2}$).

5. Work on a few skills thoroughly (Rome wasn't built in a day).

The best rule of thumb is to think as a "student" instead of a teacher when selecting objectives.

The second step in test-making is determining the layout of the test. The layout involves:

1. kinds of test questions—true-false, multiple choice, fill in the blank, matching, essay

2. number of questions

3. arrangement of test items

Let's continue the test problem by looking at a sample test designed to meet the previously stated objectives (see Figure 4-1).

The test is divided into five sections which total 100 points, not including extra credit. A summary of the test layout follows:

Section	Type	Level	Skill
I	Short-answer	Knowledge	Vocabulary, symbolism, square root, estimate
II	Short-answer	Knowledge/ Understanding	Compute third side, estimate
III	True-false	Understanding	Symbolism of the Pythagorean Theorem
IV	Essay	Knowledge/ Understanding	State the Pythagorean Theorem
V	Multiple Choice	Problem solving	Compute the hypotenuse

Notice that each section of the test has a similar test-type, but varies in level and/or skills. Sections II and III are dependent on understanding a diagram of a right triangle. In section II, the last two questions involve computing with fractions and decimals, a lot harder than using whole numbers. Even though 75 points cover computation, there is enough challenge on the test to keep all students thinking, yet not fail all the class. The extra-credit problem also offers challenge. Whether you like the sample test or not, just remember that it is an example that can be improved upon.

FIGURE 4–1. SAMPLE TEST

TEST ON PYTHAGOREAN THEOREM

Name_____

Date_____

Period_____

Directions: Place all answers on the test. Scratch work can be done anywhere on the front or back of the test. When you finish, place your test in the Test Box at the back of the room and then look at the instructions on the chalkboard.

(25 points)   I.   1. The longest side of a right triangle is called a (an) _____.

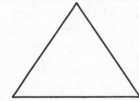

2. Find c if $c = \sqrt{2+7}$_____.

3. Estimate c to the nearest whole number if $c = \sqrt{2^2 + 7^2}$_____.

4. Find/estimate c if $c = \sqrt{144}$_____.

5. Find/estimate c if $c = \sqrt{1,000}$_____.

(50 points)   II.   Fill in the chart. Leave your answer under the square root sign unless it is a perfect square.

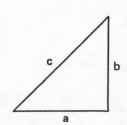

a	b	c	
3 cm	4 cm		cm
13 cm	12 in		in
5 cm	5 cm		cm
1/2 in	1/3 in		in
.6 cm	.4 cm		cm

FIGURE 4-1, Cont'd.

(10 points) III. Given the triangle below, which of the following equations are true or false. Circle your answer.

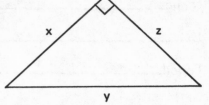

T   F   1. $x^2 + y^2 = 2^2$

T   F   2. $y^2 + x^2 = z^2$

T   F   3. $x^2 + z^2 = y^2$

T   F   4. $x + y = z$

T   F   5. $x < y$

(10 points) IV. State the Pythagorean Theorem in your own words.

_____

_____

_____

_____

(5 points) V. If 2 cm is added to each leg of a right triangle, then the length of the third side of the triangle: (circle your answer)

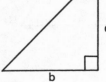

  a. Will be 2 cm longer

  b. Will be 4 cm longer

  c. Will equal $\sqrt{(b + 2)^2 + (c + 2)^2}$

  d. Will equal $\sqrt{b^2 + c^2 + 2}$

  e. Can't be predicted from the given information

Extra Credit.   Find c if:

$$c = \sqrt{(\sqrt{248})^2 + \sqrt{(92)^2}}$$ $c =$ _____

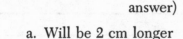

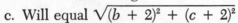

Predict your score out of 100 points: _____

Your comments about the test: _____

_____

Writing the Test

In writing any test, remember the importance of neatness, clarity, and accuracy. For example, is 3.9 really 3 and .9 or 3 times 9? Don't split items between pages if at all possible. If you are duplicating the test, remember to plan enough time to run off the copies. Save time by cutting and pasting old test questions together, and using graph paper for charts and geometric diagrams. If timing a test, a good rule of thumb to follow is: if you, the teacher, can work the test in five minutes, give the students eight to ten times that amount. Try it and see!

In general, follow these guidelines when writing tests:

1. Give clear, concise, and simple directions.
2. Group different types of items together.
3. Arrange test items from easiest to most difficult.
4. Indicate items' weight or point value relative to the entire test (number of points, percentage, etc.). For example, (10 points). Calculate the formula for the area of a trapezoid.
5. Avoid using test items that utilize answers from other items on the test.
6. Develop test items in a format similar to the way material was presented during instruction.
7. Be sure test items reflect main ideas rather then trivial details.
8. Avoid unnecessary information in a test item.
9. Allot time so that slower students are able to complete the test.
10. Avoid patterns of correct responses to item; students may use the patterns to answer questions.
11. Be sure that the test is legible.
12. Have all drawings neat and clearly labeled.
13. Prepare a test key *prior* to the time of testing.
14. Number items consecutively from first to last.
15. Avoid having part of a test item on one page and part on another.
16. Leave plenty of work space near test items so that students can show their work.
17. Be sure to designate a place for answers on the test or provide a separate answer sheet.

Scoring the Test

The scoring of the Pythagorean Theorem test is somewhat straightforward on a 100-point basis. Partial credit could be given on the essay question in part IV. Never deduct points on a test if a student tries the extra credit and fails. This discourages intelligent guessing and trying. It is a teacher decision on how many full points and partial points are to be given. When marking a test, place marks over the incorrect answer, as in the following example:

Poor Marking   Correct Marking

$$x = \sqrt{2 + 7} = \sqrt{8} \qquad c = \sqrt{2 + 7} = \sqrt{8}$$

This discourages students from attempting to change answers after tests have been returned and claiming that "you made a careless error." Record the test score on the *last* page of the test. This allows you to let a student help distribute papers without revealing grades. (An alternative method is to record the score on the inside of the first page and fold the entire test with the student's name on the outside.)

Giving and Returning the Test

Testing cannot be complete without commenting on the directions and comments before and after a test. Before giving a test, do the following:

1. Announce the test a *week* ahead of time. Don't depend solely on oral instructions. Write it on the chalkboard.
2. Tell the students what to study, what "kinds" of questions will be asked, and the points given.

On the sample test, after giving the four skill areas, you might announce the following:

Section	Points	Style
I	25	Fill in the blank
II	50	Compute-Fill in a table
III	10	True-False
IV	10	Essay
V	5	Multiple Choice
Extra Credit	?	?

When *giving* a test:

1. Make starting comments brief.
2. Let students think, so *keep quiet*.
3. Answer questions either by having students raise their hands or by having *one* student at a time come to you.
4. Be careful about explaining questions during a test. Explain problems in understanding directions, but don't give away information.
5. Stand or sit in the *back* of a room when administering a test.
6. Remember that tests make students very tense, so a kind glance, smile, or word can be helpful.

After the test has been taken, do the following:

1. Grade the papers as soon as possible.
2. Record the scores in your record book.
3. Try not to look at the student's name when grading.
4. Save time by grading each page of the test as a sequence—all page ones, then all page twos, etc.
5. Keep track of the items most frequently missed and the items everyone got right.
6. Analyze student errors and "teacher test-construction" errors.
7. Place several copies of the test and answer key in a file for make-up students or for use next year.

When you are *returning* test papers to students, try the following *before* the students see their papers.

1. Summarize and report the students' results. For example, write the distribution of grades on the chalkboard.

101		77	
100	A+	76	
98		75	C
97	A	74	
95		73	
90		70	D+
89	B	69	
87		68	D
80		Below 65 - Three	
79	C		
77			

Students should know where they stand relative to the class. Students who failed or made low grades can just be lumped together and reported as three below 65. *Never* report one below a certain score.

2. Work the most frequently missed problem(s) on the chalkboard. Leave the problem(s) on the board so students can check their work when they see their papers.

3. Write all answers on the chalkboard. (An alternative is to write the answers on a copy of the test and run off copies.)

4. Comment on strengths and weaknesses of the test.

Now return the papers to the students. Try to answer their questions, but don't let students consume your time with picayune questions. Instead of wasting time answering or arguing individual questions, ask students to return their papers with a notation for you to recheck something on their papers. Try to avoid class confrontations about test scoring, and solve any conflicts in small or one-to-one sessions. If you change your mind about "interpreting" a student response, it is wiser to make the grade change in private. If you just made a flat mistake, added incorrectly, or marked a right response as wrong, simply admit it to the student and thank him or her for bringing it to your attention. If a student brings you a paper where a test answer that is wrong is marked as right, don't penalize the student for being honest. Give the student the points and thank him or her for being honest.

Special comments are needed concerning the question of "curving or dropping" grades. Suppose you decide that a certain question on a test was unfair to all students. If the point count is 1 to 5 points, just tell the students that you think the question was your fault and concede to all the points. If the problem question involves a sizeable point spread (10 to 25), use a different procedure. Instead of "giving the students" the 25 points or throwing out the test, admit to the students that a certain question didn't give them the best opportunity to earn points and offer an extra 10-to-25 point problem in a few days or on the next test. In this way, you earn the reputation of holding your own standards but being fair. (If you are completely responsible for a bad test that's illegible, ambiguous, whatever, admit it, don't count the score, and do better!)

ASSIGNING LETTER GRADES

One of the most difficult problems you face in your evaluation is the assignment of grades. Grades are usually assigned as letters (A, B, C, D, or

F) and are intended to reflect a student's level of achievement. Plusses and minuses are sometimes used as a refinement of the grading scale.

Grades are used to make very important decisions about students. Movement to the next grade level, high school graduation, college entrance, college graduation, and job application decisions all use grades as a primary (sometimes sole) basis for a positive or negative decision.

So much emphasis has been placed on getting good grades in our society that students often resort to cheating to achieve that end. Other students have suffered severe emotional disturbances because of grades. At the same time, parents, teachers, and school administrators—and, indeed, society itself—have used fear of poor grades as a means of motivation for students to achieve.

Whether you like it or not, it does not appear that the emphasis on grades is going to decrease in importance; if anything, the emphasis will probably increase as competition for desired goals in life becomes keener. Hence, whatever system of grading you decide to use, you must feel comfortable with it and be able to defend it to students, parents and administrators. Your system must be communicated to all concerned and must be applied consistently and fairly.

In this section, alternative grading systems will be discussed and some do's and don'ts will be given to help you master the system you choose.

Deciding on a System

As a teacher you will have to decide on a system to determine grades. Even if your system uses a predetermined point or letter grade procedure, you as a teacher still decide "how hard it is to earn that 95 or A." Be sure to check with your principal or superintendent about all policies on assigning grades—Are + and − used? Are 6/9 weeks exams required?

Several systems for assigning grades are shown in Table 4-1:

TABLE 4-1

System I	System II	System III		System IV	
90–100 = A	94–100 = A	top	10% = A	270–300 points	= A
80– 89 = B	88– 93 = B	next	20% = B	240–269 points	= B
70– 79 = C	80– 87 = C	middle	40% = C	210–239 points	= C
60– 69 = C	70– 79 = D	next	20% = D	180–211 points	= D
		low	10% = F	Below 180 points	= F

Systems I and II are based on a percentage of 100 points or an average of 100 point tests. System IV is similar, except it is based on total points that could be converted to a percentage score identical to System I. System II is based on a fixed percentage receiving a certain grade regardless of scores. System III (normal distribution) is not recommended for middle school/junior high students.

Regardless of which system you use, you still must decide how to arrive at the B or 250 points, then convey this to the students at the start of the class. Some possible suggestions are given in Table 4–2 for determining a nine-week letter grade (adjustments should be made for grading over a six-week term). For simplicity, total points are reported, and then method I used for determining letter grades.

TABLE 4-2

Method I	
3 One-hour Tests	300 points
1 Cumulative Exam	100 points
Short quizzes—announced	50 points
Short quizzes—unannounced	50 points
	500 points

Method II	
Homework	100 points
2 One-hour Tests	200 points
Project	100 points
1 Cumulative Test	200 points
	600 points

Method III	
3 One-hour Tests	300 points
1 Cumulative Test	100 points
Homework	50 points
Questions in class/Attitude	50 points
	500 points

All three methods have advantages and disadvantages. Some general decisions about your scheme include:

1. How many tests? Short? Long? Announced? Unannounced?

2. Does homework count? Doing it or doing it correctly?

3. Will projects/reports be included?

4. Will evaluation be made on attitude, participation, and asking relevant questions?

There are no perfect answers to these questions. You must use trial and error and constant analysis to come up with a system that works best for you.

There are, however, some definite suggestions for grading systems. If you use homework, be sure to return papers to students even with only a check mark. Beware of cheating and copying of homework papers. If you decide to give a cumulative test, don't make this big test the last one of the six weeks. It sounds crazy, but your cumulative test should be given about three-quarters of the way through, and then the last test should cover the major mistakes diagnosed from the cumulative test. By doing this, students will avoid having all cumulative tests at the same time. (Remember students do have other classes!) A time schedule might be set up as the one in Table 4–3.

TABLE 4-3

Week	Evaluation
1	No test
2	Short daily quizzes (100 points)
3	One-hour test (100 points)
4	Cumulative test on Friday (200 points)
5	No test
6	One-hour test on Tuesday (100 points)

Another advantage of having cumulative exams earlier is you are left with more time to grade papers, to confer with students, and to avoid the last-minute computational rush.

Giving Short Quizzes

The importance of quick and frequent feedback cannot be over-emphasized. Here is a suggestion for checking daily on what students know, without overdoing the paperwork. Have students fold a piece of notebook paper on the vertical and write their names on each half; front and back. Give the students several short-answer questions on Monday for Quiz 1; collect the papers and grade. *Return* the same paper to the students, and repeat the same process. After four short quizzes, take a total score (or average) and *record* that one grade in your record book. You can vary your daily quizzes by:

1. writing problems on the chalkboard
2. writing problems on the overhead projector
3. doing problems from the textbook
4. giving an oral quiz

Determining Semester Grades

Periodically, you are asked to assign a letter grade to reflect a student's achievement. This request may occur at six weeks, nine weeks, end of semester, or some other interval.

There seems to be a tendency among teachers to simply average the letter grades and assign that grade to the student. Such a process may be relatively easy to use, but it can be quite unfair to the student because it may give a less-than-accurate assessment. For example, the average of two grades of C and a grade of A is a grade of B. But suppose that the C grades were both very close to a B grade and that the A grade was a solid one. This may mean that the student should have had a grade of B or even B+ assigned.

The point is that, on the surface, letter grades should not be considered literally. The letter grades should be closely examined so that the situation described above does not occur.

You might use a total-point system to determine six-week, nine-week, and semester grades. A student's total points for the term would be calculated and a letter grade assigned by a percentage of the total points.

When you examine the ordered point totals and find the "breaks," you may want to slightly adjust your standards. If you do adjust your standards, always adjust downward, never upward. That is, if a B is 92%–85%, then 83% could be a B, but 93% is always an A. Be sure you tell your students at the beginning of the term what your point total standards will be before assigning letter grades. Doing so will help prevent misunderstandings and possibly bad feelings about the assigned letter grade.

ASSESSING YOUR PERFORMANCE

An important part of the evaluation process is the assessment of your performance as a classroom teacher. How well did you do?

There are several areas with which you need to be concerned in assessing your performance. Figure 4–2 is a checklist you may find useful as you assess your performance.

FIGURE 4-2

Checklist for Assessing Teacher Performance

Yes	No*	
_____	_____	1. Were the goals and objectives of instruction appropriate for the students?
_____	_____	2. Did I tell the students what I expected?
_____	_____	3. Did I explain the grading system before testing?
_____	_____	4. Did I return papers within two days of testing?
_____	_____	5. Was I consistent and fair in my treatment of each student?

*For each question you checked "no," what would you do differently next time?

If you want to get an even better picture of your performance, give a short questionnaire to your students asking about your performance and asking for suggestions for improvements. As you end a semester or term, gather the ideas to improve your next year's grading system.

QUICK REVIEW

1. Describe advantages and disadvantages of using informal evaluation techniques in your classroom. Which techniques would you use? Why?

2. What are the advantages and disadvantages of using commercially prepared tests?

3. What are the advantages and disadvantages of using teacher-made tests?

4. What are the steps in preparing a teacher-made test?

5. Several systems for assigning letter grades were discussed in this chapter. Which system do you prefer? Why? Are there alternative systems you would use? If so, describe them and give a rationale for their use.

6. One way for assessing your performance as a teacher was discussed in the chapter. In what other ways might you evaluate your performance?

7. Students of the junior high/middle school age are quite capable of assessing your performance as a teacher. What are the advantages and disadvantages of student evaluations? Outline a procedure you would use for obtaining student evaluation of your performance.

8. Write a sample test item for each of these objectives.

    a. The student can express a given percent as a fraction in simplest form.
    b. The student can find the quotient of two whole numbers to the nearest tenth.
    c. The student can compute the product of any two integers.

9. Should a student be graded on effort, work quality, or a combination of these two things?

10. What are the advantages and disadvantages of using each of the following with your junior high/middle school students?

    a. open-book tests
    b. take-home tests
    c. small groups working together on a test where each group member gets the same grade
    d. semester tests
    e. test covering the entire year

11. You have caught a student cheating on a test. What would you do? Before you answer too hastily, check with your building principal to see what, if any, school policies are written for this situation.

5

The Atypical Learner

One of your major problems as a junior high/middle school mathematics teacher is how to work with the atypical learner, with atypical meaning learners who are reluctant, slow, gifted, learning disabled, mainstreamed, or physically handicapped. Working with these students is challenging yet rewarding.

After reading and studying this chapter, you should be able to:

- Identify procedures and guidelines for working with reluctant, slow, gifted and talented, and special learners in your classroom.

- Recognize characteristics and identifying behaviors of reluctant, slow, gifted and talented, and special learners.

- Describe how to keep a balance in your instructional program between the atypical learners and the other learners.

WORKING WITH RELUCTANT LEARNERS

The reluctant learner is probably more numerous than any of the other types of atypical learners. These students have had a history of frustration with mathematics, usually caused by a lack of success. They are now at a point where they see little use in trying to do the work. In some instances, they may have built a real and severe math anxiety that will keep them from performing well.

These students need your patience and understanding. The future of their mathematics education is still salvageable, but may not be for long unless you can make some headway with the students.

Here are general guidelines for working with the reluctant learner.

1. *Provide as much opportunity for success as possible*. Nothing will do more for these students than a little success. They have not enjoyed success in the past, so their barrier against learning mathematics needs to be broken. The quicker you can break down this barrier, the more likely you will be able to help them.

2. *Determine the learner's interest(s) and use activities that relate to that interest*. One good way to arouse a desire to study mathematics in a reluctant learner is to use mathematical activities that relate to the student's interest. Mathematics is everywhere and in everything, so look for the math in his or her interests.

3. *Use diagnostic techniques to determine what the student can and cannot do*. Diagnostic techniques were discussed in some detail in Chapter 4. They are especially useful here since many times a teacher begins work with a reluctant learner at a level that is inappropriate for the student's mathematical ability. The result is continued and deepened frustration.

4. *Try to make the learning of mathematics enjoyable for the student*. Successful experiences and the use of activities related to the student's interests are a good start toward making the learning of mathematics enjoyable.

5. *Tell the student what you expect to be learned*. The student should be aware of what is to be learned. Be sure that the goal or objective is appropriate for that student's ability level.

6. *Give constant and immediate feedback to the student and emphasize progress made*. Most reluctant learners are afraid or unwilling to try because they have had a long history of failure. Helping them gain confidence in their ability to do math will do more than anything else to insure progress.

WORKING WITH SLOW LEARNERS

The slow learner in your junior/middle school mathematics classroom is not able to learn mathematical concepts and skills at the same rate as other students. These students often do not have an aptitude for mathematics, so they find it very difficult to learn. They may also be reluctant to learn, a very understandable situation. Often, however, they do have a good attitude about learning math but are just not able to do it at the normal pace of your program.

In the previous section, several things were mentioned that would be helpful to a reluctant learner. All of these points also apply to the slow learner. Here are additional suggestions.

1. *Use concrete materials*. The importance of using concrete materials cannot be overemphasized. These materials will give students a chance to put the concept or skill to be learned into an understandable frame of reference.

2. *Break instruction into short steps*. A slow learner is easily overwhelmed by most instructional sequences. Since the student learns at a slower rate, break instruction into short steps to help decrease the chance of student frustration.

3. *Use different instructional approaches*. Many times, slow learners are not able to grasp the original instructional approach either because it is "too much too fast" or it does not mesh with their frame of reference. Be ready to adapt your instructional approach to meet the needs of each slow learner.

4. *Adjust your expectations of student performance*. Teacher expectations of student performance have a very powerful influence on the actual performance itself. Keep your level of expectation appropriate for the slow learner; poor motivation or frustration will result from teacher expectations that are either too low or too high.

WORKING WITH GIFTED AND TALENTED LEARNERS

You may have an opportunity to work with gifted and talented learners in your classroom. If the opportunity presents itself, don't be caught short!

It will be quite apparent when these students are in your classroom. A gifted student has superior ability to deal with facts, ideas and relationships. A talented student shows aptitude in specific areas such as mathematics or science. There is usually a great deal of overlapping between gifted and talented students.

How can you identify the mathematically gifted and talented student in your classroom? There are specific tests of intelligence, creativity, and achievement that may be used for this purpose. However, you can identify these students yourself by using a checklist. When you suspect that a student meets all or most all of the criteria listed in Figure 5-1, you should make provisions in your instructional program to help meet his or her needs.

FIGURE 5-1

Checklist for Identifying
Mathematically Gifted and Talented Students
in the Junior High/Middle School

Student Name _____ Date_____

Teacher_____ Grade_____

The student has:

_____ 1. an I.Q. of 115 or higher.

_____ 2. standardized test scores one or more years above grade level
in the areas of mathematical understanding, problem solving,
and computation.

_____ 3. standardized test scores two or more years above grade level
in the areas of mathematical understanding, problem solving
and computation.

_____ 4. had consistently above-average school marks in previous
years.

_____ 5. shown interest in mathematics and/or careers in which mathematics plays an integral role.

_____ 6. a long attention span with mathematically-related tasks.

_____ 7. facility in understanding, interpreting and completing compli-
cated directions for mathematically-related tasks.

_____ 8. good memory and recall powers.

_____ 9. eagerness to attack mathematically-related tasks.

_____ 10. intellectual curiosity, especially with cause-and-effect
relationships.

Here are some ideas for working with gifted and talented learners in
your classroom.

1. *Be sensitive to their possible presence*. Be aware that you may have
gifted and talented learners in your class. Posing open-ended and thought-
provoking questions to your class will help you identify these students.

2. *Gather challenging supplementary instructional materials*. Since
you never know when you may encounter gifted and talented learners,

build a set of resource materials to use in your classroom. These materials should be horizontal in nature to your instructional program and give the students a chance to explore and discover mathematical relationships for themselves. Laboratory-type activities are good things to have on hand.

3. *Show acceptance of gifted and talented students in your classroom.* Treat these students like other students in your classroom. Give them learning tasks that are appropriate to their ability levels.

It is often debated by educators whether or not the gifted and talented learner should simply be given more advanced materials, such as the textbook for the next grade level, for independent study. The major problem (theoretically it shouldn't be, but in reality it is) in using the vertical advancement is that future mathematical classrooms have difficulty dealing with a student who is far ahead of the curriculum in that classroom.

There is a real advantage in having gifted and talented learners stay with their peers as much as possible. They can work on other projects and materials, and the socialization process continues to develop. Many times, gifted and talented learners are found to be socially immature; a horizontal enrichment program in your classroom may help reduce the probability of immaturity. Many times gifted students are just neglected.

It is easy to fall into the trap of assuming that a student in your classroom who is gifted and talented has all of the necessary prerequisite skills and concepts to deal with mathematical ideas in your curriculum. Don't make this assumption; check it out!

WORKING WITH SPECIAL LEARNERS

There continues—and will continue—to be demands from society for schools to provide better quality instructional programs for students with special learning problems. Your school corporation may, in some cases, have special classes and teachers to work with these students. However, there is continuous effort to mainstream these students back into the regular classroom where possible, so it is quite likely that you will encounter such students in your junior high/middle school mathematics classroom.

Characteristics of Special Learners

By special learners is meant those students who are learning disabled, educable mentally retarded, emotionally disturbed, or physically handicapped. Figure 5-2 offers a description of the special terms used and some identifying behavioral characteristics. If you have a student in your class who you suspect has special learning difficulties, consult with your school counselor or principal to verify your thinking. Never label a student as "special" unless you have verification from other *reliable* sources!

FIGURE 5–2

	Definition of Term	Identifying Behavioral Characteristics
Learning Disabled	Student exhibits disorder in one or more of the basic psychological processes involved in understanding or in using spoken or written language.	Perceptual motor impairments; general orientation defects; disorders of attention, memory, thinking, speech, or hearing; specific learning disabilities in reading, math, writing, spelling.
Educable Mentally Retarded	Student has difficulty in school because he or she develops intellectually at only about one-half to three-quarters the rate of average students.	Social/emotional adjustment problems; matures slowly; poor social judgments; immature behavior; delay in visual perception and eye-hand coordination development.
Emotionally Disturbed	Student has behaviors that deviate from age-appropriate behavior, are unacceptable to society, and significantly interfere with student's growth/development and/or with lives of others.	Inability to learn which cannot be explained by other factors; inability to build or maintain satisfactory interpersonal relationships; inappropriate behavior under normal conditions; general mood of unhappiness or depression; tendency to develop physical symptoms (speech pains, fears).
Physically Handicapped	*Speech:* speech disorders are problems in the motor act of speaking, causing speech to be unintelligible	*Speech:* unintelligible speech or too fast, poor articulation; voice too high. or too low, too loud or too

FIGURE 5–2 (Cont'd.)

	Definition of Term	Identifying Behavioral Characteristics
Physically Handicapped	*Hearing:* defect in one or more parts of the ear, preventing student from hearing *Visual:* physical loss of useful vision *Physical Disability:* nervous system, congenital malformations, crippling from disease, respiratory problems.	soft, unpleasant; stuttering; shortness of breath *Hearing:* cupping hands or favoring bad ear; inattentiveness/confusion; will not participate or do school work; discipline problem. *Visual:* tilting head; squinting; rubbing eyes; ignoring and avoiding visual stimuli; awkward eye-hand coordination; complaining about not being able to see; prefers tasks that require close vision.

The learning disabled student is probably the one you are most likely to encounter in your classroom. To help you understand more about learning disabilities, below are the names and descriptions of specific learning disabilities.

1. *Dyslexia* is a disorder in students who, despite conventional classroom experience, fail to attain the language skills of reading, writing, and spelling commensurate with their intellectual abilities.

2. *Agraphia* is an inability or extreme difficulty with the formation of letters, numerals, and forms in handwriting.

3. *Aphasia* refers to a defect or loss in language, loss of expression in speech or writing, or of comprehension of spoken or written language.

4. *Dyscalculia* refers to a disorder in the ability to do or to learn mathematics. A dyscalculic youngster will show a lower than average mathematical age in relation to his or her normal mental age. Dyscalculia is characterized by severe retardation in arithmetic achievement. Dyscalculic students often display perceptual impairments. (Note: These impairments are distinct from sensory deficits in vision and hearing.)

    a. *Verbal dyscalculia* refers to the inability to identify the cardinality of sets of objects presented, or to recognize the value of written numbers, despite success in reading and writing dictated numbers.

b. *Practognostic dyscalculia* is a disturbance in the ability to manipulate real or symbolic objects for comparison of size or order.

c. *Lexical dyscalculia* is an inability to read mathematical symbols.

d. *Graphical dyscalculia* describes the inability to manipulate mathematical symbols in writing.

e. *Ideognostical dyscalculia* refers to an inability to understand mathematical ideas and relations in performing mental calculation.

f. *Operation dyscalculia* is the inability to carry out mathematical operations.

5. *Acalculia* (or "number blindness") is the failure to have acquired *basic* arithmetic concepts and skills in comparison to relative success in other academic and performance areas. Thus, acalculia is a more severe deficit than dyscalculia.

Instructional Procedures

As you plan your instructional program, there are some general points you need to keep in mind as you work with your special learners. These are listed in Figure 5-3.

FIGURE 5–3

Type of Special Learner	Educational Treatment Models/Procedures
Learning Disabled	No one procedure can be applied to all groups. Train in area of disability; continually assess to determine academic behaviors; and then respond to individual student.
Educable Mentally Retarded	Focus curriculum on practical goals to assist student in dealing with life situations in concrete terms. Use small quantities of instruction, a variety of approaches, and frequent review and reinforcement. Emphasize stronger learning modality, and provide frequent feedback to reassure and encourage.

FIGURE 5–3 (Cont'd.)

Type of Special Learner	Educational Treatment Models/Procedures
Emotionally Disturbed	**Understand and relate to student's needs. Use a consistent pattern of learning. Avoid rigidity, and behave flexibly toward feelings without oversensitivity. Never cause student to feel "cornered."**
Physically Handicapped	**Consult a specialist to create an accepting atmosphere among "normal" students. Look at total individual, not just the handicap. Don't pamper.**

As you plan your instructional program to meet the needs of your special students, make use of lots of activities. Here are general suggestions for small group or individual activities for special learners. Many of these suggestions are also appropriate for your regular students.

Preparing Activities:

1. Identify skills (concepts) as simply and precisely as possible.
2. Divide each skill activity into small steps.
3. Order the activities in planned sequence.
4. Use concrete objects (knives and forks, calendars, money, etc.).
5. Select curriculum materials that are large, easy to handle, and "uncluttered" in appearance.
6. Decide which objects (materials) are to be used (gloves, bottle caps, chalkboard, etc.) before class starts.
7. Have more materials and plans than you think you will need.
8. Plan activities for learning experiences, not just for "fun and games."
9. Prepare in advance a friendly hello and introduction.
10. Form alternative plans to be used if other activities fail.

Introducing activities:

1. Start the lesson with names, a smile, and "get acquainted" comments.
2. Don't over verbalize. Get the student to talk to you; then listen.
3. Work in areas free from distraction. (In crowded situations, have the student's back to the center of the room.)

4. Keep additional curriculum materials out of sight (under the table) until needed.

5. Stay at eye level with the student.

6. Get the student involved both verbally and physically.

Implementing activities:

1. Don't be afraid to use discipline.

2. Use short, simple sentences.

3. Use simple vocabulary words.

4. Be positive in your comments.

5. Be patient. Give the student time to use the materials and time to answer questions.

6. Don't let the student's attention wander.

7. Integrate content (language arts, reading, art, etc.).

8. Be well-planned and structured, yet flexible and adjustable.

9. Be careful in writing numerals.

Changing activities:

1. Make one activity blend to the other, if possible.

2. Change activities often.

3. Leave an activity *before* it becomes boring.

4. Each activity should have an introduction, development, and conclusion.

Ending activities:

1. Praise good behavior and responses.

2. Summarize whenever possible.

3. Let the student help in returning materials and straightening the work area.

4. Tell the student when you will be working with him or her again.

Evaluating activities:

1. Identify each activity as poor, satisfactory, or good (relative to the skill and the student).

2. Identify overall strengths.

3. Identify overall weaknesses.

4. Hypothesize learning characteristics of the student.

5. Briefly review the sequence of activities after teaching.

6. Answer this question: What should I have done if I had known what I know now?

KEEPING A BALANCE

Throughout this chapter, some of the different types of atypical learners and their learning characteristics have been discussed. You may be faced with all or some of these atypical learners in your classroom. Certainly, their needs are important. But, don't exclude the other students in the class because they also have important needs, too.

Here are some guidelines to help you keep a proper balance in your mathematics instruction program between the atypical learners and the other learners in your classroom.

1. Don't play favorites—accept all learners.

2. Don't let a small group of learners control the classroom.

3. Present lessons using different modalities (audio, visual, kinesthetic).

4. Make appropriate accommodations but not exceptions for atypical learners.

Remember that *all* of the students in your classroom are important and that you cannot and should not neglect any of them. A little common sense goes a long way.

QUICK REVIEW

1. Describe the characteristics and identifying behaviors of each of the following types of atypical learners:

   a. reluctant
   b. slow
   c. gifted and talented
   d. learning disabled
   e. educable mentally retarded
   f. emotionally disturbed
   g. physically handicapped

2. Describe appropriate instructional procedures for working with each of the seven types of atypical learners described above. Which of these procedures will also work for the other students in your classroom?

3. How do you plan to keep a balance in your instructional program between the atypical learners and the other learners in your classroom?

4. Discuss your experiences with atypical learners with fellow teachers who have had experiences with atypical learners. What would you have done in their situations? What would you have done differently (if anything) in your own situations if they were to occur again?

5. What personnel in your school system are specifically trained to work with the atypical learner? Find out who they are and consult with them on good instructional procedures for the atypical learners.

6

Computational Skills in the Junior High/ Middle School Mathematics Classroom

You are no doubt well aware of the fact that only a disproportionately small number of students ever master basic computational skills by the time they graduate from high school. This situation seems to exist despite our best efforts. It probably would not be troublesome except that so much time is spent on the development of basic computational skills in the classroom; our work and effort should show better results.

When one stops to think about it, the junior high/middle school mathematics classroom is probably the last chance many students will have to master computational skills. Little time will be spent on skill-building in high school and teachers there often do not have interest in building skills.

In the following, some ideas and suggestions are offered that you can use in helping your students develop the following computational skill areas: (1) operations with whole numbers, (2) operations with fractions, (3) operations with decimals, (4) percent, (5) operations with integers, and (6) exponents and roots.

After reading and studying this chapter, you should be able to:

- Describe the importance of checking for meaning and other prerequisites in developing algorithms.
- List general guidelines for developing algorithms.
- Identify techniques for helping students improve computational skills with whole numbers, fractions, decimals, percent, integers, and exponents and roots.
- Identify problem areas encountered by students in computation and suggest possible corrective techniques.

Many of the points made in Chapter 4 will be reinforced in this chapter as corrective techniques are examined.

CHECKING FOR MEANING AND OTHER PREREQUISITES

When students come to your classroom, there will be a great deal of variation in their level of understanding and ability with respect to the computational skills. Your problem is to sort out the various levels and help each student progress toward the mastery of each skill.

Students must have an understanding of the numbers and operations associated with computational skills. Most students will have a pretty good sense of whole numbers and the operations of addition and subtraction when they come to you. However, when it comes to the meaning of fractions and the operation of multiplication and division of whole numbers, for example, they are much less sure of themselves.

As a result, you will need to spend considerable time making sure that students have an understanding of what they are doing. You may find it very useful to use concrete materials and examples from everyday life to help students develop meaning for the symbols with which they are working. The extra time that you spend in developing meaning will pay off handsomely in terms of student retention of concepts and processes.

In addition to meaning of numbers and operations, you need to be concerned with other prerequisite skills needed for a given skill. For example, it doesn't make much sense to work with a student on addition of fractions with unlike denominators if the student cannot work successfully with equivalent fractions.

As suggested in Chapter 4, you will need to use some sort of informal or formal preassessment of a student's skill level before you proceed with instruction. You will also be able to locate errors or gaps in student thinking which can then be corrected. When the student has learned all of the necessary prerequisite skills and knowledge needed, the new skill can be meaningfully and successfully learned or mastered.

It is obvious that you as the classroom teacher must be able to identify the prerequisite skills needed to learn a specific skill. To aid you, sequential diagrams of various operations are provided in Appendix D.

DEVELOPING ALGORITHMS

Now that you have checked out your students with respect to meaning and other prerequisite skills, you are ready to move to the development of algorithms so that students will be able to successfully perform and apply the learned computational skills. Recall that an algorithm is a process for solving a computational problem. For example, the algorithm for adding two fractions is:

$$\frac{a}{b} + \frac{c}{d} = \frac{ad + bc}{ba}$$

where a, b, c, and d are whole numbers (or integers) and b and d are non zero.

Let's begin by examining some general guidelines for developing algorithms and then discuss some suggestions and ideas for specific algorithm development.

As you prepare lessons designed to develop an algorithm, keep the following in mind:

1. *Review the algorithm before presenting it to the class*. Try to anticipate where the students will likely have difficulty in understanding or following the process. Try to keep vocabulary from becoming a major problem.

2. *Prepare your examples prior to class*. A little time and effort spent before class will enable you to use examples that are less confusing and more meaningful to your presentation. Avoid using examples "off the top of your head." More often than not you will choose a poor or inappropriate example which will do little or nothing to aid your presentation, often with negative results.

3. *Go through the algorithm slowly step by step*. This will enable the students to begin to follow the logical process involved in the algorithm. Remember that what makes sense to you will seldom be viewed in the same way by the students; they will need more time to follow the process than you will.

4. ***Get the students actively involved in the presentation***. Active involvement does wonders for motivation and understanding. By being

actively involved, students are better able to internalize the algorithm, a necessity if the process is to become their own.

5. *Go through the algorithm more than once.* Repeating the steps in the algorithm will help the student who may have become confused during the first presentation.

6. *Follow the presentation with immediate practice.* Give the students one or two examples to work in class and then have one of them describe the use of the algorithm to solve the problem. A larger set of problems should be given for future practice, but be sure that each student has an understanding of the algorithm before beginning work on the larger set. If you ignore this last point, frustration will very quickly develop, usually with less than desirable results. You may find it helpful to move about the classroom answering questions and also perhaps having another student assist you in helping students who are having difficulty.

OPERATIONS WITH WHOLE NUMBERS

Most students who come to your classroom have probably stabilized or mastered the operations of addition and subtraction with whole numbers. They will need continued practice, however, in order to keep the two skills sharp. For those students who are still having difficulty, they may need additional developmental activities and certainly will need a lot of practice with the operations.

Meanwhile, multiplication and division of whole numbers have been introduced and the students will be at various levels of proficiency. During the junior high/middle school years, both multiplication and division algorithms are extended to include more complex examples. Before those extensions can be meaningful, the basic concepts of multiplication and division and the elementary algorithms must be clearly understood.

Multiplication

Your students must understand that multiplication is restated addition. They must realize that 3 x 2 is the same and gives the same result as 3 + 3. Hopefully, this is the way that multiplication was initially introduced to them, but there may be some students who did not learn it in that way. You need to return to the beginning with those students by using rectangular arrays. Excellent models for arrays are graph paper and geoboards, which usually consist of a piece of wood with nails driven into it in a regular array format. Rubber bands are used to indicate certain arrays.

For example, 4 x 3 may be pictured as:

x   x   x   x

x   x   x   x

x   x   x   x

This shows three rows with four things in each row.

The basic facts of multiplication, as well as addition and subtraction, need to be mastered by each student with a reasonable degree of speed. Students will need constant and continual practice in order to master the basic facts. Flash cards and games are especially useful here.

As your students practice multiplication with whole numbers, a problem often arises when lack of knowledge of basic facts causes students to obtain wrong answers. For students who are having this difficulty, you may want to provide a table of basic facts to assist the student. This will enable the student to practice the algorithm with a good chance of success. At the same time, of course, the student needs to work on activities to master the basic facts.

During the time that your students are working at mastery of the basic facts, they will also be working at mastery of the algorithm for multiplication. The development of the algorithm begins in its simplest form with the one-digit by one-digit (basic facts) and proceeds to the two-digit by one-digit form where no regrouping is involved, as in 23 x 3. As students work with this form, it may be necessary to rewrite the problem and solution. Thus, 23 x 3 may be written as 2 tens + 3 ones x 3 so that we get 6 tens + 9 ones or 69. Breaking down the algorithm in this way may be necessary to help your students gain an understanding of what is happening.

Two-digit by one-digit multiplication where regrouping is involved follows next with problems such as 38 x 7. A similar breakdown of the algorithm as described above may also be needed here.

The multiplication algorithm really manifests itself when you reach two-digit by two-digit multiplication. As students work with problems such as 43 x 57, they may again need to break the algorithm in component parts as before. For example:

$$\begin{array}{r} 4 \text{ tens} + 3 \text{ ones} \\ \times\ \underline{5 \text{ tens} + 7 \text{ ones}} \end{array}$$

There will be four partial products to be added together to get the final product:

$$7 \text{ ones} \times 3 \text{ ones} = 21 \text{ ones} \qquad\qquad 21$$
$$7 \text{ ones} \times 4 \text{ tens} = 28 \text{ tens} \qquad\qquad 280$$
$$5 \text{ tens} \times 3 \text{ ones} = 15 \text{ tens} \qquad \text{or} \qquad 150$$
$$\underline{5 \text{ tens} \times 4 \text{ tens}} = \underline{20 \text{ hundreds}} \qquad\qquad \underline{2000}$$
$$20 \text{ hundreds} + 43 \text{ tens} + 21 \text{ ones} \qquad\qquad 2451$$

or

$$2000 + 430 + 21 \text{ or } 2451.$$

Many of your students will already be able to solve the problem above with the standard algorithm.

$$
\begin{array}{r}
43 \\
\times\,57 \\
\hline
301 \\
\underline{215} \\
2451
\end{array}
$$

These students will need frequent short periods of practice so that the algorithm will be stabilized and accuracy maintained.

Students will need to work with examples of three-digit by two-digit and three-digit by three-digit multiplication during the junior high/middle school years. However, it does not seem appropriate to have your students spend time on multiplication problems such as 8742 x 6138. Such problems are tedious and really do not enhance the students' ability to multiply whole numbers. Plenty of practice and drill can be just as effective with examples of two-digit by two-digit multiplication problems.

One multiplication skill that is sometimes shortchanged is multiplication of a number by tens, hundreds, or thousands. Students need proficiency with these types of problems as a prelude to multiplication with decimals.

Division

Your students have basically been introduced to division of whole numbers, probably in the fourth grade. Their skills with division will, in most cases, not really be stabilized when they come to you, particularly in the early middle school years. You will probably need to spend considerable time with division of whole numbers.

Division of whole numbers should be viewed by students as repeated subtraction. For example, $8 \div 2$ is solved as:

$$
\begin{array}{cccc}
8 & 6 & 4 & 2 \\
\underline{-2} & \underline{-2} & \underline{-2} & \underline{-2} \\
6 & 4 & 2 & 0
\end{array}
$$

Two is subtracted four times, so 8 ÷ 2 = 4. When students understand division in this way, they are better able to cope with the algorithm.

As with addition, subtraction, and multiplication, students need to master basic division facts. These facts include division of numbers that have two factors that are both single-digit numbers. Plenty of drill and practice with these basic facts will be needed for student mastery.

Students will have been exposed to many variations of the division algorithm in their previous experiences, such as the following example using multiples of 10:

$$
\begin{array}{r}
60 \\
6\overline{)365} \\
360 \\
\hline
5
\end{array}
$$

(the quotient is 60 r 5)

Or students have used the "ladder" method:

$$
\begin{array}{r}
7\overline{)243} \\
210 \\
\hline
43 \\
42 \\
\hline
\end{array}
$$

7 x 30 = 210

7 x 6 = 42

"30 groups of 7 + 6 groups of 7 with 1 left over gives me an answer of 36 r 1."

Such variations of the division algorithm are useful in helping students understand the division process. However, unlike addition, subtraction and multiplication, students must learn and master the short form of the division algorithm. This is necessary because division of decimals requires the use of the short form. The short form of the addition, subtraction and multiplication algorithms is not necessary, however, to perform computations with the respective operations with decimals.

Moving to the short form of the division algorithm is difficult at best for most students, which results in frustration for both students and teachers. Here are some ideas to help you and your students.

When working with single-digit divisors, it is often helpful for students to work with exercises such as the following:

9 ÷ 3 = _____.

9 tens ÷ = _____tens.

9 hundreds ÷ 3 = _____hundreds.

9 thousands ÷ 3 = _____thousands.

and

42 ÷ 6 = _____.

420 ÷ 6 = _____.

4200 ÷ 6 = _____.

42,000 ÷ 6 = _____.

These exercises are important for two reasons. First, the student begins to look at the number to be divided in different ways and emphasizes the renaming of numbers. Second, the student gains experience in using and seeing zeroes in division problems.

After considerable work with exercises such as those above, the student should move to the next stage with problems such as: 647 ÷ 3. The procedure for solution goes like this.

1. Divide 3 into the number of hundreds and subtract

$$
\begin{array}{r}
200 \\
3\overline{)647} \\
-600 \\
\hline
47
\end{array}
\qquad 200 \times 3
$$

2. Divide 3 into the number of tens and subtract

$$
\begin{array}{r}
10 \\
200 \\
3\overline{)647} \\
-600 \\
\hline
47 \\
-30 \\
\hline
17
\end{array}
\qquad
\begin{array}{l}
\\
\\
\\
200 \times 3 \\
\\
10 \times 3
\end{array}
$$

3. Divide 3 into the number of ones and subtract

$$
\begin{array}{r}
5 \\
10 \\
200 \\
3\overline{)647} \\
-600 \\
\hline
47 \\
-30 \\
\hline
17 \\
-15 \\
\hline
2
\end{array}
\qquad
\begin{array}{l}
\\
\\
\\
\\
200 \times 3 \\
\\
10 \times 3 \\
\\
5 \times 3
\end{array}
$$

4. Combine the partial quotients and show the remainder, if any: $200 + 10 + 5 = 215$ with a remainder of 2. So, $647 \div 3 = 215$ r2.

This procedure works very well when the divisor is greater than the first digit of the dividend, as in $1267 \div 3$. The procedure for solution goes like this:

1. Divide 3 into the number of hundreds and subtract

$$
\begin{array}{r}
400 \\
3\overline{)1267} \\
-1200 \quad 400 \times 3 \\
\hline
67
\end{array}
$$

2. Divide 3 into the number of tens and subtract

$$
\begin{array}{r}
20 \\
400 \\
3\overline{)1267} \\
-1200 \quad 400 \times 3 \\
\hline
67 \\
-60 \quad 20 \times 3 \\
\hline
7
\end{array}
$$

3. Divide 3 into the number of ones and subtract

$$
\begin{array}{r}
2 \\
20 \\
400 \\
3\overline{)1267} \\
-1200 \quad 400 \times 3 \\
\hline
67 \\
-60 \quad 20 \times 3 \\
\hline
7 \\
-6 \quad 2 \times 3 \\
\hline
1
\end{array}
$$

4. $1267 \div 3 = 422$ r1

This procedure can then be simplified as follows:

1. Divide 3 into the number of hundreds and subtract. Record the number of hundreds above the hundreds digit in the dividend.

$$
\begin{array}{r}
2 \\
3\overline{)647} \\
-6 \\
\hline
4
\end{array}
\qquad
\begin{array}{r}
4 \\
3\overline{)1267} \\
-12 \\
\hline
6
\end{array}
$$

2. Divide 3 into one number of tens and subtract. Record the number of tens you find above the tens digit in the dividend.

$$
\begin{array}{r}
21 \\
3\overline{)647} \\
-6 \\
\hline
4 \\
-3 \\
\hline
1
\end{array}
\qquad
\begin{array}{r}
42 \\
3\overline{)1267} \\
-12 \\
\hline
6 \\
-6 \\
\hline
\end{array}
$$

3. Divide 3 into the number of ones and subtract. Record the number that you find above the ones digit in the dividend.

$$
\begin{array}{r}
215 \\
3\overline{)647} \\
-6 \\
\hline
4 \\
-3 \\
\hline
17 \\
-15 \\
\hline
2
\end{array}
\qquad
\begin{array}{r}
422 \\
3\overline{)1267} \\
-12 \\
\hline
6 \\
-6 \\
\hline
7 \\
-6 \\
\hline
1
\end{array}
$$

4. $647 \div 3 = 215$ r2

$1267 \div 3 = 422$ r1

A key skill for students to use this procedure and to develop proficiency in the use of the short form is the ability to identify the number of ones, tens, hundreds, etc. Give students plenty of practice with this skill.

Proficiency with the aforementioned procedure will help eliminate a common problem exhibited by students. The problem is the placement of zeroes in the quotient. For example, the procedure would apply to the following problem:

1. Divide 6 into the number of hundreds

$$
\begin{array}{r}
1 \\
6\overline{)618} \\
-6 \\
\hline
1
\end{array}
$$

2. Divide 6 into the number of tens

$$
\begin{array}{r}
10 \\
6\overline{)618} \\
-6 \\
\hline
1 \\
-0 \\
\hline
18
\end{array}
$$

3. Divide 6 into the number of ones

$$
\begin{array}{r}
10 \\
6\overline{)618} \\
-6 \\
\hline
1 \\
-0 \\
\hline
18 \\
\underline{18}
\end{array}
$$

4. $618 \div 6 = 103$

At first, students should show the fact that 6 cannot divide into the number of tens. This will help emphasize the need for 0 in the quotient. Later, students may be allowed to put the 0 in the quotient without actually showing the subtraction.

Using place value ideas to develop the short form of the division algorithm (as illustrated above) can be easily applied to two-digit divisors. Some slight changes must be made, however.

In the above examples, the principles used are: hundreds divided by ones are hundreds, tens divided by ones are tens, etc. With two-digit divisors, the following principles apply: tens divided by tens are ones, hundreds divided by tens are tens, thousands divided by tens are hundreds, etc. Students should clearly understand the principles before proceeding to the algorithms. Exercises such as the following are very helpful in helping students gain understanding:

1. 6 tens $\div$ 2 tens = _____ones

2. 12 hundreds $\div$ 2 tens = _____tens

3. 4 thousands $\div$ 2 tens = _____hundreds and

$$20\overline{)\,60} \qquad\qquad 20\overline{)1200} \qquad\qquad 20\overline{)4000} \qquad \text{or}$$

$$\begin{array}{r} \text{ones} \\ 2\text{ tens}\overline{)6\text{ tens}} \end{array} \qquad\qquad \begin{array}{r} \text{tens} \\ 2\text{ tens}\overline{)12\text{ hundreds}} \end{array}$$

$$\begin{array}{r} \text{hundreds} \\ 2\text{ tens}\overline{)4\text{ thousands}} \end{array}$$

A similar procedure to the one outlined above may now be used. The first examples should be ones where the divisor is a multiple of 10 but less than 100. For example, consider the problem $900 \div 3$.

1. Compare the tens digit in the divisor with the first digit in the dividend and identify the dividend as thousands, hundreds, tens, etc. Write the appropriate place value for the quotient.

$$\overline{\text{3 tens)9 hundreds}}^{\text{tens}}$$

2. Write the problem using numbers and perform the division.

$$\begin{array}{r} 3 \\ 30\overline{)900} \\ 90 \end{array}$$

3. Divide the number of tens in the divisor into the number of tens. Place the digit above the ones digit in the dividend.

$$\begin{array}{r} 3 \\ 30\overline{)900} \\ 90 \\ \hline 0 \\ 0 \end{array}$$

4. Multiply the divisor by the quotient to see if the product equals the dividend.

$$\begin{array}{r} 30 \\ \times 30 \\ \hline 900 \end{array}$$

Now, try 3685 ÷ 60.

1. Set the problem up to see what the quotient will be.

$$\overline{\text{6 tens)36 hundreds}}^{\text{tens}}$$

2. Divide 6 into 36 and record the answer in the tens place in the quotient.

$$\begin{array}{r} 6 \\ 60\overline{)3685} \\ 36 \\ \hline 8 \end{array}$$

3. Divide 6 into 8 since 8 is the number of tens. Record this answer in the ones place in the quotient.

$$\begin{array}{r} 61 \\ 60\overline{)3685} \\ 36 \\ \hline 8 \\ 6 \\ \hline 2 \end{array}$$

4. There are 25 ones left over, so we have a remainder of 25. Hence, 3685 ÷ 60 = 61 r25.

5. Check the work.

$$
\begin{array}{r}
61 \\
\times 60 \\
\hline
3660 \\
+ \ 25 \\
\hline
3685
\end{array}
$$

Now let's consider division which are two-digit numbers that are other than multiples of 10. Let's look at 2984 ÷ 33.

1. Set up the problem to see how the quotient will be represented.

$$
\overset{\text{tens}}{3 \text{ tens}\,)\overline{29 \text{ hundreds}}}
$$

2. Divide 3 into 29 and record the answer in the tens digit in the quotient. Multiply 33 by 9 and place this answer under the first 3 digits in the dividend.

$$
\begin{array}{r}
9 \\
33\,)\overline{2984} \\
297 \\
\hline
1
\end{array}
$$

3. Divide 3 into 1 (the number of tens) and record this answer in the ones digit in the quotient.

$$
\begin{array}{r}
90 \\
33\,)\overline{2984} \\
297 \\
\hline
1 \\
0 \\
\hline
14
\end{array}
$$

4. There are 14 ones left over, so we have a remainder of 14. Hence, 2894 ÷ 33 = 90 r14.

5. Check the work.

$$
\begin{array}{r}
33 \\
\times \ 90 \\
\hline
2970 \\
+ \ 14 \\
\hline
2984
\end{array}
$$

Students must learn to be aware of the divisor throughout the problem. A common mistake, illustrated in the previous problem, is to not take enough groups of 33 when 29 hundreds is divided by 33. This comparison can be made with the tens digits. After subtracting 297 from 298, there was 1 ten left. Since the divisor had 3 tens, as many groups of 33 were taken from the 29 hundreds.

Much drill and practice will be needed to help your students stabilize the operations on whole numbers during the junior high/middle school years. For some students, it will mean only periodic practice but for others, it will mean "starting from scratch." Make use of diagnostic and corrective procedures as outlined in Chapter 4. Also, have as wide a variety of activities as possible so that the drill and practice is as enjoyable as possible.

OPERATIONS WITH FRACTIONS

Depending upon their previous mathematical experiences, your students will probably have had only minimal contact with fractions by the time they enter the junior high/middle school years. This contact will probably have included only a study of the concept of fractions with possibly a little work with equivalent fractions.

It is safe to assume that while your students have been exposed to fractions, they probably lack necessary understanding of the concept of fractions. Before you can proceed to work with operations on fractions, you must be sure that students understand and are comfortable with the concept of fractions and equivalent fractions.

As students work with the concept of fractions, they need to see both the circle and the rectangle models, as shown in Figure 6-1. Traditionally,

FIGURE 6-1

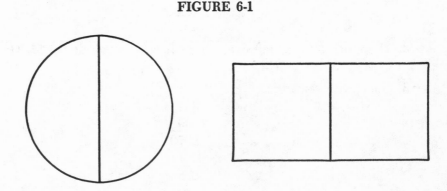

the circle model has been used, which works very well for illustrating the fractions such as halves, fourths, and eighths. However, fractions using thirds, fifths, and sixths are difficult to picture for students with the circle model. The rectangle model is much more useful for these fractions.

As you work with students to help them understand fractions, you may want to make use of concrete models and pictures of fractional parts, such as these in Figure 6-2. To this end, heavy cardboard or thin wood is good to use; while it is a little more expensive, wax paper is also good to use. The folds on wax paper appear and white lines are easily distinguishable, which is not the case with ordinary paper.

FIGURE 6-2

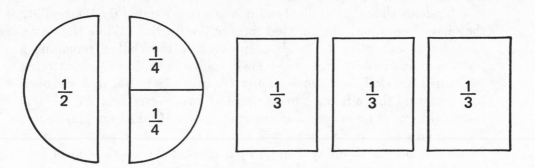

As students begin to work with the symbols for fractions, it is very helpful to think of the denominator of the fraction. For example, the fraction can also be represented with its name: 1/4 or one-fourth; 3/2 or three halves. This form seems to help students recognize and understand what fractions are.

Your students need to clearly understand and be able to work accurately with equivalent fractions. They need to realize that 2/4 is another name for 1/2 and that 6/12 is also another name for 1/2. The types of concrete models described above are good to use at this point. For example, two pieces that each represent 1/4 on top of a piece that represents 1/2 will also clearly demonstrate that 1/2 is equivalent to 2/4 or that 1/2 and 2/4 are both different names for the same thing.

Sometimes fractions that have a greater numerator than denominator are written as mixed numbers, such as 9/4 = 2-1/4. Students need to understand that 2-1/4 means the same as 2 + 1/4 and that the 2 represents 2 wholes or 8 fourths. Practice in writing fractions such as 9/4 as 2-1/4 and vice versa will be needed when students encounter those numbers in working with the algorithms for addition, subtraction, multiplication and division of fractions.

As students understand the concept of equivalent fractions, they are ready to look at the algorithm for renaming fractions; when the simplest form of the fraction is used to start with, they need to recognize that different names for 1 are being used. For example, 1/1 = 1, 2/2 = 1, 3/3 = 1. Students also need to realize that when one part of a fraction is multiplied by a number, the other part of the fraction must also be multiplied by the same number in order to keep the value of the fraction the same. Thus, 1/2 x (2/2) = 2/4.

Students should have plenty of practice in renaming fractions where they have begun with the simplest form of the fraction. When they have gained this skill, they are ready to proceed to the skill of renaming a fraction in its simplest form, traditionally known as "reducing." In working with this latter skill, for example: 2/4 = 1/2, and 3/12 = 1/4, students need to understand that a fraction in its simplest form means that the greatest common factor of numerator and denominator is 1. In the examples above, 2 is the greatest common factor of 2 and 4, and 3 is the greatest common factor of 3 and 12. Dividing 2 and 4 by 2 gives us the simplest form.

Some students may need to write down the phrase "divide by 2" or "divide by 3" beside the problem to emphasize the procedure. Encourage them to do so if necessary.

A common mistake made by students is to use a different number in dividing the numerator than in dividing the denominator. For example, a student may simplify the following way:

$$\text{divided by 2} \longrightarrow \frac{\cancel{4}\,2}{\cancel{9}\,3} = \frac{2}{3}$$
$$\text{divided by 3}$$

Another common error is to only partially simplify the fraction. For example, a student may show work like this:

$$\frac{2}{4} \quad \frac{\cancel{4}}{\cancel{8}} = \frac{2}{4}$$

Additional activities using the various fractional forms of 1 should help correct both of these errors.

The skills of renaming fractions and writing fractions in their simplest form are prerequisite to successful work with operations on fractions. For best results, these two skills need to be stabilized before proceeding with operations.

Addition

Work with addition of fractions begins with problems that have like denominators. It may be necessary to use concrete models such as shown in Figure 6-3 to illustrate the addition process. By placing the pieces on top of the model of 1, students can see how the fractions may be added.

FIGURE 6-3

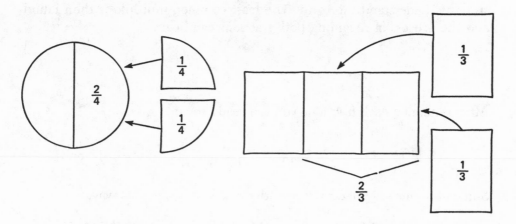

As students move toward the abstract form of addition, rewriting fractions in the form pointed out earlier in this section may be helpful. For example, 1/4 + 1/4 may be written as: one-fourth + one-fourth = two-fourths. This form emphasizes the fact that the denominator names the fraction.

This preliminary work should make it easier for students to realize that two fractions must have the same denominator in order to be added together. The skill of renaming two fractions so that their names are the same must precede the actual addition process, although students have already been exposed intuitively to addition.

One way that seems to help many students with the skill of finding a common name for two fractions is to use the least common multiple of the two denominators. For example, suppose you wanted to find 1/4 + 1/6. You can write down the multiples of 4 and of 6:

4	6
4	6
8	12
12	18
16	24
20	30
24	36
28	

Ask the student which multiples are in common to both 4 and 6 (12,24). If there is more than one common multiple, which one is the least? (12)

Breaking down the term "least common multiple" in this way helps students understand the term. The least common multiple is then found and the process of renaming both fractions can begin.

$$\frac{1}{4} = \frac{3}{12} \qquad \frac{1}{6} = \frac{2}{12}$$

After renaming each fraction, you are ready to add.

$$\frac{3}{12} + \frac{2}{12} = \frac{3+2}{12} = \frac{5}{12}$$

Some students may need to write the problem out in this way:

```
  1 fourth          3 twelfths
+ 1 sixth         + 2 twelfths              5
 ─────────        ────────────       or   ────
                    5 twelfths              12
```

There is the traditional concern that the answer to an addition problem always be written in simplest form. It is not necessary to do so from a mathematical standpoint. It is perfectly all right to require your students to do so, but, if you do, be sure you give at least partial credit for correctly doing the algorithm.

Another traditional concern has been that students must always find the lowest common denominator (least common multiple) in order to solve an addition problem with unlike denominators. This concern really has no basis. Any common multiple may be used and students should have some experience with this fact.

When your students have demonstrated proficiency in working with addition of common fractions, they are ready to work with addition of mixed numbers. If fractional numbers such as 1-1/2 + 2-1/3 are not too cumbersome, students may want to rewrite the mixed numbers as improper fractions (3/2 + 7/3) before performing the addition algorithm. Others may want to write the problem as:

$$1\frac{1}{2}$$
$$+2\frac{1}{3}$$

and solve the problem by adding the fractions together, adding the whole numbers together and then combining the answer. Students must have a clear understanding, however, that 1-1/2 means 1 + 1/2 and that 2-1/3 means 2 + 1/3.

$$1\frac{1}{2} \qquad 1 + \frac{1}{2} \qquad 1 + \frac{3}{6}$$
$$+2\frac{1}{3} \qquad 2 + \frac{1}{3} \qquad +\frac{2}{6}$$
$$\qquad\qquad\qquad\qquad\qquad 3 + \frac{5}{6} = 3\frac{5}{6}$$

Subtraction

All of the skills needed for addition of fractions are also needed for subtraction of fractions. Students must be able to rename fractions and have a clear understanding of what a fraction is. They must also, of course, be able to subtract whole numbers.

A common mistake made by many students involves the regrouping process in a problem such as the following:

$$3\frac{1}{2}$$
$$-2\frac{1}{2}$$

Students will rename the fractions correctly and realize that they must borrow

$$3\frac{2}{6} \qquad\qquad \overset{2}{\cancel{3}}\frac{12}{6}$$
$$-2\frac{3}{6} \qquad\qquad -2\frac{3}{6}$$

However, instead of regrouping 6 sixths, they regroup 10 sixths. Additional emphasis on the different names for 1 will probably help at this point. Also, if the numbers are reasonably easy to work with, the problem may be rewritten as improper fractions for solution purposes.

$$3\frac{1}{3} \qquad\qquad \frac{10}{3}$$
$$-2\frac{1}{2} \qquad\qquad -\frac{5}{2}$$

Multiplication

As with whole numbers, multiplication of fractions should be related to the repeated additional model. The first examples should be those where a fraction is multiplied by a whole number: 1/3 x 2 = 1/3 + 1/3.

At this point, the concept of reciprocal should be introduced. This can be done by first showing examples such as:

$$\frac{1}{2} \times 2 = \frac{1}{2} + \frac{1}{2} = 1$$

$$\frac{1}{3} \times 3 = \frac{1}{3} + \frac{1}{3} + \frac{1}{3} = 1$$

$$\frac{1}{4} \times 4 = \frac{1}{4} + \frac{1}{4} + \frac{1}{4} + \frac{1}{4} = 1$$

Students should then be reminded that whole numbers can be written as fractions: 3 = 3/1, 4 = 4/1. Then the examples above can be rewritten as:

$$\frac{1}{2} \times 2 = \frac{1}{2} \times \frac{2}{1} = 1$$

$$\frac{1}{3} \times 3 = \frac{1}{3} \times \frac{3}{1} = 1$$

$$\frac{1}{4} \times 4 = \frac{1}{4} \times \frac{4}{1} = 1$$

Thus, the product of a fraction and its reciprocal is always 1 (with the exception, of course, of 0).

Students are now ready to study the algorithm for multiplying fractions. The algorithm can be introduced with the renaming concept discussed earlier: 1/3 x 1. Using different fraction names for 1 and the principle that multiplying both numerator and denominator by the same number gives an equivalent fraction, you have:

$$\frac{1}{3} \times \frac{2}{2} = \frac{1 \times 2}{3 \times 2} = \frac{2}{6}$$

$$\frac{1}{3} \times \frac{3}{3} = \frac{1 \times 3}{3 \times 3} = \frac{3}{9}$$

The reciprocal concept also demonstrates the algorithm:

$$\frac{1}{4} \times \frac{4}{1} = \frac{1 \times 4}{4 \times 1} = \frac{4}{4} = 1$$

$$\frac{1}{2} \times \frac{2}{1} + \frac{1 \times 2}{2 \times 1} = \frac{2}{1} = 1$$

Students are now ready to explore the product of two fractions where neither 1 nor the reciprocal is involved as a factor: 1/2 x 1/3. To help students understand what is happening here, a diagram such as Figure 6-4 may be helpful. The rectangle represents 1.

FIGURE 6-4

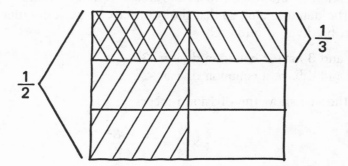

The concept of the area of a rectangle is the basis for this model. The product of 1/2 and 1/3 can be thought of as the area of a rectangle that has a length of 1/2 and a width of 1/3. Each of the parts of the whole is represented by diagonal lines. The section with both sets of diagonal lines is the one that represents 1/2 x 1/3. By comparison, the rectangle is 1/6 of the large rectangle (or 1). So, 1/2 x 1/3 can be shown pictorially to be 1/6.

The algorithm is:

$$\frac{1}{2} \times \frac{1}{3} = \frac{1 \times 1}{2 \times 3} = \frac{1}{6}$$

Many teachers and textbooks like to use the notion of cancellation in working with multiplication of fractions. For example:

$$\frac{1\!\!\!\!/2}{1\!\!\!\!/3} \times \frac{\not 3 1}{\not 4 2} = \frac{1 \times 1}{1 \times 2} = \frac{1}{2}$$

Perhaps cancellation makes the problem easier to work with, but it is confusing to many students. It does give an answer in simplest form, but, as pointed out earlier, always giving the answer in simplest form really has nothing to do with the algorithm itself. The problem can be solved without cancellation and the answer is simplified.

Confusion in using cancellation often occurs when the students do not understand the process. If you are going to teach cancellation, be sure to show students why the process works.

$$\frac{2}{3} \times \frac{3}{4} = \frac{2 \times 3}{3 \times 4}$$

Cancellation occurs when two factors are chosen, one in the numerator and one in the denominator, so that the two factors have a number in common that can be divided into each.

"3 and 3 have a common divisor--3"
"2 and 4 have a common divisor--2"

Have students show the division process:

$$\frac{2}{3} \times \frac{3}{4} = \frac{1\!\!\!\!/2 \times \not 3 1}{1\!\!\!\!/3 \times \not 4 2}$$

Some students will apply the process incorrectly as shown here.

$$\frac{2}{3} \times \frac{5}{6} = \frac{1\!\!\!\!/2 \times 5}{1\!\!\!\!/3 \times \not 6 1} = \frac{5}{1} = 5$$

The 3 and 6 were first simplified and then the factors of 2. If students continue to make mistakes using cancellation, it may be better to have them not use it, since the product can be found without it.

Be sure to help students understand that cancellation works for multiplication, but not addition. For example,

$$\frac{1 + 4}{2 + 4} \neq \frac{1}{2} \qquad\qquad \frac{1}{2} - \frac{\cancel{4}}{\cancel{4}_1} = \frac{1}{2}$$

The product of two mixed numbers is the final extension of the algorithm for multiplication of fractions. In solving the problem 4-1/2 x 1-1/3, it is probably easiest to rewrite both mixed numbers as improper fractions and then apply the algorithm.

$$4\frac{1}{2} = \frac{9}{2}$$

$$1\frac{1}{3} = \frac{4}{3}$$

$$4\frac{1}{2} \times 1\frac{1}{3} = \frac{9}{2} \times \frac{4}{3}$$

Be sure to point out to students that the process of "performing on denominators" and "performing on numerators" is a true algorithm for some operations and invalid for others. For example,

$$\frac{1}{3} \times \frac{3}{4} = \frac{1 \times 3}{2 \times 4}$$

is a correct way to multiply, but

$$\frac{1}{2} + \frac{3}{4} = \frac{1 + 3}{2 \times 4}$$

leads to an incorrect answer.

Division

It is probably safe to say that division of fractions is not well understood by either students or teachers. Division has usually been presented as a mechanical operation by saying "invert the divisor and multiply."

Actually, division of fractions can be thought of like division of whole numbers. For example, 8/2 is "How many groups of 2 are in 8?" And 3/4 ÷

1/2 is "How many 1/2s are in 3/4?" Helping your students develop an initial understanding of division of fractions will aid their proficiency with the operation.

Have you ever wondered why the old rule "invert the divisor and multiply" works?

1. $\dfrac{1}{2} \div \dfrac{3}{4}$ is the original problem

2. $\dfrac{\dfrac{1}{2}}{\dfrac{3}{4}}$ is the rewritten problem

3. Multiply 3/4 by 4/3 (the reciprocal). Do the same for the numerator so that the problem is not altered:

$$\dfrac{\dfrac{1}{2}}{\dfrac{3}{4}} \times \dfrac{\dfrac{4}{3}}{\dfrac{4}{3}} = \dfrac{\dfrac{1}{2} \times \dfrac{4}{3}}{1}$$

Note that $\dfrac{\dfrac{4}{3}}{\dfrac{4}{3}}$ is another name for 1.

4. $\dfrac{\dfrac{1}{2} \times \dfrac{4}{3}}{1} = \dfrac{1}{2} \times \dfrac{4}{3}$

5. So, $\dfrac{1}{2} \div \dfrac{3}{4} = \dfrac{1}{2} \times \dfrac{4}{3}$

Some of your students may be able to understand the steps outlined above, but it may be confusing to most of them.

Another way of viewing division of fractions may be quite meaningful to your students. Its basis is that a fraction can be thought of as a comparison of numerator to denominator. In the following example, 1/2 indicates a comparison of 1 to 2.

1. $\dfrac{3}{4} \div \dfrac{1}{2}$ is the original problem

2. $\dfrac{\dfrac{3}{4}}{\dfrac{1}{2}}$ is the rewritten problem

3. Rename both fractions to have the same name.

$$\frac{\dfrac{3}{4}}{\dfrac{1}{2}} = \frac{\dfrac{3}{4}}{\dfrac{2}{4}}$$

4. Now you have $\dfrac{3 \text{ fourths}}{2 \text{ fourths}}$ which is a comparison of 3 to 2 or $\dfrac{3}{2}$.

5. So, $\dfrac{3}{4} \div \dfrac{1}{2} = \dfrac{3}{4} \times \dfrac{2}{1} = \dfrac{6}{4} = \dfrac{3}{2}$

It will take your students some time and lots of practice to stabilize the operations with fractions before they leave junior high/middle school. Fractions are still very important in mathematics and proficiency in the operations on fractions is a desirable goal.

OPERATIONS WITH DECIMALS

As students begin to work with operations on decimals, there are two areas where skill is needed: (1) place value of whole numbers, and (2) operations with whole numbers. Your students should also realize that decimals are special kinds of fractions.

Students have been exposed to decimals in the primay grades in the study of money. The money model is a useful tool in beginning more formalized work with decimals.

The money model might be used to introduce decimals:

"There are 100 cents (pennies) in a dollar, so each penny is 1/100 of a dollar or $.01. Thus, 1/100 is the same as .01. A dime is 10 cents or 10 hundredths of a dollar. A dime is also 1/10 of a dollar. So, 1/10 = .10 = .1."

This approach does two important things: (1) the relationship between decimals and common fractions is established, and (2) the concept of equivalent decimals is introduced (1 tenth or .1 is the same as ten hundredths or .10). Both ideas are important for students working with decimals.

Students will need a great deal of practice in identifying place values of decimal numbers and in reading decimal numbers. Decimal numbers should be read in the following way:

0.32 as "thirty-two hundredths"

1.41 as "one and forty-one hundredths"

A point should be made about writing a decimal as 0.32. You may want to have your students place a zero to the left of the decimal point (when there is no whole number) to emphasize that the number is a decimal number less than 1. Students will sometimes write such a number carelessly and the decimal point will not be readily apparent. Also, the decimal point may sometimes be confused with the dot symbol for multiplication. For example: 2.3 and 2·3.

Students should demonstrate proficiency in converting fractions to decimals and decimals to fractions. This can be done initially by renaming common fractions to have names of tenths, hundredths, or thousandths.

$$\frac{1}{4} = \frac{?}{100} \qquad\qquad \frac{1}{8} = \frac{?}{1000} \qquad\qquad \frac{1}{5} = \frac{?}{10}$$

Later, as the division algorithm for decimals is introduced, the concept of repeating decimals should be introduced. This concept is, of course, the basis for the definitions of rational and irrational numbers.

Being able to round decimal numbers is a very important skill for your students. It will be especially useful in division of decimals and also in working with decimal numbers where there are several places to the right of the decimal point.

Addition and Subtraction

The algorithms for adding and subtracting decimals are essentially the same as for whole numbers. Keeping the decimal points in line will be the major problem encountered by your students (assuming that they have no difficulty with the whole number operations).

Multiplication

Multiplication of decimals is based on whole number multiplication. Your students will have most of their problems (again assuming proficiency with whole number multiplication) with the placement of the decimal point in the answer.

There are a set of principles that will help your students. For example, "tenths times tenths gives hundredths," "tenths times hundredths gives thousandths," and "hundredths times hundredths gives ten thousandths" are important in solving problems. The fraction form of these examples should be explored.

$$\frac{1}{10} \times \frac{1}{10} = \frac{1}{100}$$

$$\frac{1}{10} \times \frac{1}{100} = \frac{1}{1000}$$

$$\frac{1}{100} \times \frac{1}{100} = \frac{1}{10,000}$$

At this point, your students should explore what happens to a number (and to the decimal point) when the number is multiplied or divided by 10, 100, 1000, or 10,000. The fact that 6 is also written as 6. should also be noted.

$6 \times 10 = 60$	$6. \times 10 = 60.$
$6 \times 100 = 600$	$6. \times 100 = 600.$
$6 \times \dfrac{1}{10} = \dfrac{6}{10} = 0.6$	$6. \times 0.1 = 0.6$
$6 \times \dfrac{1}{100} = \dfrac{6}{100} = 0.06$	$6 \times 0.01 = 0.06$

The movement of the decimal point should be studied by your students in these examples. This can be done without the multiplication algorithm for decimals.

When these principles and underlying ideas have been clearly understood by your students, they will be ready to work with the algorithm for multiplying decimals. For example: 3.2 x 0.3. The same problem written in fraction form is:

$$3\frac{2}{10} \times 3\frac{3}{10}$$

$$\frac{32}{10} \times \frac{3}{10} = \frac{32 \times 3}{100} = \frac{96}{100} = .96$$

This may be helpful so that students can see how the decimal point is placed in the final answer.

Your students will have the most difficulty in placing the decimal point correctly in the final answer. Examples of the type shown above will aid in overcoming this problem.

Division

A great deal of groundwork for working with division of decimals has already been laid. The short form of the division algorithm for whole numbers is prerequisite to division with decimals.

Your students should realize that when dividing by a decimal number, such as 0.7 or 2.5, the divisor and dividend should be converted to whole numbers by multiplication using 10, 100, or 1000. The dividend must also be adjusted accordingly. For example: 75/2.5. Multiplying the divisor (2.5) by 10 means that you must also multiply 75 by 10. So the problem now reads 750/25 and the answer to both problems will be the same. Students should verify this fact by multiplying the quotient and the divisor together.

In the "box" form for division, students should realize that the decimal point is placed in the quotient immediately above the decimal point in the dividend when the divisor is a whole number. For example: 750 ÷ 25, and 9.3 ÷ 3. Division can then proceed as with the short form of the division algorithm for whole numbers. Students must be reminded that all places to the right of the decimal point in the quotient must contain a digit. Students will have a tendency to not put zeroes where appropriate, as shown here:

$$
\begin{array}{r}
.06 \\
100\overline{)6.00}
\end{array}
$$

So emphasize this point and check the answer to the problem since many mistakes will be caught.

PERCENT

As your students study percent, they should understand that percent means "hundredths." Graph paper is especially useful in helping them visualize the concept of percent.

The relationships among fractions, decimals, and percent need to be fully explored by your students. They should be able to change any of the three forms into the other two.

What is 1/4 as a decimal?

What is 1/4 as a percent?

What is 0.32 as a percent?

What is 15% as a fraction?

Being able to rewrite a number given as a percent as either a fraction or a decimal is necessary for students to solve problems involving percent.

When students have demonstrated proficiency in the skills listed above and an understanding of percent, they are ready to work with problems such as:

What is 25% of 36?

10 is what percent of 20?

25 is 50% of what number?

Such problems can be presented in such real-life situations as installment purchasing and sales taxes.

There are many ways of helping students learn to solve such problems. However, the use of proportions to solve these problems seems to be a good way to begin.

If you use proportions, be sure that your students are able to work with them. Your students may have had some prior experience with proportions when they were renaming fractions, such as:

$$\frac{1}{2} = \frac{\square}{8}$$

Using the renaming of fractions as an end task is a good way to introduce solution of proportions. Noting that the cross-products must be the same is the key to solving the proportion. This can be introduced with equivalent fractions: $1/2 = 3/6$; $1 \times 6 = 2 \times 3$. Thus, the problem $1/2 = \square/8$ can be broken down this way:

$2 \times \square = 1 \times 8$ where $\square = 4$

thus, $1/2 = 4/8$ since $1 \times 8 = 2 \times 4$

Now, your students are ready to solve the three types of problems involving percentage. They must first realize that the problem has three numbers, two of which are given. One of the three numbers is a percent while the other two numbers will make up a fraction. Let's see how the thinking might go in solving each of the three problems.

Q: What is 25% of 36?

A: Let's see, 25% is the same as $\frac{1}{4}$. I want to find $\frac{1}{4}$ of 36. I can use the proportion:

$$\frac{1}{4} = \frac{\square}{36}$$

since $\square$ will give me $\frac{1}{4}$ of 36. Working it out, I get:

$$4 \times \square = 1 \times 36$$
$$4 \times \square = 36$$
$$\square = 9$$

thus, 9 is 25% of 36.

Of course, $\frac{25}{100}$ could have been used instead of $\frac{1}{4}$. Let your students use whichever form they feel most comfortable with.

Q: 10 is what percent of 20?
A: 10 is a part of 20 and I can find that by writing it as a fraction. Now, what percent is the same as 20? I'll write the percent as:

$$\frac{\Delta}{100}$$

Working it out, I get:

$$\frac{\Delta}{100} = \frac{10}{20}$$
$$20 \times \Delta = 100 \times 10$$
$$20 \times \Delta = 1000$$
$$\Delta = 50$$

$\frac{50}{100}$ is 50% so

10 is 50% of 20.

It is important that your students verbalize and write down their solutions to the problem. Many students will give the answer as a number with no understanding of what it means.

Q: 25 is 50% of what number?
A: 50% is the same as 1/2, so 1/2 of some number is 25. I can do it this way:

$$\frac{1}{2} = \frac{25}{\square}$$
$$1 \times \square = 2 \times 25$$
$$1 \times \square = 50$$
$$\square = 50$$

thus, 25 is 50% of 50.

When and if your students encounter fractions in a given percent such as 12-1/2% or 8-1/3%, encourage them to first rewrite the numbers using 100 as a denominator. For example:

$$\frac{12\frac{1}{2}}{100} \text{ and } \frac{8\frac{1}{3}}{100}$$

To get rid of the $\frac{1}{2}$, multiply the entire fraction by $\frac{2}{2}$. Thus,

$$\frac{12\frac{1}{2}}{100} \times \frac{2}{2} = \frac{25}{200}$$

Similarly,

$$\frac{8\frac{1}{3}}{100} \times \frac{3}{3} = \frac{25}{300}$$

Now the percent can be easily used in a proportion.

Writing percents as fractions also helps students understand very large and very small percentage numbers, such as 200% and 1/2%.

As fractions, you have:

$$\frac{200}{100} = 2 \text{ and } \frac{\frac{1}{2}}{100} = \frac{1}{200}$$

Some of your students will try to tell you that 1/2% is the same as 1/2. Hence, you must be sure that they understand what percentage is, that it represents a certain number of hundredths. The graphical representation described earlier in this section will help increase student understanding of numbers such as 200% and 1/2%.

OPERATIONS WITH INTEGERS

Intuitively, your students will probably have some ideas about negative numbers when they come to you. No doubt, they will have been exposed to language such as, "It's −3 degrees this morning" or "You are now 4 points in the hole in this game." Students seem to have little difficulty in dealing with these kinds of situations, but difficulty comes when they are asked to mathematically manipulate negative numbers.

Part of the difficulty may stem from early mathematical experiences. Such an experience perhaps occurred when a primary teacher said, "You can't subtract 4 from 2—it's impossible." Such a statement was well meaning and designed to make an important point, but now you must overcome that earlier statement by showing that, indeed, you *can* subtract 4 from 2.

The thermometer model is one of the best ways to help your students stabilize their understanding of negative numbers. It also helps build the rationale for operations with positive and negative numbers.

The thermometer is useful because it uses a number line that has both positive and negative numbers (see Figure 6-5). Initial work should be done with the number line in vertical form and then shifted to the horizontal form.

FIGURE 6-5

Be sure that you make your students aware that the minus sign may mean either the operation of subtraction or opposite (additive inverse) of a positive number. For example, −3 might mean to subtract 3 or it might mean the opposite of 3. Sometimes it is convenient to write the opposite of 3 as ⁻3 when the minus sign is slightly above the center of the 3.

When your students have a good understanding of negative numbers, they are ready to study the operations of addition, subtraction, multiplication, and division with positive and negative numbers. Again, the thermometer is a useful model for developing the appropriate algorithms.

Addition

Work with addition must begin with situations such as these.

"It's 4 degrees below zero. If the temperature rises 6 degrees, what is the temperature?"

"In the game, you are 2 points in the hole. On your next turn, you score 8 points. What is your score now?"

As your students think about these problems, they can be looking at a mathematical sentence to find the solution.

$$(-4) + 6 = \square$$
$$(-2) + 8 = \triangle$$

Notice that the negative numbers in the sentences have been written with parentheses around them. This seems preferable, particularly in writing mathematical sentences, so that the negative sign is not confused with the symbol for subtraction. Also, a positive number may be written with or without the plus sign. If the plus sign is used, the number should be placed in parentheses so that there is no confusion with the operation symbol for addition. For example: $(-2) + 8$ or $(-2) + (+8)$.

The students can use the number line to solve the two sentences above. Use the number line extensively to solve these sentences.

Next, students should see some situations where the answer is negative rather than positive. For example:

"It's 10 degrees below zero. The temperature rises 6 degrees. What is the temperature now?"

"In the game, you are 5 points in the hole. You score 3 points on your next turn. What is your score now?"

Students have now had an opportunity to see that adding a positive number to a negative number may give either a positive or a negative answer. They should have plenty of practice with these two types of situations (adding a positive number and obtaining either a positive or a negative answer) so that they feel comfortable with what they are doing.

Your students are now ready to look at situations where a negative number is added. Begin with the expression: $(+4) + (-4) = \square$. Students have already seen that $(-4) + (+4) = 0$, so the commutative law is verified. Hence, $(+4) + (-4) = 0$. Adding a negative number means moving to the left on the number line (see Figure 6-6).

FIGURE 6-6

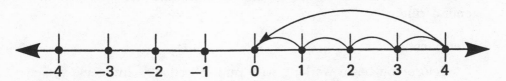

Your students can use the number line to solve the following problems.

Problem $(+3) + (-5) = \square$
Solution: adding (-5) to $(+3)$

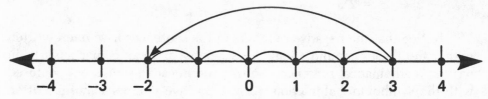

Problem: $(-2) + (-3) = \triangle$
Solution: adding (-3) to (-2)

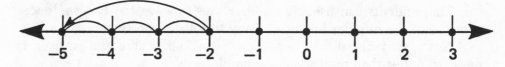

Before moving to the statement of the rule for adding positive and negative numbers, you will need to present the concept of *absolute value* of a number. At this point, it is best to simply define the absolute value of a number as its face value regardless of sign.

$$|+3| = 3$$

$$|-4| = 4$$

$$|0| = 0$$

Absolute value will be developed further in later mathematical years, but this definition is sufficient for our needs here.

The general rule for adding two integers is:

> If both numbers have the same sign, add the absolute values and give the answer the same sign. If the two numbers have different signs, find the difference of the two absolute values and give it the sign of the number with the greater absolute value.

Some students become confused in applying this rule. Thus, you may want to use the distance approach described above and not worry about the general rule.

Multiplication

Before you begin working with multiplication of integers, you may want to review with your students the fact that multiplication is repeated addition. For example, $7 \times 3 = 7 + 7 + 7$. This model can then be used to introduce multiplication of a positive and a negative number: $(-2) \times 3 = (-2) + (-2) + (-2) = 6$.

Another way to help students understand that the product of a positive number and a negative number is always negative might be the following:

"Let's see now …
$(+3)[(+2) + (-2)] = 0$,
since $[(+2) + (-2)]$ is really 0.

Multiplying it out, I have
$(+3)(+2) + (+3)(-2) = 0$.

So, $6 + (+3)(-2) = 0$.

That means $(+3)(-2)$ must be (-6)."

In $(+3) - (+7)$, the answer will have the numerical distance from $+7$ to $+3$ on the number line. If the movement on the number line is to the left, the answer is given a negative sign. If the movement is to the right, the answer is positive. In the example above, the distance from $+7$ to $+3$ is 4. Since the movement from $+7$ to $+3$ was to the left, the answer is (-4).

This reasoning also applies if the number subtracted is negative. For $(-2) - (-3)$, the distance from -3 to -2 is 1. The movement is to the right, so the answer is $+1$.

After your students understand subtraction with positive and negative numbers, they are ready for the rule.

To subtract one number from another, change the sign of the number being subtracted and then add, following the rules of addition.

Past experience indicates that your students will need lots of practice with addition of integers to stabilize their skill. The thermometer model and the number line will be useful tools for developing this skill.

Subtraction

Your first examples with subtraction should be problems where a positive number is being subtracted.

$(+3) - (+6) = \square$
$(-2) - (+2) = \triangle$

Intuitively, your students should realize that subtracting a positive number will give a lesser result. This can also be illustrated on the number line. However, when a negative number is subtracted, it is difficult for students to think of the fact that a greater answer will be obtained than the number subtracted from.

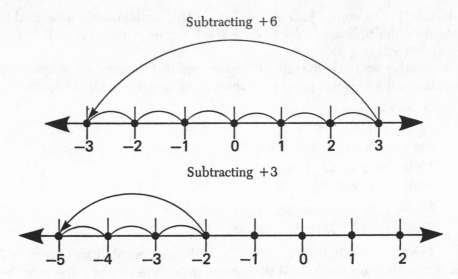

To help students picture what is happening, the subtraction problem can be viewed on the number line as the distance from the number being subtracted.

This same approach can be used to show that $(-3) \cdot (-2) = +6$.

$(-3)\,[(-2)\,+\,(+2)] = 0$

$(-3)\,(-2)\,+\,(-3)\,(+2) = 0$

$(-3)\,(-2)\,+\,(-6) = 0$

so $(-3)\,(-2)\, = \,+6$.

The obvious keys to this explanation are the renaming of zero and the distributive property. You may want to review these two things before you try this approach of explanation.

Your students should now be ready to look at the general rule for multiplication of integers.

Multiply the two numbers together. If both numbers have the same sign, the answer is positive. If the signs of the two numbers are different, the answer is negative.

Division

A good way to develop the sign designation for division of integers is to go back to multiplication of integers. For example,

$$\frac{(-8)}{(+4)} = \square \text{ and } \square \times (+4) = (-8)$$

Most students seem to have little difficulty figuring out that $\square$ is (-2).

If you are thinking of using the repeated subtraction model, be careful. As you may recall, there are two interpretations for division. Let's use 9/3:

1. How many groups of 3 are in 9?

2. I want to divide 9 into 3 groups so that each group has the same. In the example above of $(-8)/(+4)$, the first interpretation doesn't make sense. However, the second interpretation can be used if you think of the problem as what number can be subtracted from (-8) 4 times. The answer is, of course, (-2), since

$$
\begin{array}{r}
(-8) \\
\underline{-(-2)} \quad 1 \\
(-6) \\
\underline{-(-2)} \quad 2 \\
(-4) \\
\underline{-(-2)} \quad 3 \\
(-2) \\
\underline{-(-2)} \quad 4 \\
0
\end{array}
$$

Obviously, this interpretation cannot be used if the divisor is a negative number.

Your students will be delighted when they learn that the rule for determining the sign of the quotient of two integers is the same as the rule for determining the sign of the product of two integers.

After students have studied signed numbers, you might give them this "rule" to remember the rules for multiplication and division of integers.

If a good guy comes to town, that's good.
$$(+) \times (4) = (4)$$

If a good guy leaves town, that's bad.
$$(+) \times (-1) = (-)$$

If a bad guy comes to town, that's bad.
$$(-) \times (+) = (-)$$

If a <u>bad</u> guy <u>leaves</u> town, that's <u>good</u>.
$$(-) \quad \times \quad (-) \qquad = \qquad (+)$$

EXPONENTS AND ROOTS

As your students progress in their mathematical studies through the computational skills, they will encounter two very powerful mathematical concepts: *exponents* and *roots*.

Exponents

As you introduce the concept of exponents, students should understand that 5^2 is a shorthand, symbolic way of representing 5 x 5 or "two factors of 5 multiplied together."

Your students will have a tendency to look at 5^2 and write it as 5 x 2. To correct this problem, they must be reminded that the exponent of 2 simply tells how many factors of 5 are to be multiplied together. Similarly, they should see that:

$$3^4 \text{ means } 3 \text{ x } 3 \text{ x } 3 \text{ x } 3$$
$$4 \text{ factors of } 3$$

$$4^3 \text{ means } 4 \text{ x } 4 \text{ x } 4$$
$$3 \text{ factors of } 4$$

The next step in the study of exponents is to look at 2^1 and what it means. As before, it means "1 factor of 2," so 2^1 means 2.

Your students will need plenty of practice in writing expressions with exponents such as the following:

$$2^3 \text{ means } 2 \text{ x } 2 \text{ x } 2$$
$$3 \text{ x } 3 \text{ x } 3 \text{ means } 3^3$$
$$5 \text{ x } 5 \text{ x } 7 \text{ x } 7 \text{ x } 7 = 5^2 \text{ x } 7^3$$

Students should have plenty of practice writing expressions in both forms.

Q: Calculate 4^3.

Q: Write 4 x 4 x 4 using an exponent.

After the initial work with exponents and having demonstrated proficiency in manipulating expressions with exponents, your students are ready to examine operations with exponential expressions. Examples such as the following may be used to begin the work.

$$2^3 \text{ x } 2^4$$

$$(2 \text{ x } 2 \text{ x } 2) \text{ x } (2 \text{ x } 2 \text{ x } 2 \text{ x } 2)$$

$$2 \text{ x } 2 \text{ x } 2 \text{ x } 2 \text{ x } 2 \text{ x } 2 \text{ x } 2$$

7 factors of 2

$$2^7$$

so that $2^3 \text{ x } 2^4 = 2^{\,3+4} = 2^7$

After studying multiplication of expressions using exponents, your students should study division of exponential expressions. For example:

$$2^4 \div 2^3$$

$$2^4 \div 2^3 \Rightarrow \frac{2^4}{2^3} \Rightarrow \frac{2 \times 2 \times 2 \times 2}{2 \times 2 \times 2}$$

$$\frac{2 \times 2 \times 2 \times 2}{2 \times 2 \times 2} \Rightarrow \frac{\cancel{2} \times \cancel{2} \times \cancel{2} \times 2}{\cancel{2} \times \cancel{2} \times \cancel{2}}$$

$$\Rightarrow 2$$

$$\frac{2^4}{2^3} \Rightarrow 2^{4-3} \Rightarrow 2^1 \Rightarrow 2$$

When your students have established that multiplication of exponential expressions with the same base number involves addition of exponents, and division of exponential expressions with the same base number involves subtraction of exponents, they are ready to look at this expression: $2^4/2^4$.

Evaluating this expression gives us $2^{4-4} \Rightarrow 2^0$. But any number (2^4) divided by itself (2^4) is 1, so we have $2^0 = 1$.

The development of this fact should be done carefully with your students. Make full use of their intuition as they work with these exponential expressions. Be sure to compare expressions such as $3X^0$ and $(3X)^0$.

Now let's move to the study of negative exponents. The same approach as with division of exponential expressions should be used again. For example,

$$\frac{2^3}{2^5} \Rightarrow 2^{3-5} \Rightarrow 2^{-2}$$

But, $\dfrac{2^3}{2^5} \Rightarrow \dfrac{2 \times 2 \times 2}{2 \times 2 \times 2 \times 2 \times 2} \Rightarrow \dfrac{\cancel{2} \times \cancel{2} \times \cancel{2}}{\cancel{2} \times \cancel{2} \times \cancel{2} \times 2 \times 2}$

$$\Rightarrow \frac{1}{2 \times 2} \Rightarrow \frac{1}{2^2}$$

$$\text{so } 2^{-2} = \frac{1}{2^2}$$

Your students will naturally want to think that negative exponents mean negative numbers. They may need some hard convincing that negative exponents mean fractions. You may find it helpful to show them such expressions as $2^3 \times 2^{-3}$ which makes use of the multiplicative inverse.

$$2^3 \times 2^{-3} = 2^{3+(-3)} = 2^0 \text{ or } 1$$

$$\text{and } 2^3 \times \frac{1}{2^3} = 1$$

The greatest difficulty, other than the one expressed earlier, that your students will have is that they will try to use the laws of exponents on expressions where the base numbers are not the same. They may become confused with such expressions as $2^3 \times 3^2$. Remind them that they must evaluate each expression first and then find the product.

You will also want to present situations to your students such as the following:

Q: Evaluate $2^3 + 2^2$

Q: Evaluate $2^3 - 2^2$

The students' tendency will be to try to use the laws of exponents to evaluate these expressions. Watch their work carefully so that they do not make these mistakes from the beginning.

Roots

The study of roots is a natural follow-up to the study of exponents. It may be introduced with the question, "What number multiplied by itself gives 16?"

It may be helpful to have your students solve this problem by taking various whole numbers and squaring them to see if 16 is obtained.

Your students are then ready to see the symbol for root: $\sqrt{16}$ means n x $n/$ finding n where $n \times n = 16$.

The study of roots in your instructional program for junior high/middle school students will probably involve the study of *square roots*. Cube, fourth, and fifth roots will be studied at a later time.

Your students should have an opportunity to manipulate expressions using square roots. For example:

$$\sqrt{2} \times \sqrt{2} = 2$$
$$\sqrt{3} \times \sqrt{2} = \sqrt{3 \times 2} = \sqrt{6}$$
$$\sqrt{\frac{4}{9}} = \frac{\sqrt{4}}{\sqrt{9}} = \frac{2}{3}$$
$$\sqrt{2} + \sqrt{3} \neq \sqrt{2+3}$$
$$\sqrt{4} - \sqrt{3} \neq \sqrt{4-3}$$

You may also want to show your students that $\sqrt{3}$ is the same as $3^{1/2}$. The use of fractional exponents is not really necessary, but you may want to expose your students to this concept.

After their initial experiences with finding square roots which turn out to be whole numbers, the question arises about finding the square root of a number that is not a perfect square. Square root tables and approximate methods for computing square roots may be found in your textbook.

Now would be an excellent time for some estimation activities. One estimate for $3^{1/2}$ might be like this:

3^0 and 3^1 so that

3-$1/2$ is between 3^0 and 3^1. Now, $3^0 = 1$ and $3^1 = 3$, so

3-$1/2$ is between 1 and 3.

More information on the importance of estimation skills is found in Chapter 9.

There is an old method for determining the square root of a number which is seldom seen anymore. It is accurate to any desired number of decimal places and goes like this.

Q: What is 12 to the nearest tenth?

A: Let's do it like this.

1. Place 12 under the radical sign. Put in the decimal point after the number and above the square root sign. Put 2 pairs of zeroes to the right of the decimal point (two pairs so you can round to tenths). Starting at the decimal point, mark off pairs of digits to the left. The leftmost pair may consist of either one or two digits.

$$\sqrt{12.00'00'}$$

2. Find the largest perfect square less than or equal to the number in the leftmost pair of digits. Place the square root above and subtract the perfect square from 12.

$$\begin{array}{r} 3. \\ \sqrt{12.00^100^1} \\ -9 \\ \hline 3 \end{array}$$

3. Bring down the next pair of digits and draw a vertical line to the left of 300.

$$\begin{array}{r} 3. \\ \sqrt{12.00^100} \\ 9 \\ \hline 300 \end{array}$$

4. Double the digit(s) above the radical sign and place it to the left of the vertical line. Mark a place to the right of the doubled number with Δ.

$$\begin{array}{r} 3. \\ \sqrt{12.00^100} \\ 9 \\ 6\Delta \quad \overline{|\ 300} \end{array}$$

5. Find a single digit number for Δ so that 6 Δ x Δ≤ 300 (63 x 3, 64 x 4, etc.) In this case, Δ is 4 since 64 x 4 < 300 and 65 x 5 > 300. Put 4 above the pair of zeroes you brought down. Subtract 64 x 4 (256) from 300.

$$\begin{array}{r} 3. \\ \sqrt{12.00^100} \\ 9 \\ 64 \quad |\ 300 \\ |\ 256 \\ \hline 44 \end{array}$$

6. Bring down the next pair of zeroes and repeat steps 4 and 5. (Disregard the decimal point in doubling.) Δthis time will be 6 since 686 x 6 < 4400, but 687 x 7 > 4400. Put 7 above the second pair of zeroes you brought down.

$$\begin{array}{r} 3.4 \\ \sqrt{12.00^100} \\ 9 \\ 64 \quad |\ 300 \\ |\ 256 \\ 68\Delta \quad |\ 4400 \end{array}$$

7. The procedure would be repeated if you required greater accuracy. For now, $\sqrt{12}$ to the nearest tenth is 3.5.

$$
\begin{array}{r}
3.4 \quad 6 \\
\sqrt{12.00^{1}00} \\
9 \\
\hline
64 \mid 300 \\
256 \\
\hline
686 \mid 4400 \\
4116 \\
\hline
284
\end{array}
$$

Here is another worked-out example for you to go through.

$$
\begin{array}{r}
12. \quad 4 \quad 8 \\
\sqrt{156.00^{1}00^{1}} \\
1 \\
\hline
22 \mid 56 \\
44 \\
\hline
244 \mid 1200 \\
976 \\
\hline
2488 \mid 22400 \\
19904 \\
\hline
2496
\end{array}
$$

To the nearest tenth, $\sqrt{156} = 12.5$.

QUICK REVIEW

1. What are the key points to remember in developing an algorithm?

2. What are the prerequisite skills for each of the following?

   a. addition of fractions with unlike denominators
   b. multiplication of integers
   c. division with decimals
   d. finding the square root of a whole number

3. Identify the greatest difficulty your students seem to have in working with:

   a. operations on whole numbers
   b. equivalent fractions
   c. operations on fractions
   d. operations on decimals
   e. percent
   f. operations on integers
   g. exponents and roots

   What are you doing to help your students overcome these difficulties?

4. Usually the sequence for teaching fractions is as follows: concept of fractions, equivalent fractions, ordering fractions, addition, subtraction, multiplication, and division. Is there a different sequence that could also be used? Why?

5. How would you correct a student's thinking if it went like this?

   "1/3 is 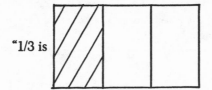   and 2/3 is

   So, 1/3 + 2/3 is 3 parts out of 6. Then 1/3 + 2/3 = 3/6."

6. What are the pros and cons of this statement?

   "Students who haven't learned their basic facts by the seventh grade should be allowed to use a calculator to do their work. If they haven't learned them by then, they never will."

7. Outline your plan for demonstrating the following algorithms. Include specific numerical examples that you would use.

   a. division of decimals
   b. division of fractions
   c. exponents
   d. addition of integers

8. What are some arguments for and against allowing students to use the product of denominators instead of finding the least common denominator?

9. Based upon your experience, how much and what types of drill do slower students need?

10. What are the pros and cons of homogenous grouping of math students according to computational skill level?

11. Does your mathematics department encourage the use of different ways of computation? Do you think it should? Why?

7

Development of Geometry
and Measurement Skills

The study of geometry and measurement has probably not received appropriate emphasis in most junior high/middle school mathematics classrooms. Some teachers feel that there are "more important things to do." However, geometry and measurement are very much a part of our everyday life and the study of these areas helps pull together concepts and skills from other areas.

This chapter examines the kind of geometry that should be taught and suggests some strategies and activities which you can use. It also looks at measurement, in particular the metric system, and how it should be incorporated into the mathematics instructional program.

After reading and studying this chapter, you should be able to:

- Describe guidelines for presenting geometric concepts.
- Describe general considerations for teaching measurement concepts and skills.
- Describe techniques for teaching perimeter, area, and volume.
- Describe techniques and activities for teaching the metric system.
- Describe a technique for teaching the Pythagorean Theorem.

STUDYING GEOMETRY

Here are some guidelines for your presentation of geometric concepts.

1. *The study of geometry should be on an informal or intuitive basis*. It is not appropriate for students to write formal geometric proofs; there will be plenty of time for that later. Rather, your students should begin to think through why certain geometric concepts happen as they do. For example, when you are talking about the fact that the sum of the angle of a triangle measures 180°, then tear off the three angles and lay them side by side, as in Figure 7-1. Your students can then easily see that the sum of the angle measures is indeed 180°. Activities like this help your students understand the concepts with which they are working.

FIGURE 7-1

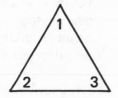 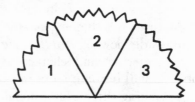

2. *Use both examples and counter-examples of geometric concepts in your presentations*. Examples of a geometric concept are very important to help your students understand a concept. However, it is also necessary to show counter-examples to help ensure understanding. For example, when you discuss examples of squares, also discuss examples of things that are not squares.

3. *Keep your students actively involved in their study of geometry*. The study of geometry should not be a passive undertaking; it must be more than simply reading a page or doing worksheets. To be understood, geometry must "come alive" for your students.

Geometry will "come alive" if you use activities that get your students involved. An example of such an activity is the one shown earlier in Figure 7-1. Encourage your students to make models of geometric figures and concepts; these models will add meaning to the study.

Paperfolding is an excellent source of many activities to demonstrate geometric concepts. These activities are best done using waxed paper, although it may be a little more expensive than you want.

Attribute pieces also present a host of opportunities for active student involvement. These pieces are various geometric shapes that usually vary in size, shape, color, and thickness. They can be used for many different things, including development of patterns such as one- or two-different sequences of the shapes.

The point is, there is a wide variety of materials and activities that will keep your students actively involved in their learning of geometric concepts. This active involvement on the part of your students will make learning more enjoyable and meaningful.

4. *Stress the relationship between two- and three-dimensional figures.* The relationship between two- and three-dimensional figures is a difficult one for many students to understand. They see little similarity between a picture of an object and the object itself.

A good way to help your students overcome this difficulty is to have them draw two-dimensional pictures of various views, such as the top view or the side view, of a three-dimensional figure. At the same time, a study of the properties and characteristics of both two- and three-dimensional objects will become more meaningful.

Making three-dimensional geometric shapes out of cardboard is also helpful. It is not a trivial activity to have your students make a network or pattern for a geometric solid such as the one in Figure 7-2 so that it can be constructed by folding.

FIGURE 7-2

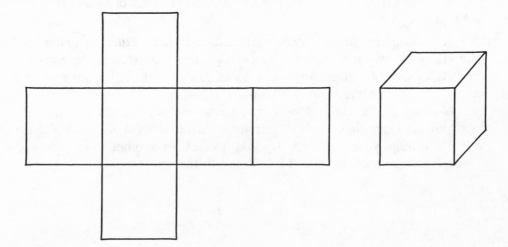

STUDYING MEASUREMENT

It is very difficult to separate the study of measurement from the study of geometry. Measurement is viewed as the assignment of a number to characteristics of a geometric shape (two- or three-dimensional) or to some quantity. As such, the act of measurement requires the use of tools.

General Considerations

When your students enter the classroom, it is safe to assume that they are not proficient in the use of measuring devices such as rulers or scales. Don't assume that the science teacher has or will teach your students how to use these devices; even if the teacher does, the additional reinforcement is good for your students.

As with geometry, your students need lots of activities that focus on their involvement with measuring devices. Traditionally, students have been given a worksheet with line segments on it and told to measure them with a ruler. This type of exercise is all right, but your measurement activities should have much more meaning. For example, measuring the heights of students in the classroom or the dimensions of a student desk or the classroom are much more meaningful.

The study of measurement also provides excellent opportunity to practice estimation skills. Being able to look at a point and estimate its distance or pick up a weight and estimate its mass is a valuable skill for later life. Take every possible opportunity to let your students work on estimation.

In studying the use of various measuring devices, the concepts of measurement to the nearest unit and precision are essential to a student's understanding of measurement. The activities for the study of those two concepts should begin with larger units and gradually work to smaller gradations.

The question of which system of measurement—metric or customary (English)—to use is one that has sharply divided opinion on the part of educators. At the present time, the United States is in a transition period to the metric system. It is not a case of *if* but *when*, but no definitive timetable has yet been set.

During this transition period, it will be desirable, perhaps necessary, to expose your students to both systems of measurement. In doing this, each system should be viewed as a separate entity. There should be *no* conversion from one system to the other; this conversion has little or no value relative to a student's understanding of either system. After students have studied both systems, it is all right to look at some rough comparisons between the two systems, such as:

a liter is a little more than a quart

a yard is almost as long as a meter

a kilogram is a little more than two pounds

However, these comparisons should be kept to a minimum.

Perimeter and Area

The concepts of perimeter and area are essential to the measurement of two-dimensional geometric figures. The concept of area will be especially troublesome for your students because of the use of a different type of measuring unit.

There are several good ways to help your students understand and work with the measurement of area.

1. *Use a geoboard*. A geoboard is a rectangular array of pegs on a board. A rubber band is stretched around the pegs to make a geometric figure, as shown in Figure 7-3. Geoboards may be commercially bought or homemade. A homemade geoboard is probably best constructed by pounding finishing nails into a piece of wood. The geoboard can be made in any size desired.

FIGURE 7-3

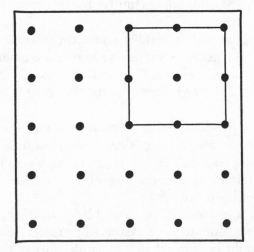

Since area is a measure of an enclosed flat suface, the student is able to count the number of square units and find the area. Initial examples should use squares or rectangles; more complex figures can be worked with later.

2. *Use graph paper.* Graph paper is really only a pictorial geoboard. It does have an advantage in that the square units are clearly marked by the lines on the paper and the square units are thus easy to count.

3. *Use square units cut from some heavy materials.* Square units cut from heavy material such as plastic coffee can lids make a good concrete way to find area. Students can place the pieces over the area in question and get an answer for the area.

4. *Use a transparent grid.* The transparent grid is easy to lay over the area to be measured and be adjusted so that it is set properly. This device is especially useful for working with circles and odd-shaped polygons where an approximation becomes necessary.

Speaking of circles, your students will quickly recognize that the area of a circle involves parts of lots of square units. The devices described above for measuring area will give an approximation; students should use these devices to find boundary areas, that is, two numbers of square units between which the actual area lies.

Formulas for areas are, of course, most often used to find area. By using figures such as squares, rectangles, parallelograms, and triangles on graph paper or a geoboard, it becomes relatively easy to find a formula to calculate area. Spend considerable time developing these formulas so that your students clearly understand why they are appropriate.

Your students will probably have difficulty using formulas where they have to "plug and chug" or substitute numbers to obtain an area. Give them considerable practice in applying formulas. Applying formulas where the answer is given and the student is asked to find a component part is especially troublesome. An example of this latter type of problem is one like this:

"The area of a rectangle is 25 square units. Its length is 8 units. What is its width?"

Have your students draw a diagram or picture of the problem to help them understand what is to be found. Figure 7-4 is often helpful in solving the problem.

A word chart notation is appropriate here. Traditionally, the label for square unit has been written as 33 square (or sq.) inches. Recently, with

FIGURE 7-4

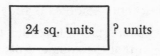

8 units

the coming of the metric system, there seems to be a tendency to write the expression as 33 in.^{2}. Be sure your students are able to work with either form.

Perimeter does not seem to be as troublesome for most students as area. The greatest difficulty will probably be the recording of the perimeter in the proper unit, especially after working with area. However, if you take the time to be sure that your students understand both area and perimeter, this improper interchange of labels will be minimized.

When introducing the notion of circumference, a good way is to use cylinders and a piece of string. Students can then physically measure the circumference of a circle. This activity also emphasizes the fact that circumference is a linear measure.

Volume

The concept of volume will also cause your students difficulty, especially in the use of cubic units. To help your students overcome this difficulty, your initial introduction of volume should be to build rectangular solids using cubes, either wooden or otherwise. Using the cubes to build the figures and then count them to find the volume, seems to help students understand the concept of volume.

You will also find that using the cubes to develop the concept will aid you in developing formulas. Asking your students to find a shorter way to find the volume than counting the cubes one by one will often result in students developing the formula themselves, a highly desirable goal.

Again, relative to notation, the traditional form has been 15 cubic (or cu.) ft. As before, it can also be written as 15 ft.^{3}, so students should be exposed to both forms.

THE METRIC SYSTEM

As you are well aware, it is only a matter of time until we are probably completely metric. The thrust for metric education will come from two sources: industry and education. You have a clear and definite responsibility to help your students learn the metric system of measurement. An appropriate motto to guide you is: "To learn and think metric, you have to *do* metric." This motto implies that your students must be actively involved in doing metric measurement so that they can learn metric measurement.

One good way to help your students gain a feeling for the metric system is to make use of references to known objects. For example, a millimeter is about the thickness of a dime. Here are some other references.

Metric Unit	*Common Object*
centimeter	width of your little finger
decimeter	width of your palm
meter	height of a doorknob
gram	weight of a paper clip
cubic centimeter	a little smaller than a sugar cube
square meter	card table top
liter	quart milk carton

Having these references in mind is a great help in making estimates in the metric system.

The best way to introduce the metric system is to relate it to money. Using the dollar as the basic unit, the penny (cent) is 1/100 of a dollar and the dime is 1/10 of a dollar. If you have introduced the mil (1/1000 of a dollar), then this is also useful.

Relationship with Money	
1000 mils	= 1 dollar
100 cents	= 1 dollar
10 dimes	= 1 dollar
10 dollars	= 1 ten dollar bill
100 dollars	= 1 hundred dollar bill
1000 dollars	= 1 thousand dollar bill

Students seem to be able to relate the money model to the metric system, so the result is quick and more effective learning.

One of the biggest problems that you will have as you approach your unit of instruction on the metric system is the lack of measuring instruments to use in class. To help you solve this problem, you and your students should make some of the aids yourselves. Here are some suggestions.

Length. To begin work in this area, you need to purchase a commercial meterstick or metric tape measure. This device will be used to make other meter measures and to check calibrations that will be made.

Wood lathe or window shade sticks may be used to make additional metersticks. Cut the sticks to a length of one meter and calibrate them in decimeters and centimeters. One way to calibrate centimeters is to lay a decimeter length at an angle across a sheet of narrow-lined notebook paper in such a way that the decimeter is separated into ten congruent segments by the lines on the paper (see Figure 7-5). Mark each of the decimeters on the stick in the same way, so the centimeter calibration will be complete.

FIGURE 7-5

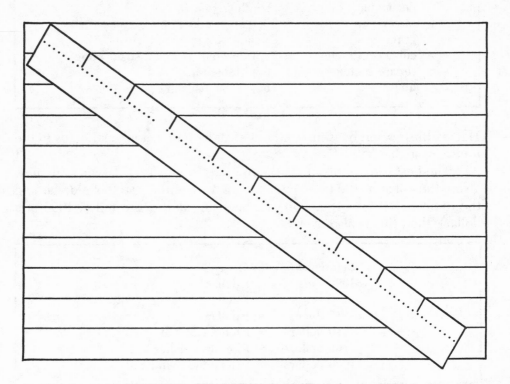

A similar technique using larger spaces can be used to calibrate decimeters. Because of their smallness, it will be more difficult to calibrate millimeters; use the commercially made meterstick or metric tape measure for millimeter measurements.

An interesting variation of the meterstick is to cut a square pole to a length of one meter. Let one side have no marks on it; this will represent a length of one meter. A second side can be calibrated into decimeters, a third side into centimeters, and so on.

Making a metric tape measure is also quite simple. Cut ribbon, twill tape, or seam tape to a length of one meter and calibrate it in the same way as the meterstick. Attach one end of the tape to an empty thread spool and roll the tape around it for easy storage. Adding machine tape may also be used to make a tape measure.

A trundle wheel may be constructed from a pizza flat, a film can, or plywood. A wheel that has a diameter of 31.9 cm will have a circumference of approximately one meter. The wheel can be rolled by attaching a handle to the center of the wheel. Marking the edge of the wheel enables a person to count the number of revolutions of the wheel and, thus, the number of meters traveled by the wheel (see Figure 7-6). Using a bolt on the edge of the wheel and a flange made of sheet metal attached to the handle so that the bolt strikes the flange makes it possible to count the number of revolutions by counting the number of times the bolt strikes the flange.

FIGURE 7-6

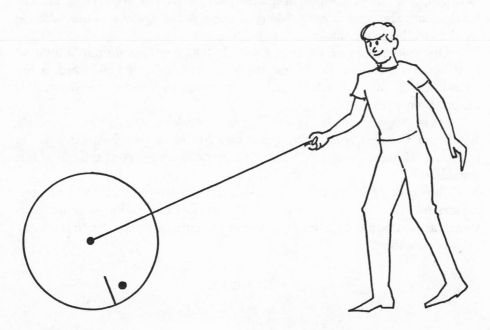

Lengths shorter than a meter may be constructed by using popsicle sticks, paint sticks, children's blocks, sugar cubes, Cuisenaire® rods, strips of checkered gingham material, or film, to name just a few. Film comes in

80, 16-, 35- and 70-mm widths; pieces of discarded film are often available from local photo-processing or television stations.

Area. The students' understanding of metric area can be greatly enhanced by letting them measure areas using square centimeters or decimeters cut from a coffee can lid, tagboard, or similar material. The students might also use a transparent centimeter grid constructed from centimeter grid paper. A geoboard whose nails are spaced one centimeter apart may also be used, with areas outlined on the board by rubber bands.

Volume. Students can make their own metric containers by calibrating any number of different containers into liters, deciliters, centiliters, and milliliters. To help in the calibration process, use discarded medical syringes, eye droppers, or clear plastic straws. A standard-size straw will hold 5 ml at a point 17.6 cm from the end.

For liters, it is possible to use containers such as coffee cans, ice cream containers, take-out chicken containers, and paint cans. A half-gallon milk carton can also be used by filling the carton with a quart of water, noting the level, and measuring up a distance of 8 mm. A mark at this new level will represent one liter. For milliliters, good containers to use are baby food jars, test tubes, half-pint or quart milk cartons, bathroom cups, aspirin bottles, and shampoo bottles. Many of these same containers may also be used to calibrate deciliters and centiliters.

Dry volume can be measured with hollow containers such as a cubic centimeter or a cubic decimeter made of styrofoam or cardboard. Dice (standard-size dice are 1.5 cm on an edge) may be used to construct and measure volume.

Mass. Working with mass will involve working with a balance scale. Ideally, a balance scale with gram weights or a pan balance will be available. However, a simple balance scale may be constructed if one is not available.

One type of balance may be made by hanging pans from a hanger, meterstick, or ruler (see Figure 7-7). Good possibilities for pans are such things as margarine containers, paper cups, cottage cheese containers, or aerosol can tops.

FIGURE 7-7

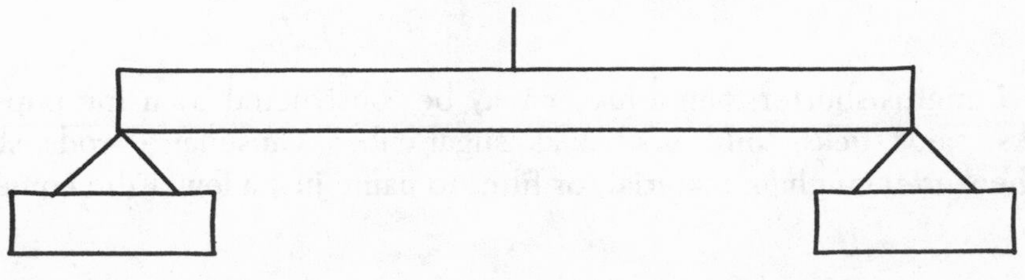

Another type of balance that can be easily constructed is pictured in Figure 7-8. The base is a small milk carton or juice container filled with sand. The arm is made from a plastic drinking straw and is fastened to the carton with a straight pin. Pins are also used to fasten the pans, pictured in Figure 7-8. Small nut cups may be used in the pans to hold water or small objects. Paper clips may be used on the arm to balance the scale when there is nothing in the pans.

FIGURE 7-8

There are many commonly found items that can be used as weights. Washers painted different colors for different weights, lumps of modelling clay, standard-size paper clips (each weighs one gram), a nickel (it weighs 5 grams), poker chips, dice, and checkers are possibilities for calibration in grams. A kilogram can be made by using a cubic decimeter made from tagboard and lined with plastic. Filling this container with water will give an object that weighs one kilogram. A bolt with several washers on it or modelling clay may also be used to make a kilogram.

Many commercial companies list the weights of their products in grams on the container. Examination of the labels of these products will show the students that the metric system is being used in everyday life.

Temperature. Celsius thermometers may be made by recalibrating Fahrenheit thermometers. The easiest ones to recalibrate are the type that hang on the wall and have their scale on the mounting which holds the thermometer. Simply change the 32-degree mark to 0 and the 104-degree mark to 40. The intervals can then be divided into degrees Celsius, at 1- or 5-degree intervals. If the Fahrenheit thermometer has the 212-degree mark on it, change it to 100 and divide the scale into degrees Celsius at 5-

or 10-degree intervals. Inexpensive thermometers that have not been calibrated may be purchased and calibrated. Boiling water and ice may be used for determining the 100 and 0 marks respectively, and the interval can then be divided into desired calibrations.

It is clear that you should not avoid study of the metric system in the classroom because of a lack of teaching aids. Whenever possible, the students should be encouraged to obtain the materials and make their own aids. In this way, the metric system of measurement will become more than something heard about or read about in a book.

EXAMPLES OF METRIC ACTIVITIES

Here are some examples of metric activities that will get your students actively involved in their learning.

Length

Activity 1: How long is a meter?
Materials: meterstick
Stand beside your seat and place the end of the meterstick on the floor so that it stands vertically. Where on your body does the end of the meterstick touch? Remember this place. How does its location compare with your classmates?

Activity 2: How long is a decimeter and a centimeter?
Materials: one orange rod and ten white rods from a set of Cuisenaire® rods

The orange rod is one decimeter long. Find objects around you or a body part that are one decimeter long. What do you find?

Place the orange rod in front of you, and next to it line up the ten white rods. The train of ten white rods should be the same length as the orange rod. Each white rod is one centimeter long. Find objects around you or a body part that is one centimeter long. What do you find?

Activity 3: Measuring parts of your body
Materials: metric tape measure 1.5 meters long

Estimate the following distances and then check to see how close you were to the actual measurement. What units of measure are appropriate in each case?

	Estimate	*Actual Measure*
a. Palm of your hand	_____	_____
b. Span (tip of your thumb to tip of your little finger when your hand is extended)	_____	_____
c. Cubit (tip of your elbow to the tip of your second finger)	_____	_____
d. Fathom (tip of second finger on left hand to tip of second finger on right hand when arms are extended)	_____	_____
e. Waist	_____	_____
f. Height	_____	_____

Activity 4: How long is your pace?
Materials: meterstick

On the floor, measure a distance that is 5 meters long. Starting at one end, walk normally to the other end, counting your steps. Using this information, find the length and width of the room and various distances outside the classroom. Check your accuracy on some of the shorter distances.

Activity 5: How big is your silhouette?
Materials: large piece of paper about 1 meter wide and 2 meters long, marking pen, piece of string 1 meter long, transparent centimeter grid

Lie on your back on the paper. With your feet together and arms at your side, have your partner trace your silhouette on the paper. Use the piece of string to find the perimeter of your silhouette. Then take the transparent grid and approximate the area of your silhouette.

Activity 6: How much carpet?
Materials: metric tape measure or treadel wheel

Someone has asked to have the student lounge carpeted. To know how much carpet to buy, you must find the number of square meters on the floor of the lounge. Compare your answers with other classmates.

Mass

Activity 7: How much does it weigh?
Materials: balance scale, centicubes, Chiclets gum, 3 or 4 each of pennies, nickels, and dimes, sugar cubes, M and M's, nut cups, small syringe, water

   Using what you know about the mass of the centicube, estimate the mass (weight) of each object below and then check your answer.

Object	*Estimated Weight*	*Actual Weight*
nickel	_____	_____
penny	_____	_____
dime	_____	_____
sugar cube	_____	_____
piece of Chiclets gum	_____	_____
one M & M	_____	_____
paper clip	_____	_____
10 cm³ water	_____	_____

   Now check your accuracy by completing the exercises below. The term "ABW" means "almost balances with."

_____ Chiclets ABW 2 nickels
_____ Chiclets ABW_____ sugar cubes
_____ pennies ABW _____ M and M's
_____ pennies ABW _____ dimes

Activity 8: How much do you weigh?
Materials: kilogram balance scale

   Weigh yourself on the scale. If you are trying to lose (or gain) weight, check yourself each week for the next several weeks to see how much you are progressing.

Activity 9: How much does a cubic decimeter weigh?
Materials: hollow cubic decimeter, balance scale, water

   Fill the cubic decimeter with water. Pick it up and estimate its mass. Check yourself by weighing the cube of water.

Activity 10: How many millimeters in a liter?
Materials: prepared game cards (thin cardboard), paper, scissors, marking
pen

Directions for playing the game:

1. Prepare for the game by cutting ten pieces of posterboard to 5 cm x 10 cm. Put each of the numerals from 0 to 9 on a different card.

2. Each player prepares the following grid on another sheet of paper:

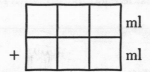

3. The ten cards are shuffled and placed face down on the table.

4. One card is turned over and each player decides where he or she wants to write that number on his or her grid. (Each player is trying to have his or her sum equal one liter.)

5. The next card is turned over and the players now place this number on the grid. The play continues until six numbers have been turned over and each player has placed the numbers on his or her grid.

6. The players now add the milliliter quantities. The player or players closest to one liter receive one point.

7. The cards are reshuffled, new grids are made, and the game proceeds as before. The winner is the first player to get ten points.

Activity 11: How big is a meter cube?
Materials: meter cube (constructed from metersticks)

This activity involves determining how many students can stand up inside a meter cube at one time. How many of your group can fit in the cube at one time?

Temperature

Activity 12: The temperature today is...
Materials: thermometer, pencil, paper

Take the inside and outside temperature in Celsius degrees before school starts in the morning, at lunch, and before going home at night. Keep a daily record.

Activity 13: Taking temperatures
Materials: thermometer, pencil, paper

Measure and record the temperature of slush, mud, the ground, the inside of a lamp shade with the lamp off, then on; measure the temperature of a refrigerator; place the thermometer on a radiator and record the temperature; measure the temperature of water from a drinking fountain of water and from a hot water faucet.

Activity 14: What's the temperature?
Materials: none

Fill in the blank beside each picture with the appropriate temperature from the following list.

B _____

C _____

A _____

D _____

37.5° C
0°C
100°C
22°C
−5°C
34°C

F _____

E _____

THE PYTHAGOREAN THEOREM

An application of both geometry and measurement is the famous Pythagorean Theorem, which refers to a property of right triangles. Students seem to have a great deal of difficulty performing the computation associated with the theorem, perhaps because of the use of squares and square roots of numbers.

However, it is also a distinct possibility that the students do not understand what the Pythagorean Theorem says. To help your students get off to a good start with the Pythagorean Theorem, use the area interpretation using graph paper, as shown in Figure 7-9.

FIGURE 7-9

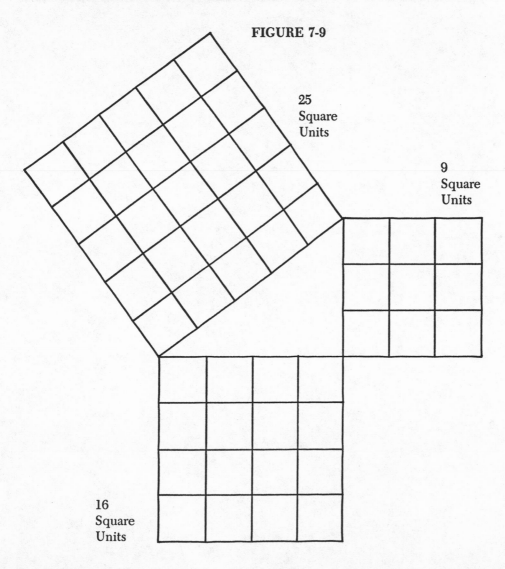

25
Square
Units

9
Square
Units

16
Square
Units

Your students should make graph paper models to check other triples of numbers to see if they satisfy the property. They can then move to the manipulation of squares and square roots of numbers.

QUICK REVIEW

1. Describe guidelines for your presentation of geometric concepts.
2. In teaching measurement, what general consideration must you keep in mind?
3. How should perimeter, area, and volume be introduced?
4. How should the metric system be introduced?
5. How was the metric system first presented to you?
6. Describe the geometric model for teaching the Pythagorean Theorem.
7. Make a list of mathematical concepts you can teach with a geoboard.
8. List some inexpensive teaching aids, other than those mentioned in the chapter, you can use to teach the metric system.
9. Describe several activities, other than those mentioned in the chapter, you can use to teach the metric system.
10. Make a list of geometric concepts you will teach at your grade level. Find or design some activities that you can use that will emphasize active student involvement.

8

Problem Solving in the Junior High/Middle School Mathematics Classroom

If you were asked which areas of the mathematics instruction cause more difficulty for you and your students, a variety of answers would be given. But one area would likely be mentioned more often than any other—problem solving.

After reading and studying this chapter, you should be able to:

- List important problem-solving skills.
- Describe appropriate classroom climate for good problem solving to take place.
- State the role of the teacher in problem-solving activities.
- Describe techniques for presenting problem-solving situations in the classroom.
- Describe techniques and activities for improving both general and specific problem-solving skills.
- Describe techniques for improving word problem-solving skills.
- Describe how estimation skills can be built by students.

WHAT IS PROBLEM SOLVING?

Most teachers associate the term problem solving with word or story problems that are found in the textbook. However, problem solving is much more than just solving word problems.

Problem solving is a process that requires an individual or a group of people to use knowledge and understanding in order to resolve a presented situation. The situation is one that has not previously been seen by the individual or group.

As such, problem solving is a skill and is, therefore, teachable. However, you will not teach problem solving to your students as a unit like you would the division algorithm or the concept of fractions. Instead, you should spend some time each day helping your students learn the skills needed to become good problem solvers. These skills will be listed in the first section of the chapter. It is also important that you realize that not all students will use the same skills in the same way as other students to solve a problem. Your instruction must be flexible enough to allow for these differences. Your job is to help each student learn to use the skills needed to become a good problem solver.

In addition, a problem for one student may not be a problem for another student because of different levels of mathematical maturity. A problem should present a new situation to the solver. Some students may have already seen or solved the problem under consideration. You should make provisions for these students who have a higher level of maturity so that they can continue to develop their problem-solving skills.

Why teach problem-solving skills in your mathematics class? The study of mathematics involves the use of quantitative thinking and is thus an excellent vehicle for the development of problem-solving skills. Problem-solving activities can also help bridge the gap between the theory of mathematics and its application in the real world. Narrowing this gap gives obvious credance to students for studying mathematics.

This chapter lists skills that students need to become good problem solvers and discusses ways for you to help students improve each skill. Also examined are the solving of word problems and the kind of classroom atmosphere necessary to foster good problem-solving skills. The last section discusses estimation, a skill that is extremely important but often ignored in the classroom.

IDENTIFYING PROBLEM-SOLVING SKILLS

It is not possible to determine a complete list of skills needed for a student to become a good problem solver. Students use different processes and skills to solve problems, so no two students will solve the same problem in exactly the same way. However, there seem to be some skills that are useful to many students:

1. *Ability to understand the meaning of vocabulary and symbols*. A student must have a clear understanding of all vocabulary and symbols

presented in a problem situation before the process of solving the problem can be begun. This understanding is necessary for the student to get a clear sense of the problem to be solved.

2. *Ability to do basic mathematical computation*. Many problems to be solved are quantitative in nature. This means that the problem solution requires a student to be able to do basic computation even if a calculator is used.

3. *Ability to estimate*. Estimation is a useful tool often neglected by the classroom teacher. It is useful because it can help students approximate the solution to a problem and may assist in determining which strategy should be used in the process of solution.

4. *Ability to organize and interpret data*. Being able to take the information given in the problem and put it into tables, graphs, or charts may be the key to solving the problem. This skill is also one that has application to everyday life outside of problem-solving situations.

5. *Ability to test the results of the problem-solving process*. The student must be able to test the adequacy of the results from the problem-solving process. It is difficult, if not impossible, to declare that a problem has been solved until the results have been checked for accuracy.

6. *Ability to ask questions that yield maximum information*. Asking good questions is very important if a student is to become a good problem solver. Students must learn to ask questions that give them needed information. Formulating such questions will give the student insight into the problem and enhance the chances of reaching a successful solution.

7. *Ability to design and use different problem-solving strategies*. Many times a student will need more than one strategy to solve a given problem. The original technique chosen may reach a dead end for one reason or another, so the student must be able to come up with a different strategy to complete the problem solution.

Now let's move to a discussion of your role as a teacher in helping students develop these seven problem-solving skills.

SETTING THE CLIMATE

The first thing you need to do as a classroom teacher to help your students develop good problem-solving skills is to create the type of classroom environment that will foster good problem-solving behavior. You must present yourself as a good problem solver and you must be able to present problems in such a way that your students will want and be able to tackle the problem to be solved. How will you accomplish these two tasks?

The Teacher's Role

There are two parts to your role in helping your students become good problem solvers. One part involves you as a problem solver yourself and the other part involves you as a manager of problem-solving activities in your classroom. These two parts are not disjoint as you will soon discover.

As a problem solver, you must exhibit a good model for your students. This means you must be able to use each of the seven skills with a high degree of proficiency. In addition, you must demonstrate to your students that you are *persistent* and *not afraid to guess,* two characteristics of good problem solvers.

Being persistent means that you do not give up easily when one strategy fails to work, and you are persistent until the solution to the problem is found. Not being afraid to guess helps give you new ideas for different strategies that may be needed to successfully solve the problem.

As the manager of problem-solving activity in your classroom, you must encourage your students to be persistent and to guess. This means you must give students ample time to solve problems and, if necessary, give some gentle guidance about new approaches to solving the problem. It also means that you need to be sensitive and careful in handling mistakes or incorrect guesses made by students. Students should feel that they will not be penalized for making mistakes and that the classroom is a place where trial and error is acceptable. Never ridicule a student for making a mistake.

Presenting a Problem

You can do much to enhance the development of good problem-solving skills by your students if you present problem situations carefully. Simply giving problems to students to solve does not mean they will be motivated to solve them.

Motivation to solve a problem on the part of the student must come from a feeling that the problem is important and worthy of being solved. When students feel there is a need to solve the problem, they will be willing to devote time and effort to its solution.

Here are suggestions for presenting problems:

1. *Present problems that are realistic and interesting to your students.* To do this, you must be aware of what your students are interested in and

concerned about. Problems that are interesting to students in an inner-city setting may be quite different from those that are interesting to students in a rural setting. You need to keep this difference in mind.

2. *Present problems in an environment where students feel free to explore.* To become good problem solvers, students must feel they are free to explore alternative solutions and to make guesses without fear of being penalized. A rigid, structured environment will soon cause students to lose motivation to solve the problem.

3. *Present problems that are appropriate for your students' levels of reading, vocabulary, and mathematical understanding.* Students must feel that they have a fighting chance to solve the problem that you pose for them. Nothing is gained by giving them problems when there is no chance that they will be able to find the solution. This does not mean that an occasional problem that is particularly challenging should not be given, but it does mean that you should not expect all students to solve the challenge.

4. *Present problems in more than one medium.* When a problem is presented in only one way, it creates a distinct disadvantage for some of your students. If you present a problem orally, you should also write it on the chalkboard or on the overhead. You may also want to present the problem through the use of visual aids such as concrete materials, pictures, or diagrams on the chalkboard or overhead. Use as many different ways as you can to present the problem so that as many students as possible will be able to understand the problem to be solved.

5. *After initially presenting the problem, give a summary of the problem.* Giving a summary of the problem gives students an opportunity to review the main aspects of the problem so that they can be sure that they understand the problem situation. If you ask for a summary from one of your students, it presents an opportunity for the student to state the problem in his or her own words, which should enhance all the students' understanding of the problem.

The climate for good problem solving to take place in your classroom is now set. You must now be concerned with specific ways to improve student problem-solving skills.

IMPROVING PROBLEM-SOLVING SKILLS

Now that you have a list of skills needed for good problem solving and have set the climate for problem solving in the classroom, you are ready to face the difficult task of improving the problem-solving skills that your students bring. Here are specific suggestions and activities for improving each of the seven skills, followed by more general suggestions for improving problem-solving skills.

Improving Specific Skills

Seven specific skills needed by students to become good problem solvers have been listed. What can be done to improve each of these skills?

1. *Ability to understand the meaning of vocabulary and symbols.* Need to improve this skill comes from the different meanings that words and symbols have when used in mathematics as opposed to their use in everyday life. For example, words such as *or, point, prime, interest, mean, product, rounding, set, adjacent,* and many others all have different meanings when they are used in a mathematical context. In everyday life, the symbol *!* is used to show strong emphasis at the end of a sentence, while in mathematics it means a particular type of multiplication: 5! = 5x4x3x2x1.

Here are two classroom activities you may find useful:

- Drill your class at every opportunity on the words and symbols being used in their work. The drill sessions may include such activities as having the students recite orally or write down the meanings of words you have given them. Exercises where the words are matched to their meaning are also good. Similar activities may be used for symbols.

- Choose a word as "Word for the Day." Write the word on the chalkboard or write it on a card for the bulletin board. Assign a student to keep track of how many other students use the word during the class that day. Periodically, have a review of past words selected as "Word for the Day."

2. *Ability to do basic mathematical computation.* There is still no substitute for drill to help students improve proficiency in this skill. As pointed out earlier, however, drill must be preceded by some understanding on the part of the student; drill without understanding will make the computation nothing but mechanical.

Diagnosis is also a very important tool you can use to help students improve computational skills. Recall the use of diagnosis discussed in Chapter 4.

As students are working to improve this skill, there should be a de-emphasis on speed and an emphasis on accuracy. It is much more sensible for a student to take a little longer to do a computation correctly than to rush through the work with the greater chance of error.

Specific activities for improving this skill have been provided in Chapter 7. Games and puzzles are also an excellent source of activities and their use will be described in Chapter 11.

3. *Ability to estimate*. By now you are well aware of the importance of this skill and specific ways of improving estimation skills will be discussed later in the chapter. For the moment, here are two activities you can use in the classroom.

- Use problems such as: "The square root of 57 is between what two whole numbers?"
- Have students estimate the number of jelly beans in a jar. Encourage them to use different methods to make their guesses.

4. *Ability to organize and interpret data*. Give students plenty of opportunities to improve this skill. A wide variety of activities can be used, four of which are described here.

- Have students collect examples of graphs and tables from newspapers and magazines. Share the collected examples with the entire class and discuss what information is given by the examples.
- Give your students the set of scores from the last math test (without names). Have them make a frequency table of the scores and a graph of the table.
- Have students make a graph or table of a set of collected data such as the daily low temperature or the results from tossing two die a certain number of times.
- Give students problems to be solved and ask them to make diagrams or drawings that illustrate the information given in the problem.

5. *Ability to test the results of the problem-solving process*. Improvement of this skill is important because it enables the student to determine whether or not the problem has been solved correctly. If the solution cannot be tested, then there is no way of knowing whether or not the problem solving has been completed. Here are two activities you can use to help your students improve this skill.

- Give students a problem and a potential solution. Ask them to verify whether or not the given solution is correct and, if not, tell why.
- Give the students problems such as, "Verify whether or not the numbers 6, 8, and 10 form a Pythagorean triple. Why?"

6. *Ability to ask questions that yield maximum information*. Good problem solvers seem to be able to decide what questions need to be asked so that the problem can be solved. Encourage your students to ask questions that seek specific information and that yield as much information as possible. The time you spend on helping your students improve this skill will pay rich dividends in terms of their ability to solve problems. Here are two activities you can use to help improve this skill.

- Pose the activity in the following way to your class. "I am thinking of a number between 100 and 1000. To guess my number, you may ask questions, one at a time, about the number. I must be able to answer the question with "yes" or "no." You have only twenty questions to guess the number, so try to ask questions that give you as much information as possible. Listen carefully to the questions being asked because, if you repeat a question, it will count as one of the twenty." As your students gain proficiency, decrease the number of questions that may be asked. You can also vary the activity by only counting questions that are answered "no."

- Present this activity to the class in the following way. "I am thinking of a three-digit number and I want you to guess what it is. You will try to guess the number by saying a three-digit number out loud. After each guess, I will give you clues about your guess and the clue will be like this. If a digit in your guess matches a digit in my number and is in the same place, I will tell you that you have a *hit*. If a digit in your guess matches a digit in my number but it is not in the same place, I will tell you that you have a *nick*. If a digit in your guess does not match a digit in my number, I will tell you that you have a *miss*. For example, suppose my number is 345 and you guess 541. I would tell you that you have 1 hit, 1 nick, and 1 miss but I won't tell which is which. If you guess 724, I would tell you that you have 0 hits, 1 nick and 2 misses. Let's count the number of guesses you need to guess my number and when we play again, we'll try to beat the record."

7. *Ability to design and use different problem-solving strategies*. This skill is important because an initially-chosen strategy may not give an acceptable result. When this happens, the student must be able to find a new strategy to solve the problem. Giving students divergent (more than one solution) problems rather than convergent (one solution) problems will help stimulate the type of thinking needed to improve this skill. Here are two activities that give examples of divergent problems.

- State the problem and place a picture of a square on the chalkboard. Then ask, "How many different ways can you divide this square in half?"
- State a problem in this way: "Use 4 twos in any way that you can to make the numbers 1 through 10. You must use all 4 twos each time and you may use any operations you want. For example, $22/22 = 1$, and $2 + 2 + 2/2 = 3$, and so on."

Now that you have suggestions for improving some of the specific problem-solving skills, let's turn to more general techniques for improving the seven specific skills. These techniques will help students improve their general ability to solve problems.

General Skill Improvement

In addition to techniques for improving the seven specific problem-solving skills, there are general techniques you can use to help students become better problem solvers. Remember that your efforts to improve your students' problem-solving skills must be continuous throughout your instructional program.

Here are some general suggestions for helping your students improve their problem-solving skills.

1. *Help students develop a basic problem-solving strategy.* As you know, some of your students are able to simply look at a problem and come up with the correct solution. The student apparently had an insight into the problem and simply "knew" the answer.

Unfortunately, most students are not able to solve problems in this manner. Many of these students may need assistance in attacking the problem. To help those students, give them a basic strategy that is given by answering five questions about the problem. The answers to the following five questions should help the troubled student solve the problem:

What is the problem about?

What does the problem ask for?

What information is given in the problem?

How can the given information be used to find the solution?

Is my solution correct?

The first question is designed to help the student get a sense of the problem to be solved. To get this sense, the student must be able to see the problem as a whole with understanding. Asking students to restate the problem in their own words is a good way to determine whether or not the student has a grasp of the problem. Diagrams or concrete materials may also be helpful to the student to answer this question.

A problem cannot be solved until the student is able to answer the second question. If a student has a sense of the problem, then it should not be difficult to answer the question.

To proceed to the solution, a student must be able to determine what information is given in the problem. In many instances, the information may be quantitative in nature. It may also be true that too little or too much information is given in the problem. The student must be able to sort out the useful information to solve the problem.

In the fourth question, the student must be able to take the given information and make a determination as to the strategy for solving the problem. This step is probably the most difficult one for students, so they will need much practice in this area. If the problem is quantitative, the student must find one or more mathematical sentences to solve the problem. If mathematical sentences are to be used, the student must obviously be proficient at mathematical computation. Give students plenty of problem situations and simply ask them to develop a strategy that can be used to solve the problem.

When the strategy has been developed and implemented, the answer to the fifth question will indicate whether or not the problem has been correctly solved. Students often neglect this last step, so you must make sure that it is not forgotten.

The above strategy may not work in all cases for all students. It does, however, give a basis for students to develop a problem-solving strategy that works for them.

2. *Practice each skill separately.* As students are improving their problem-solving skills, they will need to practice each skill separately before they try to use all of the skills to solve problems. As the classroom teacher, you must provide activities that will enable the students to practice each skill separately.

In "Improving Specific Skills," suggested activities were given for each of the seven specific skills. In the basic strategy just discussed, problems can be given to students so that there can be concentration on each of the five questions.

Once the students have demonstrated proficiency in each of the skills, situations may be given where two or more of the skills are combined for additional practice. The ultimate goal is, of course, that the students will be able to use the necessary skills to solve a given problem.

3. *Give students problems that are different in format and requested solution from those problems typically given in the junior high/middle school mathematics classroom.* After your students have demonstrated some proficiency in solving problems, begin to vary the format of the problem and/or the requested solution of the problems. These variations ensure that the students do not simply become mechanical in their problem-solving procedures. It will also enable them to be able to better deal with problems encountered in everyday life where problems are not often as "neat and tidy" as they are in the classroom.

Some possible variations and examples are given in Figure 8-1.

FIGURE 8-1

Variation	Example
1. Too little information	1. A basketball player can dribble the ball 18 times in a very short period of time. How many times can the player dribble the ball in 1 hour?
2. Too much information	2. A car is travelling at 80 km per hour. It is going to Grand City, which is 800 km away. How far will the car travel in 5 hours?
3. No numerical solution	3. Tell me how to find the area of this shaded region:

SOLVING WORD PROBLEMS

After consideration of general problem-solving skills and their improvement, let's now turn to the area of word problems. It is indeed unfortunate that such an important area in your instructional program causes your students as much difficulty as this does.

Additional Problem-Solving Skills

In addition to the seven problem-solving skills discussed previously, there are two other skills useful in solving word problems.

1. *Ability to read*. A student must be able to read to work successfully with word problems. As you will see later, you must take responsibility for helping students learn to read in math class; teaching students to read cannot be the sole responsibility of the reading teacher.

2. *Ability to write and solve a mathematical sentence for a given problem*. Most word problems, especially those of a quantitative nature, can be solved if the student can write and solve a mathematical sentence that reflects the information given in the problem. Key words in the word problem often provide the clue for writing the appropriate sentence, a topic to be discussed later in this section.

Improving Reading and Word Problem Skills

It is clear that the ability to read greatly affects your students' ability to solve word problems. But if your students are having difficulty reading, should you be expected to help them improve their reading skills?

It has been said that every teacher is a reading teacher. What can you do in your classroom to help improve student reading skills?

1. *Talk to the language arts teacher and the reading specialist*. These teachers are the reading experts. Their training programs often include word attack and comprehension skill activities that utilize vocabulary lists and reading assignments from content areas. You can provide vocabulary lists and readings from your math textbook for their use with students. These teachers may also be able to give you information about reading difficulties of particular students, so you may be able to help implement a program for a student that will be beneficial in both mathematics and reading.

2. *Point out textbook features to your students*. Your students should be aware of and know how to use such things in the textbook as the index, glossary, and chapter vocabulary lists. Often, students will be able to help themselves if they know how to use the textbook effectively. Classroom activities on using an index are helpful and can be fun, too.

3. *Diagnose reading difficulties*. As your students work with word problems, try to diagnose their difficulties. Your diagnosis will be done on an informal basis, but your findings can then be discussed with the language arts teacher or the reading specialist who will be able to suggest corrective activities.

4. *Spend class time on the meaning of vocabulary and symbols*. Vocabulary and symbols are the heart of any reading in mathematics. Be sure that your students understand the key words and symbols when they are given a reading assignment in the text. Some specific suggestions for

improving vocabulary and symbol comprehension were given in "Improving Problem-Solving Skills."

5. *Remind students that reading in mathematics is much slower than reading in other content areas*. Many students have a tendency to read math materials in the same way they read history or fiction, a tendency that often causes them to miss some of the meaning in the math material. Math materials should be read slowly, similar to the way that a foreign language is read. Students should not skim written material in mathematics.

6. *Choose word problems carefully*. Try to use problems that will be interesting and stimulating to your students so that they will want to solve them. Also be sure that the problems are matched to the reading levels of your students. In some cases, you may need or want to rewrite some of the problems so that they will better fit the needs of your students.

Avoid using problems that are nothing more than a computational exercise with a few words surrounding the numbers. Such problems are often labelled in the text as word problems, but rarely are what they are called. Students may be able to solve the problems without literally being able to read.

Read through the word problems before you assign them to your students, and discard problems that will not be of benefit to your students. Avoid the common trap of "do the evens (or odds)" when assigning problems.

7. *Use some word problems that have too little or too much information*. Students need to realize that not all word problems have the exact (no more, no less) information needed to solve the problem. These types of problems should be introduced after your students have demonstrated some skill in solving word problems.

8. *Give students a chance to practice reading·word problems*. The only way to improve student skill in reading word problems is to have them read word problems, either orally or silently. Avoid having poor readers read aloud in class. Instead, let them read aloud to a small group of classmates who have about the same level of oral reading ability or to you on an individual basis.

9. *Present word problems to students with reading difficulties in different ways*. Try to use as many different ways as possible to present word problems to students with reading difficulties. A tape recorder with the problems on tape or your reading aloud may help a student who is following the reading of the problems silently.

10. *Don't make it too easy for students not to read*. Students who have difficulty in reading will avoid the need to read at every opportunity. Don't

let this occur, if possible. It will help tremendously if you choose activities to practice reading skills that are within the grasp of the students so that the opportunity for success is maximized.

Using Mathematical Sentences to Solve Word Problems

Quantitative word problems can usually be solved by first writing a mathematical sentence about the problem and then solving it. The ability to translate a problem situation into a mathematical sentence is a very useful skill for solving many word problems.

The ability to write a mathematical sentence depends on several things. The student must be able to:

1. Identify what the problem is asking for.
2. Make a diagram or picture of or mentally visualize the problem situation.
3. Interpret the meaning and symbolism of and solve a mathematical sentence.

These three skills must be practiced separately and mastered before they can be combined so that mathematical sentences can be used to solve problems.

BUILDING ESTIMATION SKILLS

The ability to estimate has always been a useful skill in everyday life. Yet very little time is spent by classroom teachers in developing estimation skills.

Estimation is not a single skill. It is made up of many skills that can best be described in terms of situations which are presented. Let's examine these different situations and then outline some guidelines for developing estimation skills in your classroom.

Estimation Situations

There are three basic estimation situations: rounding numbers, reference point estimation, and estimated range of answers. Students need many exercises with each of the situations. The end results will be an improvement in estimation skills.

1. *Computation with rounded numbers*. You have often made guesses about the results of a computation problem by rounding numbers. For example:

Problem	*Estimate*
33 ×18	30 x 20
18)2609	2600 ÷ 20
$2\frac{1}{3} + 6\frac{7}{8}$	2 + 7

Most of the time, it is usually convenient to round numbers to the nearest power or multiple of 10. With fractions, it may be desirable to round to the nearest whole number.

Students should work with problems like the following:

a. Round out and then compute an estimated answer for 48 x 12.

b. Pick the best answer:

27 × 18 = ?

20 × 20, 30 × 20

$\frac{1}{4} + 1\frac{7}{8}$

0 + 2, 1 + 2

After students have practiced rounding skills, have classroom drills where pencils are not used. Give a problem and students are to raise their hands when they have an estimate. Do not penalize students who must use a pencil to estimate. Some can do estimates in their heads whereas others cannot.

2. *Reference point estimation.* This type of situation requires that an estimate be made based upon some reference point or standard. For example, if you are estimating the distance from your house to the front gate, you will visualize a unit of length such as a yard or a meter, and then mentally count the number of units in the distance to come up with an estimate. When you see a product marked as "3 for $2.85," you may wonder whether or not you are paying more than $1.00 for each item individually.

The types of problems that can be used for this situation might be:

a. 40 + 50 = 90. Is 42 + 49 greater than 90 or less than 90?

b. 30 × 20 = 600. Is 33 × 18 greater or less than 600?

3. *Estimated range of the answer.* This situation is especially useful because it gives parameters for the answer. The range gives upper and lower boundaries for the answer; the better the estimate, the smaller the range.

This situation also provides an opportunity for a student to declare whether or not an answer is reasonable. This type of estimation is especially useful when students are working with calculators.

Here are some examples of this situation. These examples also illustrate problems which might be given to students.

a. The square root of 78 is between what two whole numbes?

b. A house sells for $70,000. A Realtor makes 6-3/4% commission. Is the commission closer to $4,900 or $49,000?

Guidelines for Building Estimation Skills

There are some important guidelines you should keep in mind as you help your students develop estimation skills.

1. Make the building of estimation skills an integral part of your instructional program.

2. Integrate estimation with computational exercises and problem-solving activities.

3. Remember that students will estimate using different strategies. Beware of labelling one estimate wrong and another correct.

4. Stress the use of mental arithmetic and oral work in addition to paper-and-pencil activities.

5. Stress mathematical reasoning throughout estimation activities.

QUICK REVIEW

1. List seven important problem-solving skills. Why is each important?

2. What is the role of the teacher in helping students develop good problem-solving skills?

3. What points must you keep in mind when presenting a problem to your students?

4. What is the appropriate classroom climate for good problem solving to take place?

5. Describe activities that may be used to help students improve the skills you listed in exercise 1. (Your activities should differ from those given in the chapter.)

6. What can you do to help students improve their reading skills in mathematics? List specific activities you would use.

7. Outline a plan for integrating the development of estimation skills into your instructional program. List specific activities you would use.

8. Look at the word problems in one of your textbooks. Do they appear to be appropriate for helping your students become good problem solvers? Why or why not?

9. Students may bring in problems that you cannot solve. How would you handle this situation?

10. Outline a plan for teaching students to write mathematical sentences to solve word problems.

11. What can you do to help students who have an inferiority complex about mathematics become better problem solvers?

12. When you put word problems on your tests, are you interested in speed or power? Does your test construction reflect your interest? What changes might you make so that there is consistency between your thinking and the testing situation? What can you do to help students who have inferiority complexes about mathematics when they are taking your test?

9

The Laboratory Approach
in the Junior High/
Middle School Mathematics
Classroom

Like many other terms such as "modern math," "discovery approach," and "individualizing instruction," the "laboratory approach" has had many different meanings to teachers. After reviewing these different meanings, the most commonly agreed-upon definition of the laboratory approach is one in which students are actively involved in their learning. They learn by doing. It reminds us of that old Chinese proverb,

"I hear and I forget,
 I see and I remember,
 I do and I understand."

Understanding is obviously a major goal in your classroom and your use of the lab approach will aid your students in developing understanding.

After reading and studying this chapter, you should be able to:

- Apply the philosophy of the laboratory approach to the teaching of mathematics.

- Outline important considerations in setting up a mathematics laboratory.

- Describe sources for locating and criteria for selecting laboratory activities.
- Describe guidelines for managing a mathematics laboratory.
- Describe evaluation procedures for a mathematics laboratory.

USE OF A MATHEMATICS LABORATORY

Some teachers feel that a math lab must be used only with small groups or individuals. This is nonsense; your entire class can many times perform as an entire group with each student having his or her own materials. But all of your students are attacking the same problem at the same time. Hence, the number of students working on an activity is dependent upon the nature of the activity and the availability of materials for students to use.

This observation brings us to the question of materials. The mathematics laboratory is often characterized by the use of manipulative materials (things you can get your hands on), but this need not always be the case. The important thing is student involvement, whether this be accomplished through the use of manipulative materials or printed materials dealing with an abstract idea.

SETTING UP A MATHEMATICS LABORATORY

Let's turn now to the problem of setting up a math lab in your school. There are basically two possible situations: (1) have a separate room for such activities; or (2) set up the math lab in your own classroom.

If you are fortunate enough to have a separate room in your school, all of your equipment and materials can be stored there. You will probably want to use the room for two math periods per week; double periods (or back-to-back) may be desirable, if possible. There are many possible physical arangements for such a room and your own arrangement will depend on available facilities and your desires. Other classes may also want to use the lab room. This is a good selling point to your principal when you point out that many others can benefit from use of the facilities and resources.

Materials should be stored so that students have easy access to them. They should also be stored in the same place each time so that they can be easily located for use. During the lab period, it would be very desirable to have a teacher aide or a parent who can distribute and collect materials so that you will be free for consultation. It is imperative that your storage of materials and your use of them be highly organized. Lack of organization will almost surely result in chaos.

Some additional comments about materials may be in order and these remarks apply whether you have separate facilities or are conducting lab sessions in your own classrooms. There are so many commercial materials available that you could spend as much money as you want. But, realistically, your school won't have much money to spend. Thus, you and your students need to become "scroungers."

Lumber yards and hardware stores are quite willing to give you yardsticks or metersticks with their names on them, and popsicle sticks can be collected. A side benefit to this method of collection is that your students will feel much more a part of their learning situation—remember student involvement mentioned earlier? Of course, you will want to purchase some materials, but purchase only what you absolutely have to. But if you can't buy anything, you may be able to modify your desires to include something that you can get your hands on. Above all, be sure that your materials are easily accessible.

Now, suppose you don't have a separate room and must use your own. This situation is probably what most of you face. Teachers are heard saying that they can't possibly have a math lab in their classroom because there isn't room and they don't have tables. Space may be a problem, but how many of you have storage cabinets? Shoeboxes are excellent to use if you stack them in a corner or under a math table. However, such storage requires organization, so it can be accomplished only if you really want to badly enough.

Suppose you don't have access to tables in your classroom. You could use the floor, especially if it is carpeted. Here is another suggestion. Push several desks together and put a diece of dry wall or corkboard on them to make your tabletop.

Now that your physical facilities and materials have been set up, let's consider for a moment what your role in the lab situation should be. If you are the "authoritarian" type of teacher, the following may cause some discomfort or rejection: there is no place for you in the math lab if you must remain the central dominant figure. To use the lab approach effectively, your role must be that of a facilitator—to guide and assist students as they work on tasks either individually or in groups, either small or large. You must know when to act as a silent partner, when to ask questions, and when to withdraw completely. This action is not easy, but is essential to the success of the mathematics laboratory. You may have gotten the idea that operating a lab is easy, but you can see that it is not. It requires a lot of hard work and planning, but your efforts will be rewarded in terms of the progress of your students.

One aspect of the lab situation (indeed, also in the regular classroom setting) that causes teachers problems is the matter of planning and handling small groups. How many groups should there be? How do you set them up?

The secret to having groups work effectively is to help students learn to work together on a common problem. You must help them acquire skills in attacking problems and in working together. Most teachers do little or none of this and then cannot understand why students become rowdy or let one student do all the work. It is not natural for students to be able to work effectively in groups, so you must help them learn how to do so. Don't use groups until you have assessed your students' capabilities in this area and worked on strengthening them.

If you have never tried grouping, start first with one and increase the number gradually until you reach the point where you are still comfortable. Some teachers can manage a classroom situation with five or six groups; others can handle one or two. Only have the number of groups that you can comfortably handle.

Several problems connected with the mathematics laboratory have already been discussed. Cost, group management, storage and facilities, and hard work for the teacher have already been mentioned. The math lab is not designed as the cure-all to all of your instructional problems, but it can be a valuable supplement to your program of instruction. An additional point to remember is that there are some students who cannot work except in a very highly structured situation. Don't force them into a situation in which they cannot work or succeed because you will only compound your problems.

Also keep in mind that the math lab has many advantages which would make it well worth trying. Mathematics can come alive and be fun. Students have many opportunities for success and can work at their own pace and level, thereby helping you to individualize your instruction. By having your students actively involved, you can eliminate many of your discipline problems caused by boredom and frustration.

LOCATING AND SELECTING LABORATORY ACTIVITIES

A multitude of activities are available for your use with the laboratory approach. However, you must still gather and possibly modify the activities so that they will serve your purposes in the best possible way.

Your students are often an excellent source of activities; finding and developing problems which are of interest to them may provide many useful and stimulating sessions in the laboratory setting. You may also find this technique useful in other parts of your instructional program, a possibility we explored earlier in the chapter.

Your own creativity and imagination is an excellent source. Your own past experience and ideas based upon other activities will lead you further than you might think. Discuss your ideas with your fellow teachers; the discussion will likely benefit all of you.

Professional organizations such as the National Council of Teachers of Mathematics (NCTM) provide a good source of ideas. These organizations conduct meetings designed to help teachers share ideas, and also publish journals with articles written by people with excellent ideas. In particular, NCTM publishes *The Arithmetic Teacher* (grades K-8) and *The Mathematics Teacher* (grades 7-12). Both journals contain many good ideas for activities that you may be able to use.

In order to successfully use the laboratory approach, you must select appropriate activities. Here are some guidelines to keep in mind in your selection process.

1. *The materials required by the activity should be readily available.* Activities that require materials not accessible to you, either costwise or logistically, will not be useful to you. In some cases, you may be able to modify the activity to fit your materials capability, but be careful not to destroy the intent of the activity.

2. *Your students must have the prerequisite concepts and skills required to complete the activity.* The activity will be of little or no value if your students are unable to complete the activity because of a lack of prerequisite concepts and skills. Many teachers either ignore or disregard this point, usually with less than desirable results.

3. *Be sure the activity is appropriate for your classroom management system.* If the activity you choose is likely to cause a situation contrary to your classroom management needs, then choose another one. For example, if you need to keep a "tight rein" on your class, then avoid activities that tend to have the opposite effect; if you don't, the results may be disastrous.

4. *Whenever possible, the activity should have all participants actively involved at all times.* The basis of the lab approach is to actively involve your students. Activities that promote passive student involvement are not going to be useful, either to you or to your students.

5. *Your students should have a good chance of completing the activity*

successfully. As mentioned so often throughout this book, a little success goes a long way. The activities you choose should have the potential of success for each participant.

6. *The activity's purpose must be appropriate to your instructional needs.* Each activity you use must have a definite purpose that is appropriate for your instructional program. Avoid the temptation to use an activity that is very good, even though it is not appropriate for your program. There are plenty of excellent lab activities available for your use, so be sure that your choice meshes with your instructional purpose.

Within the context of your instructional needs, lab activities may be classified in a matrix format, as in Figure 9–1.

FIGURE 9–1

	Concrete	Semiconcrete	Abstract
Introductory			
Developmental			
Mastery			

The meanings of concrete, semiconcrete, and abstract were discussed in Chapter 1. By introductory is meant that the activity is designed to introduce a concept or skill. Developmental activities are designed to help gain or "handle" or stabilize the concept or skill, and mastery activities are designed to help the student practice or reinforce the concept or skill.

Most lab activities, because of the common use of manipulatives, tend to be either concrete or semiconcrete and introductory or developmental. On occasions, lab activities may be of an abstract-mastery level.

Here are some examples of lab activities and how they may be classified.

Activity 1: Area of a plane figure
Type: introductory-concrete
Grade level: 5-6
Materials: geoboard, rubber band, graph paper
Procedure:

1. Make a square that is 4 units on a side on your geoboard. The area is the number of square units inside the square. How many are there?

2. Now copy the following figure on your geoboard and find the area.

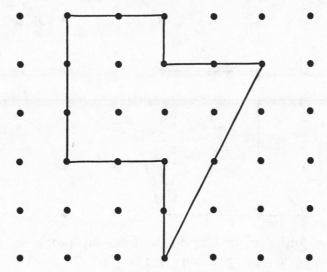

Did you find that the area is 10 square units? (Note: the diagonal of a rectangle divides its area by 2, as shown in the following example of two rectangles.)

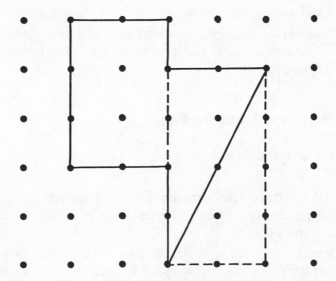

3. Find the area of the following figure.

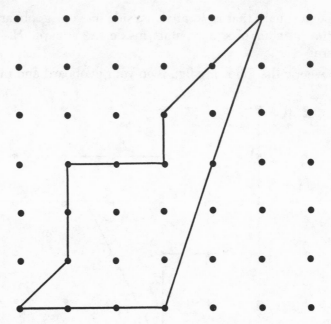

4. Use your geoboard to do the following problems. Record your answer on a piece of graph paper.

   a. Make a square with an area of 4 square units.

   b. Make a triangle that has an area of 3 square units and one that has an area of 1-1/2 square units.

   c. Make a square that has an area of 2 square units.

   d. Make two triangles, one with a base of 2 units and the other with a base of 5 units. Do it so that each triangle has an area of 5 square units.

Activity 2: Symmetry
Type: Developmental-semiconcrete
Grade levels: 5-8
Materials: Paper and pencil
Procedure:

   1. Look up the term "symmetry" in an encyclopedia. Some figures have no axes of symmetry, that is, they are unsymmetrical. Others have one or more.

   2. Draw a list of the capital letters of our alphabet that have axes of symmetry, and state how many in each case. Make each letter at

least 1/2″ high, in ink using the forms of the letters shown, and sketch in its axes of symmetry in pencil, as in the following:

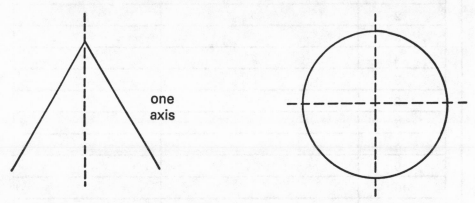

Capitals: A B C D E F G H I J K L M N O P Q R S T U V W X Y Z

Activity 3: Tossing dice
Type: Introductory-concrete
Grade level: 5-8
Materials: pair of regular dice, graph paper
Procedure:

1. Make a table showing the various ways that the sums of 2 through 12 can occur if two dice are tossed.

2. How many ways can each sum occur? (A 2 on the first die and a 3 on the second is different from a 3 on the first and a 2 on the second.)

3. The probability of obtaining a sum of 7 if two dice are tossed is represented as a fraction, as follows:

$$\text{Probability (sum of 7)} = \frac{\text{number of ways the sum of 7 can be obtained}}{\text{total number of different possibilities}}$$

What is P9 (sum of 7)? P sum of 8?

4. Toss the pair of dice 36 times. Record your results and make a graph of the frequency distribution. From your results, compute the fractions indicating the number of times the sum of 7 *actually* occurred. How does this answer compare with your result in question 3?

5. Complete the following table:

Sum	Theoretical Probability	Actual Results
2		
3		
4		
5		
6		
7		
8		
9		
10		
11		
12		

6. Now on the same graph that you made in question 5, make another graph to indicate the *theoretical* number of times each sum should occur. Use a different colored pen or pencil to draw this graph.

Activity 4: Geometry patterns
Type: Developmental-semiconcrete
Grade level: 5-8
Materials: paper and pencil
Procedure:

1. Find the total number of triangles in the following figure. Try to find a systematic way of counting them.

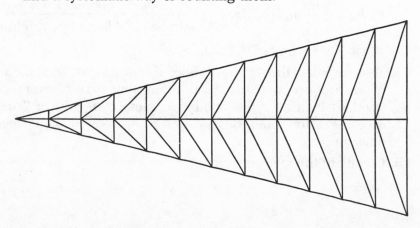

2. Find the total number of squares in the following figure. (Squares can be 2 units on a side, 3 units on a side, etc.)

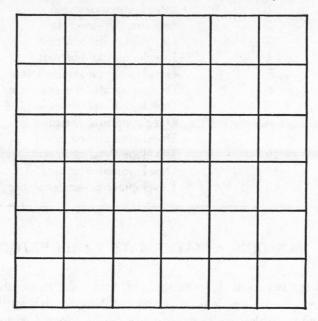

3. Find the number of squares in the following figure.

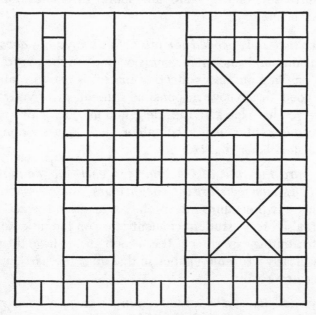

For some other examples of lab activities, refer to the section on the metric system in Chapter 7. The following chart indicates which type each activity is.

Activity	Type
1	Introductory-concrete
2	Introductory-concrete
3	Developmental-abstract
4	Developmental-abstract
5	Developmental-semiconcrete
6	Developmental-semiconcrete
7	Developmental-concrete
8	Developmental-abstract
9	Developmental-concrete
10	Developmental-abstract
11	Developmental-concrete
12	Developmental-semiconcrete

MANAGING A MATHEMATICS LABORATORY

Good management is essential to the success of the laboratory approach. As pointed out earlier, implementing the lab approach is hard work, but its possible results in terms of student learning and motivation make it worth the effort. Here are some guidelines for managing a mathematics laboratory.

1. *Have materials needed for lab activities readily accessible*. There should be a minimum amount of confusion both on the part of students and yourself in handing out and collecting materials used in lab activities. It would be a good idea to have responsible students assist you in this task. In cases where you have lab activities designed for one or two students, such as in a learning center, use a container such as a shoebox to store all necessary materials for that activity.

2. *Be sure that the instructions for each lab activity are clearly understood by students before they begin work*. Unnecessary interruptions caused by activity procedure interpretation result in the activity not going smoothly. It also breaks student concentration on the task at hand and may result in a frustrating experience. It is a good idea to have the procedure for the activity clearly written on paper so that all of the participants can refer to the procedure easily.

3. *Have activity participants turn in a record of their results*. There are two advantages to this technique. First, some participants do not take

the activity seriously unless you have some way to check on them. You also have an idea whether or not the activity is achieving its intended purpose. Second, you can use the results for diagnostic purposes if you suspect that the participants are having difficulty.

4. *Be sure that the activity is appropriate for the ability level of the participants.* Lab activities require different levels of ability. A participant soon loses interest in an activity that requires either a higher or lower ability level. When interest is lost, the activity has no chance of achieving its purpose.

5. *Go through the activity yourself before using it in class.* Sometimes you will find that the procedure is confusing or that the level of the activity is inappropriate for your students. These potential problems may not become apparent if you simply look over the activity quickly.

6. *Be aware of social factors as well as ability in forming groups to work on a lab activity.* It is not clear what is the best way to form groups so that they will work together effectively. Voluntarily-formed groups may result in one or more groups of the class "rowdys" and chaos may occur. It may also result in the "I-ain't-gonna-do-nothing" group or a group of friendless students. Instead, make the group assignments yourself and use a sociogram for guidance.

To make a sociogram, tell your students that they will soon be working in groups. Ask them to write on a piece of paper the names of two or three other students with whom they would like to work in a group situation. Be sure to remind them that your group assignments may not perfectly match their desires. This technique may take a little extra time to administer and analyze, but its information will be useful to you, both in the present and in the future.

7. *Change group composition periodically.* The obvious advantage is that each student will get an opportunity to work with many other students in the class. It also gives you a chance to try different students together in group situations; such group composition may not have occurred to you earlier. It also helps reduce the chance of a stigma caused by homogenous group composition, such as the "dummy" group. Many times, a student of lesser ability can learn from a student of higher ability.

8. *Appoint a group leader for each group.* Choose your leaders carefully. They should possess leadership characteristics, and this will give them an opportunity to develop these characteristics. Your sociogram will help you identify your class leaders. Your class will go much more smoothly if you have your class leaders working for you and not against you.

EVALUATING A MATHEMATICS LABORATORY

There are many ways to evaluate students' performance in a mathematics laboratory. Techniques such as observation of the students at work, study of written work, or a periodical check of the student's progress may be used in a lab situation. You will need to decide on the best way(s) to evaluate your activities.

As discussed earlier in Chapter 5, each lab activity must have one or more objectives as its basis. Evaluation is used, then, to determine whether or not the objective(s) has (have) been achieved.

Performance Tests

Since students are actively involved in a lab activity, it seems reasonable that a performance test based on physical involvement in a problem situation is appropriate to use. In such a test, a student may be given a set of manipulative materials and asked to respond to a set of questions, either in oral or written form. The idea of the performance test is that students use the materials, if they desire, to answer the questions, or, the students may be required to use the physical materials to perform a specified task.

Recordkeeping

One of the important parts of the evaluation process is recordkeeping of the results of the evaluation. So that the information may be readily available to both you and the student, use a card such as the one shown in Figure 9–2.

At times, you will not find it possible to observe each individual student or group during work on an activity. In such cases, a brief discussion with the student or group can accomplish the same purpose as the observation. If at all possible, complete a card for each student every one or two lab periods.

You will find that a review of the cards over a period of time can be very helpful in making educational decisions about the student. It is impossible to remember all that you have observed about a particular student, so the cards will assist you in reconstructing your thoughts.

FIGURE 9–2

Student Name   Lesson or Activity

Date started   Date completed   Lesson Number
Areas of Strengths   Area of Needed
                                               Improvement

Annotated Comments: 1.
                    2.
                    3.
The next activity should be:

Lesson or Activity Name

Number

Teacher

QUICK REVIEW

1. What is the philosophy of the laboratory approach to learning mathematics?

2. What are the potential problems in using the lab approach? How can you resolve these problems in your own teaching situation?

3. How would you go about setting up a mathematics laboratory in your teaching situation?

4. Make a list of three specific sources of lab activities. Find two activities from each source that you could use in your classroom.

5. What are the criteria for selecting lab activities. What other criteria should also be considered?

6. List six specific guidelines for managing a mathematics laboratory.

7. Write down the names of each of your students. Next to each name, write the names of two other students you think would choose to work with that particular student. Now make a sociogram and compare your results. Do you know your students as well as you think you do?

8. What techniques would you use to evaluate a lab situation in your classroom?

9. Make a performance test for two of the activities you selected in exercise 4 above.

10. Outline a recordkeeping procedure that you would use in your classroom. Show it to a fellow teacher who has used the lab approach and discuss ways that your procedure could be improved. Ask your fellow teachers to do the same thing.

11. Describe what is meant by introductory, developmental, and mastery activities. Do the same for concrete, semiconcrete, and abstract activities. Give an example for each of the six types. Now give an example for each cell in the matrix as pictured on page 188 of this chapter.

10

Games in the
Junior High/Middle School
Mathematics Classroom

The use of games as a teaching tool in the mathematics instructional program has become popular in recent years. Classroom teachers have found that games, properly chosen and used, can be very beneficial to the learning of mathematics. In this chapter, how games can best be used in the classroom, the different types of games and how they may be selected, and guidelines for managing games in the classroom are examined. Finally, some examples of games which you can use in your classroom are given.

After reading and studying this chapter, you should be able to:

- Describe various uses of games in your classroom.
- Describe potential dangers of the use of games in your classroom.
- Classify games according to type.
- State and use criteria for selecting games.
- State guidelines for managing the use of games in your classroom.

TEACHING THROUGH GAMES

Games are like any other teaching tool; they can be misused. Games are not a panacea to solve your problems as a classroom teacher but, if properly used, they can be beneficial to your mathematics instructional program.

What are some of the uses you can make of games in your classroom? Games may be used to:

1. *Reinforce skills which your students have learned*. Drill and practice is often boring to students. Games can help disguise the drill and practice needed to stabilize, maintain, and hopefully improve students' skill levels.

2. *Help improve student attitude*. Games provide an excellent opportunity for your students to enjoy success in their mathematical learning. The importance of success in improving student attitude cannot be understated. Games that have the element of chance in determining a winner are especially useful here.

3. *Actively involve students*. Active student involvement is psychologically desirable for your students. Your students are much more likely to learn and maintain needed mathematical concepts and skills if they are actively involved in the learning situation.

4. *Add variety to your instructional program*. An effective instructional program in mathematics has a wide variety of learning experiences. Games help add to this variety.

5. *Promote healthy competition*. Some competitive experiences are good for your students. As long as the competition is kept in perspective and at an appropriate level, it can be an excellent motivational device for your students. The question of competition will be discussed in more detail later in this chapter.

6. *Help your students learn to follow directions*. Failure by students to follow directions is probably one of your biggest classroom problems. Games require that students follow directions and this reinforcement should be helpful in other phases of your instructional program.

7. *Help your students learn to verbalize*. It seems that many students in the junior high/middle school have difficulty verbalizing their thoughts because of a fear of being wrong. Games require verbalization and this practice in a nonthreatening situation may be very beneficial to your students.

8. *Enrich or challenge your students*. You are always looking for things to enrich or challenge your students. Games that require the use of thinking skills and the planning of strategy will be excellent for your students.

Like anything else, games can be detrimental to the effectiveness of your instructional program. Most of these can be entirely avoided if you plan carefully enough ahead of time and if you are aware of their potential danger. Potential dangers include these:

1. *Games can encourage meaningless play.* A game that is used for "its own sake" with no real purpose can turn into chaos and disaster. The game must have a clear purpose, be appropriate for the level of your students, and monitored by you to see that the game achieves its avowed purpose.

2. *Some games may take too much time to play.* Your entire instructional program is important. Games that are too time-consuming cause other, perhaps more important parts, of your program not to be implemented. If you are not careful, some of your students will take much more time than necessary to play a game so that they will not have to do something else.

3. *Games can be too expensive.* If you are not careful, games can be very expensive to purchase or replace. You do not need to purchase lots of expensive games; some of the best ones for your purposes will cost you little or nothing.

4. *Games can create discipline problems in your classroom.* The use of games must be tightly managed and controlled by you so that chaos does not result. Excessive emphasis on winning is one of the biggest classroom disrupters. Also, perhaps there are some students who should not play in the same game because of personality conflicts; watch for these situations and don't allow them to happen.

5. *Games can promote too much competition among your students.* Games in which the emphasis is on winning or where the reward for winning is inappropriately high have no place in your instructional program. Too much competition destroys the chance that the game will achieve its intended purpose and may be psychologically damaging to some of your students.

6. *Games can encourage cheating on the part of your students.* When the pressure of or the emphasis on winning is too great, your students will likely resort to cheating. Nothing more needs to be said.

SELECTING GAMES

Once you have decided to use games, you need to select games that are appropriate for the purpose and concept or skill you want your students to learn. Avoid the common mistake of using a game that does not fit into your program appropriately. In this section, the various types of games basic in criteria which you should use for selecting games are discussed and some examples of games which will be useful to you are given.

Types of Games

Games may be classified into different types according to several characteristics. As you choose games to use in your classroom, you may need to choose games according to these types. Games may be classified by:

1. *Style of play.* Style of play means such things are board games, matching games, dice games, chalkboard games, relay games, games such as Bingo or Lotto and domino games. Classroom management should be a definite consideration here.

2. *Number of players.* Many games that you will want to use will be designed for a single player or for a small group of 2 to 4 players. In some situations, a game played by the entire class at the same time may be appropriate.

3. *Medium.* Medium means the type of communication used in playing the game. Communication may take the form of paper and pencil, use of special manipulative materials, visual, movement, or oral.

4. *Areas of concepts or skills.* Broad concept or skill areas are a good way to help classify games. These are the areas of multiplication, division, fractions, decimals, percent, measurement (including metrics), geometry, problem solving, and vocabulary among others.

5. *Level of concept or skill development.* Chapter 9 mentioned that the level of concept or skill development may be classified as introductory, developmental, or mastery. Games may also be classified in this manner. The vast majority of games, however, that you will select will be at the mastery level.

As an example of the three levels, let's look at a game you have, no doubt, heard of or maybe even used. For convenience sake, the game will be used at the mastery level and shows how it may be varied for the introductory and developmental levels. Remember, however, that such variations are not always possible nor necessarily desirable because of the nature of the game.

Name of game: Duplicate

Purpose: To provide practice in recalling multiplication facts for 8 and 9

Grade level: 5-8

Number of players: 2

Materials: deck of 36 prepared cards: the cards are made in pairs with the product (64) on one card and the problem (8 x 8) on the other card; the facts for 8 include 8 x 1 through 8 x 9 and the facts for 9 include 9 x 1 through 9 x 9.

Game Directions:

1. Shuffle the deck of cards. Then place them face down in a rectangular fashion with six rows of six cards each.

2. Each player turns over a card. The player with the greater product starts the game. Both cards are then returned, face down, to the arrangement.

3. The first player chooses two cards and turns them over. If the cards match (problem with product), the player keeps both cards and gets another turn. If the cards do not match, they are turned over and it is the other player's turn.

4. Players alternate turns until all of the cards have been matched. The player who has the greater number of cards is the winner.

The same game format can be used for a game at the introductory level. Again, 36 cards would be used, but the respective pairs would look like this:

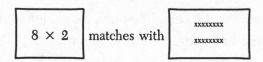

At the developmental level, the matching cards might look like this:

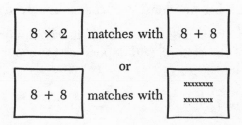

Each of the five classifications above will be important in your choice of a game. For example, you may want to use a mastery-level chalkboard game for two players where answers will be given orally in the area of fractions. Systematically examining these types *before* you make your final choice will ensure the best possible choice of a game for the situation in question.

Criteria for Selecting a Game

In addition to considering the type of game you use, there are other criteria you must consider. Use the following checklist:

1. The game is appropriate for your instructional objective.
2. Your students have the necessary prerequisite skills to play the game.
3. Little time is needed to make the game.
4. The game is inexpensive.
5. The game is easy to supervise.
6. Your students enjoy playing the game.
7. The instructions for the game are clear and easily understood by your students.
8. Your students are actively involved in each play of the game.
9. The game enables you to maintain good classroom control.
10. The game is self-checking if played by a single player or a small group of players.
11. The game can be completed in a reasonable amount of time.
12. The game has a variety of uses or variations.
13. The game promotes good sportsmanship and does not over-emphasize competition.
14. The game can be easily stored.
15. The game has an element of chance involved in winning.

The first criterion mentioned is obviously important. Beyond that, your weighting of the criteria will depend on your own teaching situation and teaching style.

Examples of Games

The following games meet a high percentage of the game selection criteria. Most of these games can be easily duplicated so that the entire class can play at the same time. (Hint: You will get a lot of "mileage" out of having a classroom set of dice and a set of regular playing cards.) In their present form, these games are all of the mastery level.

You will no doubt think of others and also of variations to these games. Hopefully, you can use some of them in the near future!

Name of game: Double Trouble
Purpose: To practice column addition
Grade level: 5-8
Number of players: 2
Materials: two regular dice, game sheet, 2 pencils
Procedure:

1. Each player rolls the two dice and adds the numbers. The player with the greater sum takes the first turn.

2. Each player takes five turns, using the game sheet shown. At the end of a turn, the player records his score (addend). Turns alternate between players. The player with the larger sum of five scores (addends) is the winner.

Player 1	Player 2
Addend 1 _____	Addend 1 _____
Addend 2 _____	Addend 2 _____
Addend 3 _____	Addend 3 _____
Addend 4 _____	Addend 4 _____
Addend 5 _____	Addend 5 _____
SUM _____	SUM _____

3. To determine a score (addend) for a turn, a player rolls the dice and verbalizes the sum $(3+5=8)$. He then rolls the dice again $(6,5)$ and adds the new sum (11) to the previous sum (8) for a total of (19). The player keeps rolling the dice and adding the sum verbally to his previous total. The adding is stopped whenever a player *decides to quit* or *when he rolls doubles* $(1,1)(2,2)(3,3)(4,4)(5,5)(6,6)$. If a player decides to quit (before he rolls doubles), he records the accumulated total as his score for a turn. If a player rolls doubles, he must quit for that turn and record a zero for his score.

4. Double trouble occurs if a player rolls double ones. The player not only takes a zero for that turn, but must take a zero for each of his *previous* scores (addends). A score sheet might look like this:

	Player 1		Player 2
Addend 1	24	Addend 1	97 0
Addend 2	0	Addend 2	142 0
Addend 3	37	Addend 3	85 0
Addend 4	0	Addend 4	0 (Double Ones)
Addend 5		Addend 5	25
SUM		SUM	

Variation:

Keep the same rules except multiply the numbers appearing on the dice. Add the products to get a score for a turn.

Name of game: Roll-a-Digit
Purpose: To practice addition of decimals
Grade level: 5-8
Number of players: 2
Materials: one die marked with 100, 10, 1, .1, .01, and choice; game sheet (see Figure 10–1), 2 pencils
Procedure:

1. Each player rolls the die. The player with the greater number decides if the five games will be played for the *greater* or *lesser* sum. She also takes the first turn of the game.

2. The first player rolls the die and records the number with a tally mark on the game sheet. If a player rolls choice, she may then

	GAME ONE
100.	1
10.	
1.	
.1	111
.01	
SUM	100.31

	GAME ONE
100.	1
10.	11
1.	1
.1	1
.01	
SUM	121.10

FIGURE 10–1

GAME SHEET FOR ROLL-A-DIGIT

Circle One:
Greater Sum
Lesser Sum

	GAME ONE	GAME TWO	GAME THREE	GAME FOUR	GAME FIVE
100.					
10.					
1.					
.1					
.01					
SUM					

Tournament Total [   ]

Circle One:
Greater Sum
Lesser Sum

	GAME ONE	GAME TWO	GAME THREE	GAME FOUR	GAME FIVE
100.					
10.					
1.					
.1					
.01					
SUM					

Tournament Total [   ]

select a value that she wants. Players alternate turns until each has had five turns.

3. After each player completes five turns, she totals her score to determine the winner (see the sample game sheet on page 206).

4. The game is repeated five times and scores recorded in the tournament total. If a player adds incorrectly at anytime, the other player gets to add her opponent's score to her total.

5. A calculator may be used to check answers.

Variations:

Instead of rolling the die five times, roll the die ten times. Change the decimal representations on the die. Here are some examples:

Die: 10^2, 10^1, 10^0, 10^{-1}, 10, choice

Die: 10^0, 10^{-1}, 10^{-2}, 10^{-3}, 10^{-4}, choice

Die: Ten, One, One-tenth, One hundreth, One thousandth, choice

Name of game: Fraction Baseball
Purpose: To reduce fractions to lowest terms; to determine if a fraction is more or less than 1/2
Grade level: 4-8
Number of players: 2
Materials: two regular dice, game sheet (See Figure 10–2), 2 pencils, 4 markers each for two players
Procedure:

1. Each player rolls the two dice and calculates the fractional number by placing the *lesser number over the greater number.* The player with the greater fraction goes to bat first.

2. The first player puts his marker on home plate. He then rolls the dice and verbalizes the fractional value in lowest terms. He moves his marker around the bases according to the rules shown in the Game Sheet (Figure 10–2). (A single advances all markers one base, a double advances all markers two bases, etc.)

3. The first player continues to roll the dice and moves his markers around the bases to score runs. When the first player makes three *outs,* his turn at bat is over. The second player then takes his turn.

4. Each player has nine turns (innings) at bat. (There are no balls or strikes in this game.) The player with the greater score wins.

FIGURE 10–2

GAME SHEET FOR
FRACTION BASEBALL

Dice Value	Move
1	Single
1/2	Double
1/3	Triple
1/4	Home Run
Between 1/2 and 1	Out
Less than 1/2	Roll Again

	Player 1		Player 2	
Inning	Runs	Outs	Runs	Outs
One				
Two				
Three				
Four				
Five				
Six				
Seven				
Eight				
Nine				
TOTAL				

FIGURE 10–2 (Cont'd.)

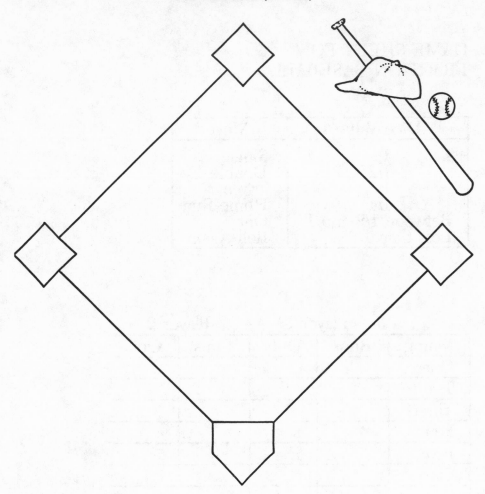

Name of game: Computo
Purpose: To add ten (one- or two-digit) numbers
Grade level: 5-8
Number of players: 2
Materials: regular deck of cards, two different markers (old chess pieces, tiny cars, party favors, etc.), paper and pencil
Procedure:

    1. Make a gameboard by dealing out 12 cards face up in the square as follows:

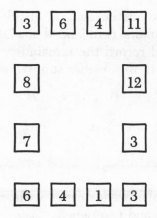

2. Each student places her marker on any card on the gameboard.

3. A deck of cards is placed face down in the center of the gameboard. (The remaining cards from the deck will not be used.)

4. Each player draws a card. The student with the larger number will play first.

5. The first player draws a card and moves her marker the appropriate number of spaces. She moves in a clockwise direction and *records* the numeral (on her paper) of the card she landed on.

6. Repeat this process until each player has moved her marker ten times.

7. At the end of ten rounds (or when the deck is turned up), each player adds up her score. The player with the larger sum wins the game.

8. If one player lands on another player's card at the same time, she adds ten points to her score and subtracts ten points from her opponent's score.

Variations:

1. Vary the number of turns to make the game easier or harder.

2. Arrange the cards in a circle instead of a square.

3. When a student turns over a card, she may move her marker clockwise or counterclockwise to give her a better score.

4. Instead of adding, multiply the *number of spaces moved* by the *number on the card* where the marker lands. Then find the sum of the ten products.

5. Change the computation again. Consider the numeral card turned over and the numeral card landed on. Divide the larger number by the smaller and record the remainder. Then *add* the remainder. The student with the *smaller* sum wins.

Name of game: Choose Your Space
Purpose: To divide decimals
Grade level: 5-8
Number of players: 2
Materials: deck of regular playing cards (without tens, queens, and kings), work sheet, and two pencils
Procedure:

1. Shuffle the cards. Each player draws a card. The player with the greater number decides if the game is for the greater or lesser quotient. This player also takes the first turn of the game.

2. The first player draws a card from the deck and chooses his space (records the numeral in any digit position in the dividend or divisor). A jack will represent zero. The player then places the card in a discard pile. The second player draws a card and records the number on his division problem. Play alternates until each player has six turns. The following is a sample game sheet:

Player 1   Player 2

· □ ⟨3⟩ □ ⟍ · □ □ □   · □ □ ⟨9⟩ ⟍ · □ □ □

3. Both players calculate their quotient. If a player makes a mistake, he automatically loses the game.

4. A calculator can be used to check decimal answers.

Variation:

Change the work sheet to any operation with any desired number of digits. Try the following examples using decimals and fractions.

(6 Turns)   (4 Turns)

☐ . ☐ ☐   ☐ ☐ . ☐

☐ . ☐ ☐   ×   . ☐
_____   _____

(4 Turns)   (4 Turns)

☐   ☐   ⎛ ☐   ⎞ ☐
_____ + _____   ⎝ ___ + ☐ ⎠
☐   ☐   ⎝ ☐   ⎠

Name of game: Slap-a-Prime

Purpose: To identify the prime numbers within the sequence 1,2,3, ... 11,12,13

Grade level: 4-6

Number of players: 2

Materials: regular deck of cards

Procedure:

1. Shuffle the deck of cards and deal out half the deck (26) cards face down to each of two players.

2. Each player holds her deck in one hand, not letting the other player see her cards.

3. At the *same* time, each player places one card from her deck in the center of the table so that both players can see both cards.

4. The first player to slap the two cards while verbalizing the prime number(s) takes both cards.

5. If neither of the cards names a prime, both players turn over additional cards. Players repeat this process until a prime appears. When one player correctly slaps a prime, she takes all cards (4,6,8,etc.).

6. The game ends when each player has turned over all her cards from the deck.

7. The winner is the player with more cards.

Variations:

1. Instead of slapping a prime, the student may call out the word "primo" or "prime."

2. Change the slapping for primes to *slapping* for another reason. Write the new condition on a card. Below are some possible conditions:

   a. Slap if *one* number is divisible by *3*.

   b. Slap if the *sum* of the two numbers is *even*.

   c. Slap if the *sum* of the two numbers is divisible by *4*.

   d. Slap if the *product* of the two numbers is *odd*.

   e. Slap if the *fraction* (smaller over larger) is in reduced form.

   f. Slap if the *decimal* equivalent of the fraction (smaller over larger) is less than *.4*.

   g. Slap if the *greatest common divisor* (G.C.D.) of the two numbers is 2.

   h. Slap if the *least common multiple (L.C.M.)* of the two numbers is *greater than 20*.

Name of game: Putt-Putt
Purpose: To perform operations with whole numbers, fractions, decimals, and percents
Grade level: 5-8
Number of players: 12
Materials: score sheet (See Figure 10–3), two regular dice, 2 pencils
Procedure:

1. Each player rolls the dice. The player with the greater sum "tees" off first.

2. The object of the game is to advance through Holes A through F with the lesser score. The first player rolls the dice and continues to roll the dice until he satisfies the condition of Hole A (sum is less than six). He records the *number* of times he rolled the dice as his score for Hole A. The second player rolls the dice and records his score for Hole A.

3. Play continues in a similar manner through each hole. If a player has not met the condition by his tenth roll, he may quit and record ten as his score for that hole. He then moves to the next hole. At the end of Hole F, each player totals his score.

4. In figuring a difference, always take the lesser number from the larger. In figuring fractions (quotients), divide the lesser number by the greater number.

Variations.

Change the conditions of each hole to any desired computational outcome. To make the exercise more challenging, use math symbols and two dice (red and green). Let X represent the number on the red die and Y represent the number on the green die. Here are some examples.

Hole	Condition
A	$x + y < 6$
B	$x - y < 2$
C	$x/y > 40\%$
D	$x + 1/y < .75$
E	$x + y/xy < 1/2$
F	$x^2 + y^2 < xy$

FIGURE 10–3

PUTT-PUTT
SCORE SHEET

Hole	Condition	Par	Score
A	Sum is less than six	3	
B	Difference is less than two	2	
C	Product is between 10 and 19	3	
D	The fractional value is more than 3/5	2	
E	The fractional value is between .65 and .85	4	
F	The fractional value is 100%	6	
		20	

MANAGING GAMES IN THE CLASSROOM

Good management of games in your classoom is very important. Here are some suggestions for their physical and instructional management.

1. *Have games stored in an easily accessible area.* There should be a minimum amount of confusion involved in passing out and returning the game. This will result in better classroom management.

2. *Be sure that game instructions are clearly understood by each player before the game is begun.* Lack of understanding of the rules is likely to cause disagreements among the players. The playing of the game will go much more smoothly if there are no unnecessary interruptions for rule interpretations.

3. *Appoint one of the players to see that all pieces (if appropriate) are returned to the game box and the game put in its proper storage area.* It is very easy to lose vital game pieces if care is not taken. Having one student responsible avoids confusion and also helps develop a sense of responsibility among your students.

4. *Have game players turn in a record (if appropriate) to you of the results of their play.* There are two advantages to this technique. First, students sometimes do not take a game seriously unless you have some way to check on them. You also have an idea of whether or not the game is achieving its intended purpose. Second, you can use the score sheets for diagnostic purposes if you suspect the players are having difficulties.

5. *Make the playing of the game accessible to all students in the class.* Games should not be played as a reward for completing other work first. If the game has instructional value, then all students in the class should have an opportunity to play.

6. *Be sure that each player knows the purpose of playing the game.* Students should be aware of the objective or purpose of the game. If the purpose is known by the players, the game has a much better chance of achieving its purpose.

7. *Be sure the game is appropriate for the ability of the players.* Games require different levels of ability. A player soon loses interest in a game that requires either a higher or a lower ability level. When this interest is lost, the game has no chance of achieving its purpose.

8. *Play the game yourself before using it in class.* Many times, you will find confusion in the rules or that the game is inappropriate for your students. These potential problems may not become apparent if you simply look over the game quickly.

9. *If the game involves the choosing of teams, choose the teams yourself or use some random method of choosing teams.* Selecting the teams yourself will help ensure that the game will be evenly matched. Players soon lose interest in a game that becomes one-sided. Teams may also be chosen by "counting off" or some other such technique. There should be provision to change team membership, however, if the game shows indication of being one-sided.

10. *Settle ahead of time with your class how you will handle situations of cheating.* There should be a penalty for cheating. Students should be aware of this penalty ahead of time so that they will know the consequences for their actions. Also, knowing the penalty ahead of time may deter some students from cheating.

11. *Do everything possible to reduce over-competition.* Over-competition can cause a game to not achieve its purpose. One good way to help minimize this potential problem is to be sure that the reward for winning a game is not too high. This will also help reduce the incidence of cheating and help you maintain good classroom control.

12. *Give encouragement to the player who is the perpetual loser.* Students who continually lose sometimes develop a defeatist attitude. Encouraging these students will help them want to continue to play the game and give their best effort. Using games that have a high degree of chance will help you in your encouragement efforts.

13. *Watch for ideas for new games.* There are literally millions of ideas for games. You never know when you may run across a game that is "just right" for your students.

In summary, the wise management of games in your classroom will help your instruction program. Beware of using a game simply as "play time" and, whenever possible, require that score sheets be turned in to you. Make the playing of games an extension of your instruction program, not an excuse for goofing off and wasting time.

QUICK REVIEW

1. What uses can you make of games in *your* classroom?

2. List some potential dangers of using games in your classroom. If you have used games, have you been confronted with any of these dangers? If so, how did you handle the situation?

3. How can games be classified?

4. What criteria should be used for selecting a game? What other criteria can you think of that might supplement the list given in the chapter?

5. List guidelines for managing games in your classroom. Are there other guidelines that should be considered? If so, what are they?

6. Go through some of your professional magazines. Write for catalogs from companies that list games you could use in your classroom.

7. Your principal thinks that "games are just play" with no instructional value. How would you respond to this statement? How would you respond if a parent raised the same point with you?

8. Outline a plan for using and managing games in your classroom.

9. Select ten games you would use with your students. Be sure that each game meets most of the criteria for selecting games.

10. What are some ways of choosing teams for group games in your class? What are advantages and disadvantages of each?

11

Calculators and Computers in the Junior High/ Middle School Mathematics Classroom

The last decade has seen a tremendous proliferation in the use of calculators and computers in our everyday lives. It is safe to say that there is at least one hand-held calculator in each of our families and, with the purchase price decreasing steadily, the number will continue to grow. At the same time, a growing number of people have purchased computers for the home and the use of computers in industry increases at nearly an exponential rate.

What all this means to you as a classroom teacher is that you need to begin (or continue) to include both calculators and computers in your mathematics instructional program. In the following chapter, how this can be done will be discussed and examples of curricular activities which you can use in your classroom are given.

After reading and studying this chapter, you should be able to:

- Describe a rationale for and various uses of calculators in the classroom.
- Describe and use criteria for selecting a calculator.

- Effectively manage the use of calculators in the classroom.
- Demonstrate complete computer literacy.
- Plan and implement a unit on computer literacy.
- Describe basic components of the BASIC language.
- Write a simple BASIC program.

USING CALCULATORS IN THE CLASSROOM

There are many parents and teachers who do not believe that students should be allowed to use the hand-held calculator in the classroom. They believe that no mathematics will be learned and that the students will do nothing more than punch buttons. In addition, they believe students will become mentally lazy and their education less than adequate.

There is a distant possibility that the above concerns are valid *if* there is not a careful effort made by the classroom teacher in planning the use of the hand-held calculator and in choosing activities for the calculator.

As a teaching tool, the hand-held calculator can be invaluable. But it is like any other tool—it can be greatly misused.

A widely accepted use of the calculator in the classroom is the checking of work done by paper and pencil. There are several advantages for this use.

1. You need not check every answer on a student's paper.
2. The student receives immediate feedback and reinforcement.
3. The student may develop self-confidence by being able to check work for accuracy before it is turned in to you.

Another valuable use of the calculator is in helping students debug problems when they have a wrong answer. For example, in a multiplication or division problem, the student can use the calculator to check each of the individual steps. This use also helps reinforce the process or algorithm for solving the problem.

Another use you may want to make of the calculator is with problems when there is the application of a formula(s) to solve the problem. Allowing the student to use the calculator in these types of situations does not force the use of tedious and time-consuming computation. The student is thus free to concentrate on the problem to be solved and the application of the formula.

Many teachers have used calculators as a motivational device. Students are allowed to "mess around" with the calculator when they have earned some free time. Such spontaneous play with a calculator has a place in the very beginning, but there is a better use for the free time. If you feel that such play is important, then include *all* of the students in some carefully planned activities that utilize this play.

The following guidelines are recommended for using the calculator in your classroom.

1. Introduce the use of the calculator *after* the class has a thorough understanding of the mathematical processes they are to learn.

2. Keep the calculators under your control by determining when they will or will not be used.

3. Allow students to use the calculators for drill and practice, but be sure they give an oral answer to the problem before checking it with the calculator.

4. Be sure students have appropriate mathematical skills before using the calculator.

There are other guidelines for the physical management of the calculator in the classroom and these will be listed in "Managing Calculators in the Classroom."

In what mathematical areas will students need skills to effectively use a calculator? There are at least four areas.

1. *Problem Solving.* Students need problem-solving skills such as those listed in Chapter 8. It is very easy for students to become involved in using a calculator in a problem which they do not understand. For example, they must be able to interpret the meaning of a negative number when a greater number is subtracted from a lesser number. The calculator is of no use if students do not have a sense of the problem and the solution.

2. *Estimation.* Students must be able to estimate if they are to effectively use the calculator. For some reason, many students have developed a "blind faith" in the calculator; whatever answer is shown on the display must be correct because calculators don't make mistakes. They do not realize that there may have been a mistake in entering data on the calculator. If they have good estimation skills, such mistakes will nearly always be caught. A calculator with a weak battery may give faulty answers but, with proper maintenance procedures, such a mistake should almost never occur.

3. *Decimals.* Students must be proficient with all phases of decimals, including the reading, writing, and understanding of decimal notation. The ability to change fractions to decimals is also important because many application problems from everyday life will contain fractions.

The use of rounding and significant digits is also a part of a student's work with decimals. There is seldom a need to report all eight digits shown on the display, so students must be able to round to whatever accuracy is required.

4. *Place Value.* Skill in working with place value is important in all operations at all levels of mathematics. On the calculator, you can check the expanded form of a number by listing digits with the appropriate number of zeros after them and then performing whatever operation you want.

SELECTING A CALCULATOR

Let's assume that you have the opportunity to purchase calculators for your classroom. Selecting the right calculator for your classroom use can be confusing because there are a wide variety of brands, types, prices, and features available to you. Here are some guidelines for selecting a particular calculator for use by your students.

1. For most purposes, students through the eighth grade need only the four basic functions. You might want to consider, however, various other keys such as memory, square root, constant, change sign, and add-on percent.

2. The read-out display should be clearly legible when classroom lights are on.

3. The keys should be large and well spaced so that the mistake of hitting an adjacent key is not easily made.

4. The calculator case should be made of hard, durable plastic.

5. The minus or negative sign should appear immediately to the left of the number on the display rather than on the far left of the display or indicated by a separate light on the display. This placement is more natural for students since they learned about the sign in this position.

6. A symbol or other means to indicate "overflow" should be clearly visible on the display when a number is too large to fit the display.

7. The display should accommodate at least eight digits.

8. The display should have a floating decimal point rather than one that is fixed.

9. The algebraic logic approach to computation is recommended. This means that if you push the keys 4, +, 6, = in that order, you will get 10.

10. Avoid calculators that have more than one function on a single key.

11. The calculator should use a long-life battery. There should also be provision for recharging the battery with an ordinary wall socket. The necessary adapter for this purpose should be provided with the calculator.

12. Symbols should be notched on the face of each key.

13. The calculator should have an automatic shut-off so that the batteries will not run down if someone forgets to turn off the calculator.

14. The clearing key should be able to erase only an erroneous entry so that an entire process does not have to be repeated.

Of course, most calculators will have all of the things suggested. However, you need to consider those suggestions that are most important to you and pick the calculator that most closely suits your purposes.

MANAGING CALCULATORS IN THE CLASSROOM

Good management of calculators in your classroom is very important. As pointed out earlier, they can be an excellent teaching tool if used correctly. You have already seen how calculators can be used in your instructional program; here are some suggestions for their physical management.

1. *Put an identifying label and number on each calculator.* Your calculators should be clearly identifiable so that they cannot be confused with a student's own personal calculator. Hopefully, the calculator case will be of hard durable plastic. Ask your school librarian for the white paint that is used for putting call numbers on books. Print the school's initials and a number on the case and then cover it with a coat of shellac, fingernail polish, or some other substance that won't react with the plastic. If your school has an imprinting machine for labelling, use it.

2. *Have an easily accessible storage area for the calculators.* The area should be easily accessible during class and in a place where you can keep an eye on it. A cabinet or set of shelves that can be secured would be good to use.

3. *Appoint responsible students to assist in passing out and collecting calculators.* These students would be responsible for passing out and collecting the calculators from other students. Each of your assistants should be responsible for five or six calculators. They should be sure that

each calculator has been turned off before storage. They should also check to see that all calculators that have been passed out are also returned.

4. *Use a checkout sheet for individual students who want to use a calculator.* The checkout sheet should ask for the date, student's name, calculator number, time signed out, and time signed in. The sheet should be taped to your desk. Be sure that all calculators signed out during a class period have been returned by the end of class.

5. *Be aware of your calculator's battery life.* If you have provisions for recharging batteries, then be sure to do so before the battery becomes too weak to function properly. Have a student be responsible for checking batteries. Keep a supply of new batteries available in case they are needed.

Good physical management and maintenance of your calculators will ensure maximum use in your classroom. It will also allow their life to be as long as possible.

TEACHING COMPUTER LITERACY

The rapid growth of the use of computers in the past two decades is well known to all of us. It has technologically enabled us to do things that were considered impossible not long ago.

The computer's impact means that the education of your students is not complete without an awareness of the computer, what it can do and what it can't do. Your instructional program in mathematics must include a unit on computer literacy for your students if they are to be well prepared for their adult lives. Additionally, many of your students already have a microcomputer in their home, and the number of homes with their own computer will continue to increase at a rapid rate in the next few years.

In this section, the concept of computer literacy will be discussed. In addition, it outlines the components of a unit on computer literacy that you can use in your classroom.

Since you may not be familiar with current computer jargon, a glossary of computer terms can be found in Appendix D.

What Is Computer Literacy?

Simply stated, computer literacy means being aware of the computer, its operation and uses, what it can do and what it cannot do. It means being aware that the computer is *not* able to think for itself, a popular myth for many people. And it means being aware that the computer is a very useful tool for some tasks, but quite inappropriate for others.

There are several components to computer literacy. To be computer literate, a person must have knowledge of the basic parts of the computer, how it operates, its uses and misuses, simple programming techniques, computer occupations, and the history and development of the computer industry. These components will form the basis for a unit on computer literacy that you can use in your classroom.

A Unit on Computer Literacy

The unit consists of five parts:

1. basic parts and operation of a computer

2. computer uses and misuses

3. simple programming techniques

4. computer occupations

5. history and development of the computer industry

Each component may be expanded to suit the needs of your students.

Basic Parts and Operation of a Computer. The basic purpose of a computer is to solve problems. To solve problems, the computer must be told what to do and when to do it. In order to complete its task of solving problems, the computer must receive information (input), process the information (central processing unit), and give results (output).

Each of the three main parts of a computer is needed to solve problems. Figure 11–1 shows the main parts of the computer. The arrows indicate directions in which information flows within the computer.

FIGURE 11–1

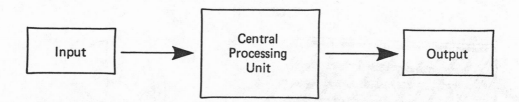

After information is given to the computer through input, it is acted upon by the computer following a set of prescribed instructions called a *program* that has also been given through input. After the computer has processed the information, the results are given through the output.

The central processing unit (CPU) has three parts as shown in Figure 11–2. The information is in the *control* received from the input. Control decides whether the information should go to *memory* for storage or to *arithmetic* for calculators. A program tells control what to do with the information and when to do it. When the instructions for processing the information have been completed, control sends the results to output.

FIGURE 11–2

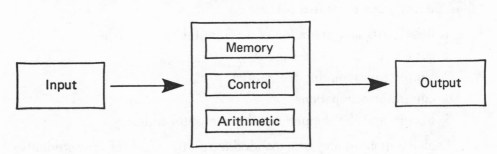

Information (data) is given to the computer through input by using one of four methods: electric typewriter, magnetic tape, magnetic disc or punched cards, shown in Figure 11–3. The electric typewriter sends the data in typed form exactly as it would appear on a piece of paper. The magnetic tape has the data imprinted on it magnetically and looks like recording tape. The punched card has data in coded form on it; letters, numbers, and symbols are coded by punching the appropriate holes on the card. The magnetic disc unit is a metal disc or drum that has the data placed on it magnetically and looks like a phonograph record.

FIGURE 11–3

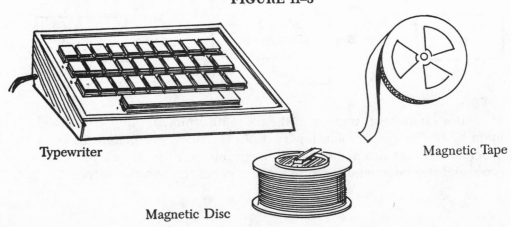

Typewriter

Magnetic Tape

Magnetic Disc

There are several pieces in input equipment or devices that are needed to feed data to the CPU; three pieces of equipment are connected to the CPU via cable. A *card recorder* is used to reach punched cards. A *magnetic tape unit* which looks like a giant tape recorder is used to read the magnetic tape. The *magnetic disc unit* uses an arm much like a phonograph to read the data from the magnetic disc. The *electric typewriter* transmits the data when keys are struck and is part of a *terminal (CRT)* that may be located some distance from the CPU. The terminal may be connected to the CPU by telephone or cable and shows the user on the screen what data is being typed into the computer. The terminal may look like a typewriter or like a television screen; the latter type of terminal is called a *cathode ray tube (CRT)* and is pictured in Figure 11–4.

FIGURE 11–4

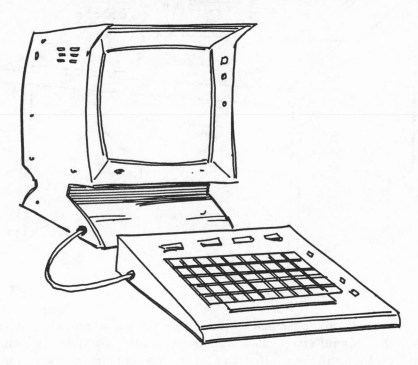

There are several types of output devices a computer may use. The magnetic tape and the magnetic disc unit may be used for output purposes as well as input. Most of the time, a *printer* is used to give output. The printer is a machine that types the output on paper at a speed of more than 1200 lines per minute. Another frequently used output device is the terminal screen, but it does not give a permanent record of output unless the results are also routed through the printer. In addition, the electric typewriter and card reader may be used as output devices.

A piece of equipment that is not directly tied into the computer is the *keypunch machine*. The machine is used to make the punched cards that are used for input. The keypunch machine is located near the computer and is pictured in Figure 11–5.

FIGURE 11–5

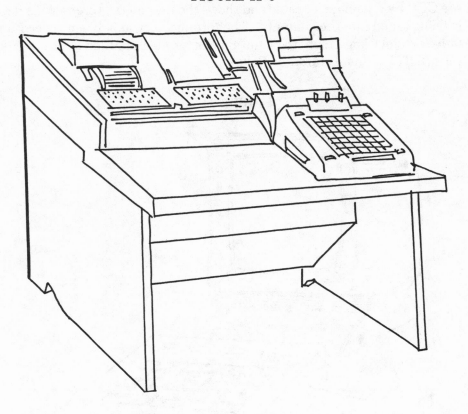

Now that you are familiar with the basic parts of a computer, let's look at how the computer operates. Suppose you have a problem which you want to solve on the computer. To prepare the problem for the computer, you must write a *program*. A program is a special set of instructions that tells the computer how to solve the problem. As you write the program, you break down the problem into a step-by-step procedure that is called *logic*. You begin the process of writing the program by making a *flowchart*, which is a map showing the steps needed to solve the problem. Next, you code the program into a language that the computer can understand. Finally, you *debug* the program, which is a process for finding and removing errors in the program. When this process has been completed, you are ready to feed the program and data into the computer so that the solution can be obtained.

It was mentioned earlier that you must code a program into language that the computer understands. FORTRAN (Formula Translation) and PASCAL (a high-level language) are two languages used by scientists and mathematicians. COBOL (Common Business Oriented Language) is the primary computer language for business. BASIC (Beginners All-purpose Symbolic Instruction Code) is used by beginning programmers for mathematical problems. The home or microcomputer, which is rapidly growing in popularity, uses BASIC as its language. There are many other languages, of course, but these are the most widely known.

There are many times when you may want to reuse a program several times to solve problems as the data changes. To avoid having to put the program into the computer each time you want to use it, put the program into the computer's memory. It can then be simply recalled from the memory each time you need it.

Whenever words, symbols, or numbers are stored in memory, they are recorded by using a series of switches and the binary number system. The binary number system uses the digits 0 and 1. The switches have two positions: "on" and "off." Usually 1 represents "on" and 0 represents "off." The computer translates each word, symbol, and number into its unique binary code for purposes of storage.

Since the binary number system uses only the digits 0 and 1, it has place value just as the base ten system (see Figure 11–6).

FIGURE 11–6

Base Ten				Base Two			
10^2	10^1	10^0		2^3	2^2	2^1	2^0
100	10	1		8	4	2	1

In base 10, 101 is one more than 100. In base 2, 101 represents 5. In base 2, 10 represents 2, as shown in the following two columns.

Base 10 Numbers	Base 2 Numbers
1	1
2	10
3	11
4	100
5	101
6	110
7	111
8	1000
9	1001
10	1010

Computer Uses and Misuses. Whether you realize it or not, the computer affects you in some way every day of your life. And, new ways of using computers are being discovered daily.

How does society use the computer? Your bank keeps track of your money with the computer, which also prints your monthly savings and checking statements. Department store billing and inventory records are mostly done by computers. Cash registers in the supermarket tell the clerk how much change you should receive and sometimes actually counts it out for you. Your doctor uses the computer to help diagnose your illness and may indicate what medicine should be prescribed. Law enforcement officials make heavy use of the computer in their work. And, of course, all levels of government use the computer for their handling of data, including your tax returns. Machines in many industrial plants operate automatically; the automation is possible because of a computer program. Even some of the larger commercial airplanes take off and land by using a computer program rather than a pilot. There are probably thousands of other examples you can think of.

Education is beginning to make greater use of the computer both for instructional and recordkeeping purposes. Student records are kept on a computer in many school systems and in almost all colleges. Transcripts and report cards are printed by a computer program.

In the classroom, computer-assisted instruction (CAI) has been introduced in recent years. CAI allows a student to sit at a terminal and interact with a computer. The computer is programmed to help the student learn something and is able to adjust instruction according to student response. Computer-managed instruction is a system for the use of the computer in management aspects of teaching. For example, daily and weekly records of student performance on quizzes and homework may be kept on the computer.

Data processing has become an integral part of most industrial operations today. The computer is able to organize and analyze vast amounts of data and return it to the user in nearly any form desirable. This task often could not be physically done by people or it would take so long that the results would be of no use. Not only is the task able to be completed, but it usually saves the company a great deal of money in terms of manpower. Without data processing and the computer, we would never have been able to make our manned space flight to the moon.

Unfortunately, there are many ways in which the computer can be misused. There is a great deal of confidential information about many things and people which is stored on computers. This information can be accessed just as easily as it can be stored and, in the hands of unscrupulous people, can be very damaging. Passwords and codes are used to try to control this potential danger, but there is no guarantee of security. For example, there have been cases where money in a bank has been stolen by someone who transferred funds from one account to another. Complexity of programs and the amount of data involved makes detection of crimes by computers almost impossible to detect and solve.

Many people have the fear that the computer has robbed them of their privacy. So much information about a person, especially on government computers, is on the computer that could be accessed by anyone that their fear cannot be disregarded. Information required for credit purposes is so extensive and easily available that privacy is a real problem.

Simple Programming Techniques. In order to solve a problem, the computer must be given the procedure for solution on a step-by-step basis. The computer is told what to do and when to do it with a *program*. In writing programs, programmers use *flowcharts* to map out the strategy for solving the problem.

In flowcharting, certain geometric shapes and symbols are used to indicate particular instructions. The shapes and symbols used are pictured in Figure 11–7.

FIGURE 11–7

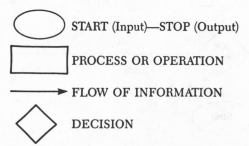

START (Input)—STOP (Output)

PROCESS OR OPERATION

FLOW OF INFORMATION

DECISION

Let's illustrate how a flowchart may be used to eat a hot dog (see Figure 11–8).

FIGURE 11–8

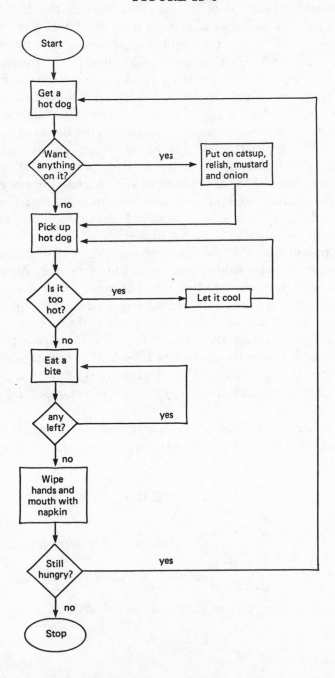

Figure 11-9 is an example of a flowchart for sharpening a pencil.

FIGURE 11–9

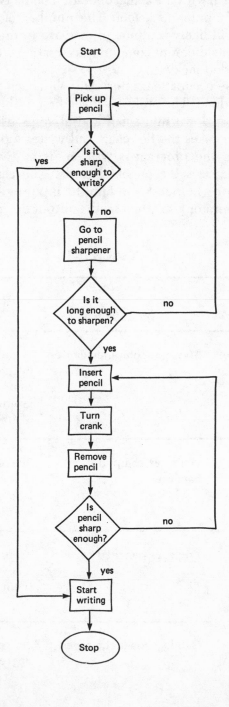

Computer Occupations. The growth of the computer has created many new occupations for people. Some of the occupations require a great deal of training, while others require very little. The occupations range from those that deal with the actual operation of the computer to those that deal with the computer as a tool. The number of job openings in the computer field will likely continue to increase in the next decade.

Table 11–1 lists different computer occupations, their responsibilities, and training needed for each.

How do these occupations interrelate with each other? Suppose there is a project to be done. The project is given first to the systems analyst who breaks the project down into small logical steps using a flowchart. The programmer then takes the flowchart and writes a program to do each of the steps. When the program is written, it is given to the keypunch operator who prepares the punched cards. The cards are given to the computer operator who puts them into the input device on the computer. The computer operator also monitors the output device. While all of this is

TABLE 11–1

Occupation	Responsibilities	Requirements and Training
Computer center director	Manages computer center	Training and experience in the operation of the computer and programming. College degree desirable.
Computer operator	Operates computer hardware	Training in the operation of a computer, but college degree not required.
Keypunch operator	Prepares punched cards	Training in operation of a keypunch with good typing skills. College degree not required.
Tape librarian	Catalogs magnetic tapes	No special training or degree required.

TABLE 11–1 (Cont'd.)

Occupation	Responsibilities	Requirements and Training
Programmer	Writes programs	College degree or certificate required with good knowledge of at least one computer language. Ability to think logically required.
Systems analyst	Designs plans to use the computer	Knowledge of computer operation, programming, and specialized field of involvement. College degree required.

going on, the computer center director oversees the work of the keypunch operator and the computer operator. If the program is to be run again but not stored in the computer memory, it is put on magnetic tape and given to the tape librarian. The print-out of the program is then given back to the systems analyst who then decides whether or not the project has been completed.

History and Development of the Computer Industry. From the beginning of time, man has used computers in primitive forms. Fingers were probably the first form used and they were used for counting purposes. The early Chinese and Japanese used the abacus for their computation and, in fact, still use it today (See Figure 11–10).

FIGURE 11–10

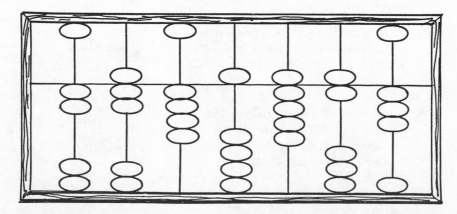

The operations of addition, subtraction, multiplication, and division were invented long before the year 1600, but except for the abacus, few computing aids were available. Finally, in 1600, some people began trying to build machines that could do arithmetic quickly. A list of these inventions and their dates of invention are outlined in the following list.

1614	Napier's Bones were rods used for quick multiplication.	
1620	The slide rule used numbers represented by distances on a scale and could solve multiplication and division problems.	
1642	Pascal's calculator could add a column of eight figures, but could only do addition and subtraction.	
1671	The Leibniz wheel could do addition, subtraction, multiplication, and division.	
1801	Jacquard's Loom punched cards to weave designs into fabric.	
1889	Hollerith's punch card machine was a digital computer that could sort, count, and tabulate data from punch cards.	

1944	Aiken's Mark I was developed. It was the first large-scale automatic digital calculator.
1946	The ENIAC computer was developed by Edkert and Maachly. It was designed to develop mathematical tables for firing projectiles. ENIAC was very large in size and used the vacuum tube.
1951	The Universal Automatic Computer (UNIVAC I) was developed as the first commercial computer. It was capable of addition in two micro seconds and could multiply in ten micro seconds.
1959	Computers entered their second generation. Computer size became much smaller with the invention of the transistor. The number of computers produced began to increase. FORTRAN was developed as a computer language. Mass storage (2,000,000 characters) became a reality.
1965	Computers entered their third generation. The use of miniature electronic circuits made faster, more reliable, and less expensive computers possible. More programming languages were developed.
Future	Future generations of computers will be marked by greater use of magnetic tapes and discs, video and audio response units, and more circuits. Computers will continue to decrease in size and cost. There will be increased use of home computers for more and more purposes.

INTRODUCTION TO BASIC LANGUAGE

As a part of computer literacy, you may want to introduce your students to the BASIC language. This language is the easiest to learn and is the one found on the microcomputer (with variations among brands) that many of your students may have at home.

In this section, an introduction to BASIC is presented. In addition, suggestions for teaching BASIC in your classroom are offered.

BASIC in the Computer

As you write your program from the flowchart, you will use *statements*. Statements serve two purposes: (1) to tell the computer what to do, or (2) to give information about your program which you can use or which can be used by someone who is reading your program. Statements that are designed to give information to the *user*, writer, or others are called *REM statements* (REM stands for "remark"). REM statements will not be acted upon by the computer. For example, you may want to say REM PRO-GRAM WRITTEN BY G.R. DOE or REM PROGRAM DESIGNED TO SOLVE PROBLEM #347. Notice that the REM statements are written in all capital letters. No lower case letters are used in writing BASIC programs.

Variable names are used to represent data in BASIC. These variable names are addresses in the computer's memory (storage) and tell the computer where to go to find a particular piece of data. A variable name may be given by a single letter of the alphabet or by a letter followed by a single digit 0 through 9. (Zero is often printed by the computer as $\emptyset$ to distinguish it from the letter O.) Examples of variable names might be A   B   J3   X4   T6 and so on.

Mathematical symbols do not always have the same meaning in BASIC as the one to which you are accustomed. For example, the symbol " = " does not mean equal. It means something *quite different*. That symbol tells the computer to assign to the variable on the left the value of the expression on the right of the " = " symbol. Only one variable can appear on the left of the " = " symbol. For example,

Y = 3 The value of 3 is assigned to Y.

X = Y The variable X is given the same value as the variable Y. If you had entered Y = 3 before X = Y, then X would now have the value of 3.

X = X + 2 The variable X is now assigned a value that is two more than the assigned value. From above, X now has a value of 5.

Mathematical operations do not always use the conventional symbolism to which you are accustomed. Table 11–2 shows the operational symbols used in BASIC.

TABLE 11–2. Operational Symbols for BASIC

Operation	*Symbol*	*Example*
Addition	+	A = B + C
Subtraction	−	A = B − C
Multiplication	*	A = B * C
Division	/	A + B / C
Exponentiation	↑	A = B ↑ 2
Root	^	(the square of B)

There are some fundamental rules in writing BASIC programs that must be observed.

1. Two variables may not be written next to each other, but must be separated by an operation sign. For example, you can never write XY.

2. Two or more operations signs cannot be written consecutively. Use a parentheses to separate the operations. For example, if you wanted to multiply 3 by -2.7, you would write: $A = 3 * (-2.7)$, not $A = 3 * -2.7$.

3. Computation is an expression that contains two or more operations and is performed from left to right in the following order:

   a. operations in parentheses

   b. exponentiation

   c. multiplication and division

   d. addition and subtraction

If the computer is given the expression $3 * (3 + 1) - 2 \uparrow 3$, it will perform calculation in the following steps:

Step 1:	$3 * 4 - 2 \uparrow 3$
Step 2:	$3 * 4 - 8$
Step 3:	$12 - 8$
Step 4:	4

There are some typical system commands that will cause the computer to do certain things in your BASIC program. Table 11–3 lists these and describes what happens.

TABLE 11–3

Command	Use Tells Computer to:
RUN	execute program
LIST	list your entire program to that point
LIB	list names of the programs stored in memory

The commands are executed when you hit the carriage return key. (R is the usual key.)

Some typical program commands used in BASIC are in Table 11–4.

TABLE 11–4

Command	Tells Computer
PRINT " "	to print whatever is between quotation marks.
PRINT A	to print the value of A.
END	there are no more instructions in the program.
READ	to look at a list of information (a READ statement is a program requirement when you have a DATA statement in the program).
DATA	there is information coming that should be read.
INPUT	that data will be coming from user to execute program.
LET	that value is to be assigned to a variable.

Each line in a BASIC program must be numbered. It is most convenient to number your lines using multiples of 10, especially if you have a short program. This allows you to insert other lines between two lines if you choose to do so. For example, if you want to add an additional line between lines 10 and 20, it would be easy to do so by simply choosing a line number such as 11 or 17 or whatever. There is no way to add a line between 10 and 11 without renumbering. Line numbers are needed only for program commands.

Let's see what it's like to write a program in BASIC. Suppose you wish to print your name. The flowchart for the program looks like Figure 11–11. To the right of the flowchart is the program as it would be written in BASIC.

To enter this program into the computer:

1. Type 10 PRINT "TOM JONES" and hit return key.
2. Type 20 END and hit return key.
3. Type RUN and hit return key. (No line number is needed for a system command.)

The computer would then print TOM JONES and stop.

Figure 11–12 shows some more examples of simple computations. The flowchart is on the left and the BASIC program is on the right.

You may want to have your program do a series of calculations before it finishes. This may be accomplished by including a *loop* in your program.

FIGURE 11–11

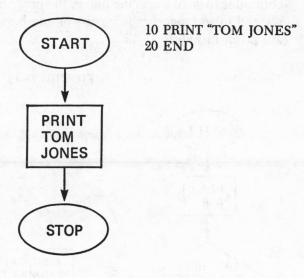

10 PRINT "TOM JONES"
20 END

FIGURE 11–12

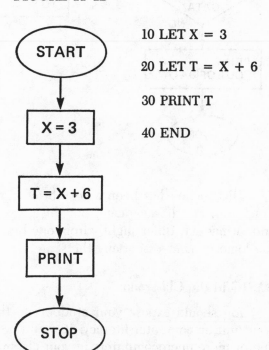

10 LET X = 3

20 LET T = X + 6

30 PRINT T

40 END

The command *GO TO* is one way of including a loop. GO TO tells the computer to go to a specific line in the program. For example, suppose you wanted to add together five pairs of numbers. The flowchart and program are given in Figure 11–13.

FIGURE 11–13

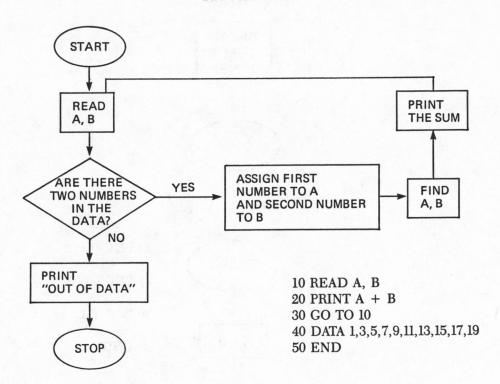

10 READ A, B
20 PRINT A + B
30 GO TO 10
40 DATA 1,3,5,7,9,11,13,15,17,19
50 END

This section has been a very brief introduction to BASIC. There is much more to the language, but this gives you the idea. The commands and format may differ slightly from one brand of computer to another, but the logic remains essentially the same.

BASIC in the Classroom

You should expose your students to the fundamentals of BASIC in your unit on computer literacy. It would be desirable if you had access to one or more microcomputers in your classroom so that students could try some very simple programs.

Your students should have plenty of opportunity to flowchart problems and solutions. Not only is this appropriate to learning programming techniques, it also helps them develop the kind of logic that will help improve their problem-solving skills.

USING COMPUTERS IN THE CLASSROOM

As stated in the section on Computer Literacy, one of the major goals of your instructional program should be the development of computer literacy by your students. Ideally, you will have access to microcomputers for the computer literacy component but, even if you don't, the topic should not be ignored.

However, the development of computer literacy is not the only use for computers in your classroom. In this section, other instructional uses for the computer that you can incorporate into your instructional program will be examined. This examination, of course, assumes that microcomputers are available for your use, either in your classroom or in another location in your building. These uses of the computer in the classroom also depend upon the availability of software, either commercial or teacher-made.

Simulations

The term "simulation" means many things to many people so that a precise definition is difficult to agree upon. Let's assume that a simulation situation is a problem-solving situation that can be presented to your students for their action and reaction. The situation may be scientific or social in scope and be either real-life or make-believe in nature. Simulation is useful in helping your students develop problem-solving skills and in giving meaning and relevance to your instructional program.

Simulation activities can be used not only in your mathematics instructional programs, but also in other curricular areas. Investigating changes in profit or loss in a manufacturing situation caused by economic and other conditions is an example of simulation activity you could use. Looking at the mathematics involved in weather prediction or bank transactions are other examples of simulation. The point is that simulation activities can be an integral part of your instructional program that will be enjoyable and meaningful to your students.

How does the computer help with simulation? The computer can be programmed with a simulation situation to which students can respond and get immediate feedback. Because of its capabilities, the computer can handle simulation situations that are too complex or time-consuming to do by hand. The result is increased student learning and motivation.

More and more simulation programs on a wide variety of topics are being developed commercially every day. The chances are excellent that you can find one or more simulation programs that will fit your instructional needs at a reasonable cost. Some teachers have decided to write their own simulation programs with varying degrees of success. Before you attempt to undertake this task, be advised that there is a tremendous investment in time and effort needed to successfully write a simulation program for the computer.

Games

When the topic of computer games is mentioned today, there is always mixed reaction as to their value on the part of parents and teachers. Computer games, when properly used, can have a very positive influence on your students. The points for using computer games successfully in your classroom are essentially the same as the ones for games outlined in Chapter 10. The following reasons strongly support the use of computer games in your classroom.

1. Students like them.
2. Games help develop thinking and decision-making skills.
3. Games can be used to introduce new ideas and skills.
4. Games can be played in groups that can emphasize group collective effort to solve a problem situation.
5. Games can be used to spark an interest by your students in a new area.

There are literally hundreds of computer games commercially available today. Choose a game carefully and you will be pleased with the results.

Tutorial

A third use for computers in the classroom is tutorial activities. As the term "tutorial" implies, these types of activities can be used to either help a student acquire a new skill or maintain an already-existing one through drill and practice. There have been many forms of tutorial computer programs introduced over the years including, among others, computer-assisted instruction (CAI) and computer-assisted learning (CAL).

The primary advantage of tutorial programs is that a one-to-one teaching situation is provided for the student that can be completed at his or her own rate. These programs usually include good audio and visual stimuli and, while not as effective as the human teacher, do provide an adequate substitute for most students.

As with simulation activities and games, there are many commercially-available tutorial programs. Your professional judgment will be required so that appropriate choices can be made for your students.

A Final Word

Ideally, you would have enough microcomputers so that there would be one machine available for every two or three students. In reality at the present time, you probably will not have the ideal situation. Hence, you must adapt the suggestions made in this section to meet your microcomputer availability. But, keep plugging and you will find new and varied ways to incorporate microcomputers into your instructional program. Your students will clearly benefit from greater exposure to the microcomputer.

SELECTING COMPUTER HARDWARE AND SOFTWARE

Selecting appropriate computer hardware and software is of paramount importance to the successful use of computers in your classroom. The selection process is time-consuming but, properly done, will pay rich dividends both to you and your students. A good rule of thumb for most situations is to select appropriate software and then select the hardware.

In this section, criteria for selecting computer hardware and software will be discussed. These criteria are appropriate for the microcomputer because it is the most widely-used computer for junior high/middle school classroom purposes. These criteria may also be used if you have the opportunity of purchasing a microcomputer and accompanying software for your own personal home use. You may want to consult the "Glossary of Computer Terminology" in the Appendix if some of the terminology in this section is unfamiliar to you.

Selecting Hardware

Selecting appropriate hardware is not an easy task. In some sense, the selection task is analogous to that of selecting a new automobile. There are a great many brands and types of microcomputers available and you can literally spend as much money as you want. Remember that microcomputer sales are highly competitive, so beware of sales personnel; take your time and shop wisely.

As you shop for a microcomputer, there are several steps you need to follow.

1. Identify the objectives of the learning environment. (Who will be the audience? What are the skills to be learned?)

2. Identify the necessary content/presentation modes (audio/visual, motion/still, illustrative/verbal, etc.).

3. Identify constraints (economic, learner, physical facility, qualified teacher availability).

4. Identify features of the microcomputer in terms of *must* have, *should* have, and *like to* have.

5. Select the microcomputer based on the information gathered in steps 1 through 4.

These five steps will give you a systematic approach to the selection of the appropriate hardware.

Some of the features alluded to in step 4 above might include such things as the following:

1. color
2. audio
3. voice recognition
4. touch panel (light pen) input
5. printer
6. graphics output/input
7. alternate character sets
8. music
9. memory size (RAM and ROM)
10. external memory (cassette/disk drive)

You must establish your priorities relative to *must* have, *should* have, and *like to* have.

As you are pondering the available information about the various microcomputers you are considering for selection, there are qualities about the microcomputer with which you must consider. Information about these qualities can be gained from brochures and sales personnel, but talking to other people who have knowledge of or have purchased the equipment may be the most beneficial.

1. durability/reliability
2. expandability
3. interface capability with other brands of input/output devices
4. simplicity of operation
5. memory size
6. keyboard type (touch panel or key)

7. availability of software and documentation support by the manufacturer
8. output quality of text and/or graphics
9. availability of local service

Don't be bashful about asking pertinent questions. After all, you are making a significant financial investment and you need to be as sure as possible that you are getting the best quality and quantity for your money.

There are two common errors usually made by purchasers of microcomputers. One is the failure to recognize that microcomputers are machines and must, therefore, be routinely maintained (at additional cost). More than one school corporation has purchased microcomputers and failed to budget money for maintenance and repair. The result is that an expensive piece of equipment lies idle because there is no money for repair.

The other error occurs when random-access-memory (RAM) is too small to be useful. The latter error usually occurs because of a desire to lower the cost of purchase, which is understandable. However, the RAM size should be at least 48 to 64 kilobytes. A smaller RAM eliminates the opportunity of using many programs because they are too long.

Selecting the appropriate hardware is not an easy task. It is time-consuming at best. But, properly done, your shopping efforts will be greatly rewarded, both in usability and enjoyment. To further help your deliberations, look at the checklist in Appendix E.

Selecting Software

The usefulness of the hardware you select will only be as good as the software you select. The hardware can do nothing without software.

The selection of software involves much of the same type of consideration that you would give to selection of a textbook or other supplementary instructional materials for your classroom. The major obstacle you will encounter is the reluctance of commercial software companies to let you preview software before purchase. Their reluctance is understandable because of the ease of copying a preview program, a problem that does not exist with textbooks or other instructional materials.

The only ways to overcome the previewing obstacle are to seek software products that can be evaluated at a local store or to consult independent evaluation groups for their opinions. Quite frankly, there is a proliferation of "garbage" software on the market today, so you must be very careful before you pay good money. This money will not usually be refunded once you break the seal on the disk, so be sure to check return provisions *before* the purchase is made.

When you have the opportunity to preview and evaluate software programs before purchase, there are several criteria you need to consider. For ease of application, the criteria is divided into three classes: technical, educational, and management.

The technical area refers to the software as it relates to the microcomputer and the microcomputer's execution of the software. The following questions should be asked about the technical area.

1. *Does the software utilize your microcomputer's capabilities?* A good piece of software is one that does something different because of the microcomputer that could not normally be done otherwise. For example, a simple drill sheet where the student simply gives the answers is not really an appropriate exercise for microcomputer software. However, if the software gives immediate feedback and/or branches to a tutorial situation, then the software is using the unique capabilities of the microcomputer.

2. *Is the software "bomb proof"?* Good software should provide for student responses other than the correct response. These responses should branch meaningfully to another part of the software program that will assist the student in "getting back on track."

3. *Does the software have pleasing graphics and/or sound reproduction?* Nothing will turn students off more quickly than graphics or audio provided by the software that are not pleasant to see or hear. A flickering screen or raspy audio is sometimes found on software. Another problem commonly encountered are software time delays that do not give adequate time for the student to read a message on the screen before the software progresses to the next phase.

The educational area refers to the educational quality of the software. Software that is not educationally sound will be of no benefit to you whatsoever. The following questions should be asked about the educational area.

1. *Is the software technically correct?* Many times you will find software that has incorrect grammar or spelling or has mathematical mistakes. Occasionally, you will find software that will develop a skill in a sequence that is not appropriate. Avoid software that is not educationally correct.

2. *Does the software provide assistance to the student in understanding incorrect answers?* Some software will simply tell the student that a response is incorrect with no help or explanation. Good software guides the student toward a correct response.

3. *Does the software specify necessary prerequisite skills needed by the student?* It is not always obvious what prerequisite skills are needed by the student to successfully use the software. Be sure you determine what the prerequisite skills are and that the student has those skills before using the software. A lot of frustration will be avoided if you do this important task first

4. *Does the software have clear and appropriate objective(s)?* The software objectives should be clearly stated so that you can easily determine what the objectives are. Also, the objectives should be appropriate for your instructional program. If the objectives are not appropriate, the software will not be of use to you.

5. *Does the software encourage learning through feedback?* One of the main advantages of a learning tool is that it can give immediate feedback to student response. But, this feedback must encourage the student to continue. Positive reinforcement is the kind of feedback you should look for.

The management area refers to how easily the software can be used in a classroom situation. Software that cannot be easily managed in your teaching situation will be of no help to you. The following questions should be asked about the management area.

1. *Does the software have directions that are easy to understand and follow?* The directions should be easy to understand and follow for *both* you and your students. Confusion about directions causes frustration and negates any instructional benefits the software might have had.

2. *Does the software assist in tracking student progress?* It is very helpful if the software gives a summary at the end of how well the student performed. This summary will give beneficial feedback to the student and also assist you in assessing student performance.

3. *Is the software flexible to meet different student needs?* Software that has different levels of difficulty that can be chosen by the student will be of most benefit to your instructional program.

A Final Word

Selecting appropriate hardware and software is the key to the successful use of the microcomputer in your classroom. Common sense and comparison techniques will help you get the most appropriate and best equipment for your money. For your convenience, evaluation forms for selecting hardware and software may be found in Appendix E.

QUICK REVIEW

1. What appropriate uses can be made of hand-held calculators in the classroom?

2. What uses would *you* make of calculators in your classroom?

3. Taking the set of criteria for selecting a calculator from the chapter, rank in order the criteria for your use. What other criteria would you use? How would these other criteria fit into your ranking?

4. Gather information and/or literature about hand-held calculators available on the market. Which calculator(s) appear to meet your needs if you were to purchase some for your classroom?

5. You want to approach your principal about purchasing a classroom set of calculators. Outline your proposal to present to him or her. Include the brand and cost of the calculator you want to purchase, along with your rationale for purchasing a classroom set.

6. Your principal has purchased a classroom set of calculators for you. Devise a plan for managing the calculators.

7. Define computer literacy.

8. Name the basic parts and describe the operation of a computer.

9. State some computer uses and misuses.

10. Name six computer occupations, the responsibilities of each occupation, and the training required for each occupation.

11. Make a flowchart of your actions as you prepare to drive your automobile. Start from the time you decide to leave the house until you pull out of your driveway or parking lot.

12. List the five parts of the computer.

13. Trace the history and development of the computer industry.

14. Construct a flowchart from the following list of instructions.

    a. START   c. C = A + B   e. STOP
    b. INPUT A,B   d. PRINT C

15. What results are printed out for X, Y and Z from this program?

    10   X = 6
    20   Y = 3*X + 4
    30   Z = 2*X
    40   W = Y + 2

```
50   PRINT Y, Z, W
60   END
```

16. Code the following as valid BASIC statements:

   a. $Y = 2A + 3B$

   b. $A = \dfrac{Y}{x + 2}$

   c. $R = 8 + \dfrac{X}{2} - Z$

   d. $A = 3.14R^2$

   e. $K = (3X - 7)^2 - 2X$

17. Each of the following BASIC statements may contain an error. Rewrite each correctly, if necessary. If the statement is correct as is, mark it "OK."

   a. $Y = 6 X$

   b. $A = 3$

   c. $A + B = C$

   d. $C = 4 + 5 + 7$

   e. $X = 3 (A + B)$

18. Write the BASIC program shown in the flowchart in Figure 11–14.

FIGURE 11-14

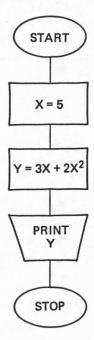

19. Gather information and/or literature about microcomputers that could be purchased by your school. Which computer(s) appear to meet your needs in developing a unit on computer literacy for your students?

20. Your principal has asked you to take charge of five new microcomputers that have been purchased for your building. Outline the steps that you would take to implement their use.

21. Your principal has asked you to make a recommendation on the purchase of a microcomputer system for your building. Use the microcomputer evaluation form from the Appendix and visit some local computer stores. Which system would you recommend? Why?

22. What sources are available to you for the purchase of software for the microcomputer you recommended in the previous exercise in the following areas?

    a. simulation
    b. games
    c. tutorial

    Which software pieces from these sources would you purchase? Why? (Use the software evaluation form found in the Appendix, and consider cost as a factor.)

23. Find out which area school corporations have implemented microcomputers into their junior high/middle school(s). Contact them and find out how the microcomputer has been implemented. What was done right and what was done wrong during the implementation phase? How would their plan need to be modified to fit your situation?

12

Survival and Growth as a Junior High/Middle School Mathematics Teacher

Throughout this book so far, your survival and growth have been focused in terms of your instructional program in mathematics. All aspects have been looked at: the learner, how you organize and work with the learner, and various curriculum components. Now let's turn our attention to *you;* your survival and growth.

After reading and studying this chapter, you should be able to:

- Describe different techniques for coping with stress.
- Describe the need for and ways of building relationships with parents, fellow teachers, other school personnel, and your principal and other administrators.
- Describe techniques for improving the classroom through improving your performance as a teacher.
- Describe the importance of supporting your school system.
- Describe the benefits of joining professional organizations.
- Describe the need for continuing inservice and formal education.

COPING WITH STRESS

One of—if not the biggest—problems that you face as a classroom teacher today is how to cope with stress. The increasingly rapid pace of our society has placed a great deal more burden on you as a classroom teacher. Your ability to keep this burden from getting the best of you will, in part, determine your effectiveness as a classroom teacher and probably whether you opt to continue teaching as a career.

Stress comes from many directions. Students, colleagues, community, and your own self are all potential sources of stress. Clearly, you must control or eliminate this stress or you will not be able to survive as an effective teacher of junior high/middle school mathematics.

Student Stress

As you are well aware, the pre-teen years are very difficult for your students. They want to behave as adults, but are not quite mature enough to deal with this desire. Here are some tips to help you deal with students.

1. *Don't overreact*. Sometimes this is easier said than done. Remember that you are the stabilizing influence for many of your students. They will present situations to you that you won't believe. Many of them are frustrated academically and personally, so if you overreact, the situation could blow up in your face. In a sense, it's better to underreact, but this does not imply that you should become passive or a "milque toast." Try to get to the cause of the students' difficulties and help them deal with their problems. However, recognize that there will be some problems for which you can do nothing; accept that fact and go from there.

2. *Don't take student remarks personally*. At times, your students will say some very cruel and cutting things to you. In many cases, they do not mean to say those things, so keep this in mind.

3. *Avoid the use of sarcasm with your students*. Sarcasm has never been an appropriate method for dealing with students. Students soon lose respect for you and when this happens, you will no longer be effective as a classroom teacher.

4. *Work to gain the respect of your students*. Classroom management, as pointed out earlier, is much easier to maintain when you have the respect of your students. Consistency, fairness, and compassion in the way you treat your students will go a long, long way towards gaining the respect of your students. Maybe that "golden rule" has some real merit to it!

5. *Find an outside release for your frustrations*. Leave your problems with students at school. Develop some interests or hobbies that you can pursue during out-of-school hours. Physical activity and sports work for many people. You will find that you will be much more ready to tackle the problems when you return to school if you have been doing something else. Recognize that there has to be a time to get away from student problems.

Colleague Stress

It is naive to assume that your colleagues, fellow teachers, and administrators will always behave in a professional manner. Colleagues may become jealous of you if they think you are more effective as a teacher than they are or if they think you are being favored by the principal. Be aware, too, of the politics of the situation and deal with them. If there is a problem with a colleague, confront the problem with that individual directly and attempt to resolve it in the open. Never be guilty of backbiting. This also helps keep frustration from building inside of you.

Community Stress

Communities today are placing added responsibility on you as a classroom teacher. Many of the things that your students are supposed to be learning at home are not being taught there. You must recognize that your role is more than just a teacher of junior high/middle school mathematics, and you really have no choice but to accept that additional responsibility. However, recognize that there will be some things you will have no control over; do *what* you can *when* you can.

Try to understand your community and its politics. Becoming active in community affairs is a good way to do this. Also, your community will expect certain behaviors from you, a fact you cannot ignore. Your outside releases for your frustrations must be within the parameters of your community's expectations. Learn those parameters and respect them.

Your Own Stress

You will face many personal stresses from family, friends, and your own person. These stresses must be left at home in the same way that school stresses must be left at school. Don't keep the stress pent up inside of you, but find appropriate and continual release for it. Whatever that release is, it must work for you.

It is also helpful if you develop friendships and activities away from the school setting. Having only professional colleagues as friends or activities that are school-related makes it much more difficult to leave your problems at school.

Above all, if you feel unable to cope with your stress, seek outside help. Your minister or a close friend may be the one who can help you. In any case, don't keep that stress pent up inside of you; the end result may be disastrous.

BUILDING ADULT RELATIONSHIPS

Your survival as a junior high/middle school mathematics teacher is also dependent on the types of relationships you build with other adults: parents, fellow teachers, school personnel, and administrators. These relationships must be based on mutual respect and understanding of the other person and his or her role.

Parents

In general, you will probably find most of your students' parents fairly cooperative. They are interested in their youngster's progress both academically and socially. There are, however, parents who feel that their youngsters can do no wrong and that if there is a problem, it's because you have not done your job. This latter type of parent is usually the one who has youngsters giving you the most difficulty. Here are some thoughts on building positive relationships with parents.

1. *Be accessible*. When a parent calls and wants to come in to see you, don't put the parent off. Be as accommodating as possible in setting up a scheduled visit.

2. *Keep parents informed about good as well as bad student progress*. Parents like to know when their youngster is doing a good job as well as when they are doing poorly. Let them know that you are interested in their youngster. A short note sent through the mail, with a copy to your principal, lets the parent know you care—it doesn't hurt the involved student's morale, either.

3. *Inform parents as soon as possible if you feel the youngster is in danger of failing a term*. A common, in many cases valid, complaint from parents is that they had no idea their youngster was failing. Don't depend on the student to convey the message home, because it simply won't get there. A telephone call or a brief note may gain parental support to help the student.

4. *Attend parent-teacher meetings if your school has such a group*. Sometimes these meetings may seem a waste of time, but you should make

every effort to attend and participate. This shows that you are interested in your students and their progress.

5. *Treat your parents as a professional should*. Sometimes teachers have a tendency to display a "know-it-all" attitude or to talk down to parents and students, especially if the teachers are frustrated. Keep a calm attitude and listen to what the parents have to say. They know the student as well or better than you think you do, especially when you see the youngster for probably only an hour a day.

6. *Be accountable for your behavior outside of school hours*. Like it or not, you are expected to maintain a higher standard of behavior in your community than are other adults. This does not mean that you can't "kick up your heels," but use good common sense in when, where, and how you do it.

Fellow Teachers

Your fellow teachers can be a real source of ideas and inspiration to you as a classroom teacher. Many of them will have more teaching experience than you, so you can learn from that experience. Showing a genuine interest in the teaching area is a good way to build strong professional relationships.

Avoid the gossip in the faculty lounge about fellow teachers or about students. This gossip can be nothing but detrimental to the esteem that other teachers hold for you.

It is also very helpful if you take your share in assigned responsibilities. Don't be the person who always has an excuse for why he or she can't do hall or lunchroom duty. It is proper to expect others to carry their fair share but, unfortunately, this will not always happen.

If you perceive a problem with a fellow teacher, try to work it out directly. Don't be sneaky in your handling of the situation.

Other School Personnel

It is important to your effectiveness as a classroom teacher that you have a good working relationship with other school personnel, such as the counselor, school secretary, and custodian. These people have a definite role to fulfill in the school, just as you do, and their jobs are no less important.

The counselor is an excellent support for you in dealing with problems of your students. Seek his or her advice and counsel when a student has you frustrated. The counselor also has access to student records; information within the records may enable you to work more effectively with a particular student.

The school secretary is your chief clerical support. Try to give the person as much lead time as possible in doing clerical tasks for you. Let the secretary know when a good job or a favor has been done for you; a little praise or a "thank you" goes a long way. The secretary is also a person with a finger on the pulse of the politics of the school staff. Never underestimate the secretary's role in this regard.

Custodians are your source of help in the physical maintenance of your classroom. Have a kind word for them now and then, and you'll be surprised at the little extras they will do for you. As with the secretary, never underestimate the custodian's role in school politics.

Principal and Other Administrators

Some of the most important people you must work with are those who are directly in charge of you as a classroom teacher. There are two basic axioms in working with the administrators.

1. *Remember the "chain of command."* There are established procedures within your school system, so never deviate from these or you may no longer be teaching in that system. Always start with your building principal in requests for anything related to your instructional program.

2. *Keep your principal informed.* Never let your principal be embarrassed because you did not inform him or her about a situation which has occurred or will occur. Keep the principal informed of your dealings with students and parents, and send him or her copies of notes sent home.

Try to handle difficulties with students in the classroom rather than in the principal's office. The office should be the last resort when all else has failed. However, do keep your principal informed about actions you have taken in dealing with students. Your principal will appreciate (and so will you) documentation, including dates and times, of these student dealings.

Your principal will also appreciate your sharing the responsibilities for the more unpleasant tasks, such as hall or lunchroom duty. Like it or not, this is part of your role as a teacher and as a professional.

IMPROVING THE CLASSROOM

As pointed out in Chapter 4, there are three basic factors that determine the effectiveness of the classroom. These factors are:

1. student performance
2. student attitude

3. your performance as a teacher

As you consider ways to improve your classroom, you must seek improvement in all three areas. However, in a sense, the first two factors cannot improve unless you improve your own performance.

Some pertinent questions relative to assessing your own performance were suggested in Chapter 4. There may be others, but these, at least, get at the basics of assessing your performance.

In addition to your own personal evaluation, ask your principal, fellow teachers, and your students for feedback about your performance as a teacher. Their views should give you a good cross section of opinion.

Your principal obviously plays an important part in the evaluation process. Decisions on whether or not you continue in your present teaching position rest almost completely with your principal. Take an offensive tact with your principal by issuing an open invitation to visit your classroom and give you feedback on your performance. Don't wait for your principal to inform you of a visit for evaluation purposes. More and more frequently, teachers are being asked to prepare objectives and lesson plans in advance. Ask your principal to review these materials and give you feedback.

Have you ever considered asking fellow teachers to come into your classroom and observe your teaching? Why not? They are trained professionals just as you are and they may have some valuable assistance for you. Offer to return the favor to them. It also gives you a chance to share ideas about teaching methods with your fellow teachers, something that is, unfortunately, seldom done. It just seems that, many times, teachers go into their classroom, close the door, and dare any outsider to invade their domain. This may be caused by insecurity. If teaching performance is to improve, you may well encounter some feelings of jealousy from fellow teachers because of your efforts at improvement. But this should not and cannot deter you from your goal. If some of these feelings surface, try to deal with them directly. The net result may be that one of your fellow teachers may improve his or her own performance.

Few teachers, if any, consider the gathering of feedback from their students. Students at the junior high/middle school age are quite capable of giving you meaningful feedback about your performance as a mathematics teacher. Devising some sort of simple questionnaire may be a good start. It need not be sophisticated, but designed to be completed relatively quickly. Figure 12–1 is an example of what such a questionnaire might look like.

The questionnaire could be given after each unit or after each grading period. The student responses might surprise you!

FIGURE 12–1

Yes	No	What Did You Think?
_____	_____	1. Did you know what I expected of you?
_____	_____	2. Did you know how you were going to be graded?
_____	_____	3. Did I treat you fairly?
_____	_____	4. Did I give you good explanations of the material?
_____	_____	5. Were my tests fair?
_____	_____	6. Did I treat other students fairly?
_____	_____	7. Did you learn the material from the way I taught it?

You do not need a word of warning on the above suggestions for obtaining feedback about your teaching performance. Not all of the feedback is likely to be positive. Avoid the temptation of becoming defensive if you receive some criticism. Consider the criticism carefully before you reject it as being invalid. It takes a strong person to even consider trying these suggestions and if you really feel uneasy, don't do it. However, if you are truly interested in improving your own performance in the classroom, you will try those suggestions and/or others you may be able to think of.

SUPPORTING YOUR SCHOOL SYSTEM

As a professional, you have a responsibility to support the rules and policies of your building and the school board. There may be things you don't like, but that is not the question; your obligation is to support the rules and policies until they are changed. If there are things about the rules and policies that are objectionable, work to get them changed, but don't abandon your responsibility in the meantime. If no change is forthcoming, then you have two choices: live with it or resign.

JOINING PROFESSIONAL ORGANIZATIONS

Professional organizations are an excellent way to help you grow professionally. Whichever organizations you join, participate in their activities; don't join just for the sake of a membership card. This participation will give you maximum opportunity to benefit fully.

As a junior high/middle school mathematics teacher, there are two types of professional organizations you should consider joining. The first is the general education organization. Nationally, the list of possibilities includes the National Education Association (NEA), the American Federation of Teachers (AFT), Phi Delta Kappa (PDK) and Association for Supervision and Curriculum Development (ASCD). There are also state educational organizations and local classroom teacher groups. Joining the local group should be a "must."

The second type of professional organization is the one devoted to the improvement of the teaching of mathematics. The most notable ones here are the National Council of Teachers of Mathematics (NCTM), School Science and Mathematics (SSM), and The Research Council for Diagnostic and Prescriptive Mathematics (RCDPM). There are also state and local organizations, most of them affiliated with NCTM.

These organizations usually publish periodical journals which keep you abreast of current trends in general and mathematics education as well as ideas and techniques for teaching. Many of the organizations also sponsor conferences throughout the country on a national, regional, state, and local basis. These meetings provide an excellent opportunity for you to share problems and ideas with fellow professionals; the end result is likely to be professional growth for all concerned.

Since it is expensive to join professional organizations, don't try to join every organization. Instead, choose the ones you feel are most appropriate and useful for you. Once you join, become active in that organization's affairs. The time and money you invest will pay rich dividends to you as a professional, and the organization and others will benefit from your efforts.

Check into the possibility of having your school system help share the expenses for your travel to professional meetings. The chances of getting assistance will never be known unless you ask.

CONTINUING INSERVICE AND FORMAL EDUCATION

One of the best ways to grow professionally is to continue your education, on both an inservice and formal basis. Local inservice and credit courses from colleges and universities give you an opportunity to focus on aspects of mathematics teaching as they relate to your own classroom. Take advantage of these opportunities when they arise.

Encourage your local school corporation to provide strong and continuous inservice programs. In fact, this should be an integral negotiated contract package with your school board. Be sure to make your suggestions for inservice programs known to the appropriate people and give your full support to the programs that are presented.

In addition, you may want to continue your formal education at an area college or university. In some states, you are required to hold an advanced degree to keep a teaching certificate valid. In other states, you are required to take some amount of formal education periodically to keep a valid certificate. Take advantage of the courses offered at colleges and universities. In addition to learning from the classes, you will meet fellow teachers with whom you can share ideas on the improvement of mathematics teaching.

QUICK REVIEW

1. Describe different ways of coping with stress. What other ways not mentioned in the chapter seem to work for you?

2. What are some effective ways of building relationships with:
   a. parents
   b. fellow teachers
   c. other school personnel
   d. your principal and other administrators

   List some specific examples of things you have done that have either worked or not worked.

3. What are the pros and cons of feedback from students, fellow teachers, and your principal about your performance as a teacher?

4. Design a comprehensive plan you would use to gain feedback about your teaching performance.

5. Are you familiar with your school system's rules and policies regarding student conduct and your responsibilities? If not, review them. While doing this, it might be a good idea to review *all* rules and policies.

6. Which professional organizations do you belong to? Which ones should you belong to? Investigate the "should" group and review the benefits of membership.

7. What are the inservice and formal education opportunities available to you?

8. Find out who is in charge of inservice programs for your school system. What is the procedure for making suggestions for future inservice programs?

9. Survey the other junior high/middle school mathematics teachers in your school system. Compile a list of possible inservice topics and present it to the administration.

Appendices

This section provides a number of ready-to-use aids to help you in selecting instructional materials and assessing students' needs as well as a handy glossary of common computer terms. It includes the following:

Forms for Evaluation of Textbooks and Commercial Games

Since you often need to evaluate textbooks and commercial games for possible purchase, we have included two forms for such evaluation (see pages 267-274). Properly selected, these materials can be one of the strongest assets of your mathematics program.

List of Commercial Sources of Instructional Materials

The list provided on pages 275-287 is not exhaustive nor do we necessarily recommend the source's products. For your convenience, we have indicated the general nature of each source's product line. The classifications used are listed below:

Computational Skills (CS)

Measurement and Geometry (M&G)

Metrics (M)

Problem Solving (PS)

Math Labs (ML)

Games and Puzzles (G&P)

Calculators and Computers (C&C)

We suggest that you write to the sources in which you are interested for current product lines and price lists.

Student Assessment Instruments

These include ready-to-use instruments for assessing your students' attitude towards mathematics, their self-concept, and their learning style(s). They are intended to help you learn more about your students and their needs and to help you plan and implement a more effective mathematics instructional program in your classroom (see pages 288-295).

Glossary of Computer Terminology

As you begin to work more and more with microcomputers, there are some common computer terms that you will be likely to encounter. The glossary provided here, beginning on page 296, includes some of the most common ones. It is by no means exhaustive, but should give you a good start toward an understanding of computer jargon.

Microcomputer and Software Evaluation Forms

The forms included will assist you in purchasing the appropriate microcomputer and accompanying software for your home and/or classroom use. (See pages 302-306.)

Answer Key to Quick Reviews

Beginning on page 307, this section includes chapter-by-chapter answers to the quick reviews in some of the chapters, in any cases where they are required.

APPENDIX A-1: TEXTBOOK EVALUATION FORM

Textbook_____

Publisher_____

Evaluator_____Date_____

To use this form, rate each following item by indicating whether or not you agree that the item is a characteristic of the textbook. If you agree that the textbook reflects the item, mark the item rating as +1. If you disagree that the textbook reflects the item, mark the item rating as −1. If you are not sure, mark the item rating as 0. Then decide what the priority of the item is to you. If the item has high priority to you, mark the priority rating as 3. If the item has low or no priority to you, mark the priority rating as 1. If the item is medium, mark the priority rating as 2. Multiply the item rating by the priority rating and enter the answer in the item total. After each item has been totaled, add these totals to obtain a grand total. The highest possible score on the form is 42 and the lowest possible score is −42.

For example, suppose that, for a given criteria, the textbook definitely meets that criteria and that the criteria has a high priority to you. You would score it as follows:

$$\underset{\substack{\text{item}\\\text{rating}}}{\underline{\quad 1 \quad}} \quad \text{X} \quad \underset{\substack{\text{priority}\\\text{rating}}}{\underline{\quad 3 \quad}} \qquad \underline{\qquad 3 \qquad}$$

The higher the score, the better the textbook meets the criteria of being a good textbook. You, however, must make the final decision on purchasing the textbook.

1. The textbook is geared to the interests, needs and abilities of my students.

$$\underset{\substack{\text{Item}\\\text{rating}}}{\underline{\qquad}} \quad \text{X} \quad \underset{\substack{\text{Priority}\\\text{rating}}}{\underline{\qquad}} \qquad \underline{\qquad\qquad}$$

2. The language of the textbook is appropriate for the reading level of my students.

_____ X _____   _____
Item   Priority
rating   rating

3. The textbook's presentation of concepts and ideas is mathematically correct.

_____ X _____   _____
Item   Priority
rating   rating

4. The textbook develops concepts and skills in a spiral manner.

_____ X _____   _____
Item   Priority
rating   rating

5. The textbook contains sufficient and appropriate examples of the concepts and skills presented.

_____ X _____   _____
Item   Priority
rating   rating

6. There are an adequate number and variety of practice exercises for each concept and skill presented.

_____ X _____   _____
Item   Priority
rating   rating

7. The textbook is free of sexism and discrimination.

_____ X _____   _____

Item   Priority
rating   rating

8. The textbook emphasizes the development of problem-solving skills.

_____ X _____   _____

Item   Priority
rating   rating

9. The physical construction of the textbook is durable and long lasting.

_____ X _____   _____

Item   Priority
rating   rating

10. The textbook provides for alternative teaching strategies.

_____ X _____   _____

Item   Priority
rating   rating

11. There is a comprehensive and useful teacher's manual for the textbook.

_____ X _____   _____

Item   Priority
rating   rating

12. The textbook and/or teacher's manual provides suggestions and materials for the atypical learner.

_____ X _____   _____

Item   Priority
rating   rating

13. There are adequate and appropriate supplementary materials available for the textbook.

_____ X _____   _____
Item   Priority
rating   rating

                                              Total Score
                                                                _____

The textbook should be adopted: _____yes_____no

Comments:

APPENDIX A-2: COMMERCIAL GAMES EVALUATION FORM

Name of Game _____

Publisher _____ Price _____

Evaluator _____ Date _____

    To use this form, rate each item below by indicating whether or not you agree that the item is a characteristic of the game. If you agree that the game reflects the item, mark the item rating as +1. If you disagree that the game reflects the item, mark −1. If you are not sure, mark the item rating as 0. Then decide what the priority of the item is to you. If the item has high priority to you, mark the priority rating as 3. If the item has low or no priority, mark the priority rating as 1. If the priority is medium, mark the priority rating as 2. Multiply the item rating by the priority rating and enter the answer in the item total. After each item has been totaled, add these totals to obtain a grand total. The highest possible score on the form is 42 and the lowest possible score is −42.

    For example, suppose that, for a given criteria, the game definitely meets that criteria and that the criteria has a high priority to you. You would score it as follows:

$$\underset{\substack{\text{Item} \\ \text{rating}}}{\underline{\quad 1 \quad}} \quad X \quad \underset{\substack{\text{Priority} \\ \text{rating}}}{\underline{\quad 3 \quad}} \qquad \underline{\quad 3 \quad}$$

The higher the score, the better the game meets the criteria of being a good game. You, however, must make the final decision on purchasing the game.

1. The game is appropriate for my instructional objective.

$$\underset{\substack{\text{Item} \\ \text{rating}}}{\underline{\quad\quad\quad}} \quad X \quad \underset{\substack{\text{Priority} \\ \text{rating}}}{\underline{\quad\quad\quad}} \qquad \underline{\quad\quad\quad}$$

2. My students have the necessary prerequisite
   skills to play the game.

   _____ X _____   _____
   Item   Priority
   rating   rating

3. The cost of the game is reasonable.

   _____ X _____   _____
   Item   Priority
   rating   rating

4. The game is easy to supervise.

   _____ X _____   _____
   Item   Priority
   rating   rating

5. My students will enjoy playing the game.

   _____ X _____   _____
   Item   Priority
   rating   rating

6. The instructions for the game are clear and will
   be easily understood.

   _____ X _____   _____
   Item   Priority
   rating   rating

7. My students are actively involved in playing the
   game.

   _____ X _____   _____
   Item   Priority
   rating   rating

8. The game enables me to maintain good class-room control.

_____ X _____   _____
   Item   Priority
  rating   rating

9. The game is self-checking.

_____ X _____   _____
   Item   Priority
  rating   rating

10. The game can be completed in a reasonable amount of time.

_____ X _____   _____
   Item   Priority
  rating   rating

11. The game has a variety of uses or variations.

_____ X _____   _____
   Item   Priority
  rating   rating

12. The game promotes good sportsmanship.

_____ X _____   _____
   Item   Priority
  rating   rating

13. The game can be easily stored.

_____ X _____   _____
   Item   Priority
  rating   rating

14. The game has an element of chance.

_____ X _____   _____
Item   Priority
rating   rating

Total Score _____

The game should be purchased: _____yes_____no

Comments:

APPENDIX B: LIST OF COMMERCIAL SOURCES OF INSTRUCTIONAL MATERIALS

	CS	M&G	M	PS	ML	G&P	C&C
Acme United Corporation Bridgeport, CT 06609			X				
Action Math Associates, Inc. 825 Monroe #10 Eugene, OR 97402			X		X	X	
Activity Resources Co., Inc. P.O. Box 4875 Hayward, CA 94540	X	X	X	X	X	X	X
Aero Educational Products Limited P.O. Box 71 St. Charles, IL 60174			X				
Apple Computer, Inc. 10260 Bandley Drive Cupertino, CA 95014							X
Arthur J. Gude 845 Dudley Street Lakewood, CO 80215		X					
A. Balla and Company P.O. Box 24200 Ft. Lauderdale, FL 33307			X				

	CS	M&G	M	PS	ML	G&P	C&C
Borg-Warner Educational Systems 600 West University Drive Arlington Heights, IL 60004	X		X				
Cambridge, The Basic Skills Company A New York Times Company 488 Madison Avenue New York, NY 10022							
Camelot Publishing Company P.O. Box 1357 Ormond Beach, FL 32074							X
Cassettes Unlimited Roanoke, TX 76262	X	X	X		X		
The Center for Applied Research in Education P.O. Box 130 West Nyack, NY 10994			X				
The Class Roomservice Co. P.O. Box 146 Campbell, CA 95008			X				
Computer Design Corporation 12401 West Olympic Boulevard Los Angeles, CA 90064							X

Publisher							
The Continental Press, Inc. P.O. Box 554 Elgin, IL 60120							X
Creative Educational Services, Inc P.O. Box 663 Bloomfield Avenue West Caldwell, NJ 07006						X	
Creative Publications P.O. Box 10328 Palo Alto, CA	X	X		X		X	X
Creative Teaching Associates P.O. Box 293 Fresno, CA 93708		X				X	
Cuisinaire® Company of America, Inc. 12 Church Street New Rochelle, NY 10805	X	X	X	X	X	X	X
Dale Seymour Publications P.O. Box 10888 Palo Alto, CA 94303				X			
Damon/Educational Division 80 Wilson Way Westwood, MA 02090		X	X		X		X

	CS	M&G	M	PS	ML	G&P	C&C
Davidson Films, Inc. 3701 Buchanan Street San Francisco, CA 94123			X				
Didax 3 Dearborn Road P.O. Box 2258 Peabody, MA 01960		X	X				
Digital Equipment Corp. 146 Main Street Maynard, MA 01754						X	
EDITS Publishers P.O. Box 7234 San Diego, CA 92107	X						
Edmund Scientific Company 300 Edscorp Building Barrington, NJ 08007			X				X
Educational Activities, Inc. P.O. Box 392 Freeport, NY 11520	X		X	X			

The Education Center 1411 Mill Street Greensboro, NC 27408		X			X	
Educational Teaching Arts A. Daegger & Company 159 West Kinzie Street Chicago, IL 60610		X	X	X	X	
Educational Tools, Inc. 901 West Douglas Wichita, KS 67213					X	
Electronics Futures, Inc. 57 Dodge Avenue North Haven, CT 06473						X
Electronic Learning, Inc. 50 Glen Street Glen Cove, NY 11542						X
Enrich, Inc. Sunnyvale, CA 94086	X			X	X	
ESP, Inc. P.O. Box 5037 Jonesboro, AR 72406				X	X	X

	CS	M&G	M	PS	ML	G&P	C&C
Fearon Pitman Publishers 6 Davis Drive Belmont, CA 94002	X		X	X	X	X	X
General Learning Corp. Morristown, NJ 07960		X	X		X		
The George F. Cram Co., Inc. P.O. Box 426 301 South LaSalle Street Indianapolis, IN 46206	X			X			
Great Ideas, Inc. 40 Oser Avenue Hauppage, NY 11787	X				X		
Heathkit Benton Harbor, MI 49022							X
Hewlett Packard Advanced Products 10900 Wolfe Road Cupertino, CA 95014							X
Ideal School Supply Company 11000 South Lavergne Avenue Oak Lawn, IL 60453		X	X		X	X	

	1	2	3	4	5	6	7
Incentives for Learning, Inc. 600 West Van Buren Street Chicago, IL 60607		X	X				X
Imperial International Learning Corporation P.O. Box 548 Kankakee, IL 60901							X
The Instructor Publications, Inc. P.O. Box 6108 Duluth, MN 55806					X	X	
International Minicomputer Accessories Corporation 2465 Augustine Drive Santa Clara, CA 95051	X				X		
Lansford Publishing Company P.O. Box 8711 San Jose, CA 95155							
LaPine Scientific Company Department D4 6009 South Knox Avenue Chicago, IL 60629	X	X	X	X	X	X	X

	CS	M&G	M	PS	ML	G&P	C&C
Learning Research Assoc., Inc. 1501 Broadway New York, NY 10036	X				X		
Leicestershire Learning Systems Hill Mill Chestnut Street Lewiston, ME 04240		X	X		X	X	
Mafex Associates, Inc. 90 Cherry Street Box 519 Johnstown, PA 15907			X				
Markline P.O. Box 1705P Waltham, MA 02254							X
The Math Group, Inc. 396 East 79th Street Suite 28-5 Minneapolis, MN 55420			X			X	
Math House Div. of Mosaic Media, Inc. Dept. C980, P.O. Box 711 Glen Ellyn, IL 60137	X			X			

Math Master P.O. Box 1911 Big Spring, TX 79720	X	X		X	X
Metrix Corporation P.O. Box 19101 Orlando, FL 32814				X	
Midwest Publications Co. P.O. Box 448 Pacific Grove, CA 93950		X	X		
Monroe, The Calculator Co. 550 Central Avenue Orange, NJ 07051	X				
National Bureau of Standards U.S. Department of Commerce Washington, D.C. 20234				X	X
National Semiconductor/NOVUS Consumer Products Division 1177 Kern Avenue Sunnyvale, CA 94086	X				
Ohaus Scale Corporation 29 Hanover Road Florham Park, NJ 07932				X	

	CS	M&G	M	PS	ML	G&P	C&C
Pathescope Educational Films, Inc. 71 Weyman Avenue New Rochelle, NY 10802			X				
Polymetric Services, Inc. 18314 Oxnard Street Tarzana, CA 91356			X				
Real-T-Facs 26 Overlook Drive P.O. Drawer 449 Warwick, NY 10990			X				
Rowsey Enterprises P.O. Box 666 Friendswood, TX 77546			X				
Sadlier/Oxford 11 Park Place New York, NY 10007	X		X	X			
Schloat Productions 150 White Plains Road Tarrytown, NY 10591			X				
Scholar's Choice Limited 50 Ballantyne Avenue Stratford, Ontario N5A 6T9			X				X

Company						
Science Research Assoc., Inc. 259 East Erie Street Chicago, IL 60611			X	X		X
Scott Resources, Inc. 1900 East Lincoln Ft. Collins, CO 80522		X			X	
Sharp Electronics Corp. 10 Keystone Place Paramus, NJ 07652	X					
Society for Visual Education 1345 Diversey Parkway Chicago, IL 60614				X		
Spectrum 8 Denison Street Markham, Ontario L3R 2P2				X		
Swani Publishing Division Regal-Beloit Corporation P.O. Box 248 Roscoe, IL 61073				X		
Tarmac 71 North Market Asheville, NC 28801						X

Company	CS	M&G	M	PS	ML	G&P	C&C
Teaching Resources Corporation 100 Boylston Street Boston, MA 02116					X		
Telex Communications, Inc. 9600 Aldrich Avenue South Minneapolis, MN 55420			X				
Texas Instruments, Inc. 13500 North Central Expressway P.O. Box 5012, M/S 54 Dallas, TX 75222			X			X	X
Tuf P.O. Box 173 Rowayton, CT 06853							
Visual Materials, Inc. Redwood City, CA 96099	X	X	X				
W. H. Freeman and Co. 660 Market Street San Francisco, CA 94104				X			X
Walker Educational Book Corp. 720 Fifth Avenue New York, NY 10019		X			X		

Walt Disney Educational Media Company
500 South Buena Vista Street
Burbank, CA 91521

Ward & Sons
Spartanburg, SC 29304

Weber-Costello
1900 North Narragansett Ave.
Chicago, IL 60639

Western Learning Laboratories
11923 Venice Boulevard
Los Angeles, CA 90066

Westinghouse Learning Corp.
5005 West 110th Street
Oak Lawn, IL 60453

J. Weston Walch, Publisher
Portland, ME 04104

Wff'N Proof
Box 71-RT
New Haven, CT 06501

Xerox Education Publications
1250 Fairwood Avenue
P.O. Box 444
Columbus, OH 43216

APPENDIX C-1: STUDENT ASSESSMENT INSTRUMENTS —MATH ATTITUDE

Student Name_____

Date_____

Score_____

Read each of the following statements and decide how you feel about each one. Then circle the corresponding letter (D) Disagree, (U) Undecided, (A) Agree.

1. Math class is really a strain for me.

    D   U   A

2. Math is very interesting to me.

    D   U   A

3. I don't like math at all.

    D   U   A

4. Math is fun.

    D   U   A

5. Math makes me feel good.

    D   U   A

6 . I can't think very well when I'm doing math problems.

    D   U   A

7. Everybody else is better in math than I.

    D   U   A

8. Doing math problems makes me feel uncomfortable and frustrated.

> D   U   A

9. I feel good about math.

> D   U   A

10. I get very lost when I'm doing math problems.

> D   U   A

11. I enjoy doing math problems.

> D   U   A

12. I get a bad feeling when I hear the word "math."

> D   U   A

13. I'm afraid to do math problems because I don't think I'll be right.

> D   U   A

14. I really like math.

> D   U   A

15. I have always enjoyed taking math courses.

> D   U   A

16. I get nervous just thinking about math.

> D   U   A

17. I dread taking math classes.

> D   U   A

18. I am happier in math class than in any other class.

> D   U   A

19. I feel at ease in math class.

        D   U   A

20. I feel very positive about math.

        D   U   A

NOTE TO TEACHER:
You may want to fold this part of the page under while the student is responding.

Scoring: Positive Questions are 2, 4, 5, 9, 11, 14, 15, 18, 19, 20
         Negative Questions are 1, 3, 6, 7, 8, 10, 12, 13, 16, 17

1. If the question is of a *positive* nature, score $D = -1$, $U = 0$, $A = +1$
   If the question is of a *negative* nature, score $D = +1$, $U = 0$, $A = -1$

2. Total the number values for the items and divide by 20 (carry your answer out two decimal points).

3. This converted number should lie between -1.00 and $+1.00$, expressing a negative to positive attitude respectively. 0 indicates a neutral attitude. Record this converted score on the space provided at the top of the first page.

For example: A raw score of -8 would be calculated as $-8 \div 20 = \underline{-0.40}$
             (converted score)
             A raw score of $+3$ would be calculated as $+3 \div 20 = \underline{+0.15}$
             (converted score)

APPENDIX C-2:
STUDENT ASSESSMENT INSTRUMENTS—
SELF-CONCEPT

Name _____

Date _____

Score _____

Below is a list of words that might describe how you feel about yourself. Place a check under the column you think best describes how you feel.

I think I am:	Like me	Sometimes Like me	Not Like me	Score
1. lazy	___	___	___	___
2. shy	___	___	___	___
3. cool, very good	___	___	___	___
4. bad	___	___	___	___
5. popular	___	___	___	___
6. honest	___	___	___	___
7. good at making friends	___	___	___	___
8. sad	___	___	___	___
9. afraid to take chances	___	___	___	___
10. good looking	___	___	___	___
11. happy	___	___	___	___
12. good at sports	___	___	___	___
13. a failure	___	___	___	___

Total _____

Scoring

Like Me

If you marked "like me" for items 3, 5, 6, 7, 10, 11, or 12, you score 3 for that item.

If you marked "like me" for items 1, 2, 4, 8, 9 or 13, you score 1 for that item.

Sometimes Like Me

Score 2 for each item you marked as "sometimes like me."

Not Like Me

If you marked "not like me" for items 1, 2, 4, 8, 9, or 13, you score 3 for that item.

If you marked "not like me" for items 3, 5, 6, 7, 10, 11, or 12, you score 1 for that item

NOTE: The highest possible score is 39 and the lowest possible score is 13. The average is 26.

TEST OF LEARNING STYLE

This test will give you an idea of the learning styles of your students. To give the test, you need:

1. A group of not more than 10-12 students since it is difficult to observe more than that number of students at one time.

2. A copy of the Learning Style Sheet for each student so that you can mark as you observe their reactions:

V = Visual learner
A = Audio learner
K = Kinesthetic learner

Look for these student reactions:

VISUAL LEARNERS will usually close their eyes or look at the ceiling as they try to recall a visual picture.

AUDIO LEARNERS will move their lips or whisper as they try to memorize.

KINESTHETIC LEARNERS will use their fingers to count off items or write in the air.

The student with a photographic mind will repeat things exactly in the order they are given and will be disturbed if someone changes the order.

Begin by telling your students that you are going to give them a test to determine what kind of learners they are: VISUAL, AUDIO or KIN-ESTHETIC. Tell them that you are going to ask them to help you remember a list of numbers.

Part One

1. Write the numbers 17, 25, 12, 3, 7, 4, 26, 35, 1, 8 on the chalkboard. The students may watch you, but cannot write anything.

2. Erase the chalkboard. Then read the same list of numbers orally to the students; again, they cannot write the numbers.

3. Read the list again orally and tell the students to write the numbers on their paper.

4. Tell the students to turn over their papers and write as much of the list of numbers as they can. Observe their reactions as they rewrite the list and record your observations on the Learning Style Sheet.

Part Two

1. Use a new list of numbers—19, 9, 12, 10, 6, 24, 2, 8, 36, 5—and read the list orally to the students. They cannot write the list.
2. Read the list again.
3. Tell the students to write the list on a sheet of paper. Observe their reactions as they write the list and record your observations.

Part Three

1. Use another list of numbers—8, 11, 52, 3, 23, 7, 5, 27, 18, 2—and tell the students to write the list as you read it orally.
2. Tell the students to rewrite the list next to the list they just wrote.
3. Tell the students to study the list they have just written. Allow about one minute for them to study the list.
4. Tell the students to turn the paper over and rewrite the list. Observe their reactions as they rewrite the list and record your observations.

After you have finished all three parts, summarize your observations for each student. Write any particular comments that seem appropriate.

LEARNING STYLE TEST

Student's Name _____ Date _____

Teacher's Name _____

PART ONE:

   A   V   K

PART TWO:

   A   V   K

PART THREE:

   A   V   K

Observations and Comments:

APPENDIX D: GLOSSARY OF COMPUTER TERMINOLOGY

alphanumeric. A term used to indicate a combination of letters, numbers, and special symbols such as punctuation or mathematical notation.

arithmetic unit. That portion of a computer processing unit that performs addition, subtraction, multiplication, and division.

auxiliary storage. Any storage device in addition to the main storage of a computer; for example, magnetic tape, disk, or drum.

binary number system. An internal numbering system incorporated by computers that uses the number two as a base (as opposed to the decimal system which uses the number ten).

bit. A contraction of Binary Digit, a single pulse in a group of pulses. It is a single hole in a punched tape or card. Bits comprise a character, and characters comprise a word.

branching. A method of selecting the next instruction for the computer to execute, based on the results of previous operations.

buffer. A device that compensates for speed differences between two machines, permitting them to operate together.

bug. A mistake or malfunction in the design of a program or computer.

byte. A measure of computer memory that contains eight bits and holds a single character or number.

card punch. A machine that encodes data into tabulating cards in the form of a pattern of round or rectangular holes. Card punches may be activated by a computer or from a keyboard.

card reader. A machine that transcribes data from punched cards to a computer or magnetic tape.

cathode ray tube (CRT). A device similar to a television screen upon which data can be stored or displayed.

central processing unit (CPU). That portion of a computer containing the arithmetic, logic, control, and, in some cases, main storage units.

character. A single letter, number, or symbol that a computer may read, write, or store.

COBOL. Common Business Oriented Language is a computer programming language using basic English phrases designed for business applications.

code. A system of rules for using a set of characters to represent data or instructions.

compare. To examine two *numeric* data items to find if one is equal to, smaller, or larger than the other. To examine two *alphabetic* data items to find if one is the same, earlier, or later than the other in sequence.

compile. To prepare a machine language program by translating each symbolic coded instruction into two or more machine language instructions.

compiler. A set of instructions enabling the computer to automatically carry out the "compile" function.

console. The part of a computer that is used for manual control and observation of the computer system.

control unit. That part of a computer system containing the circuits for interpreting and controlling the execution of instructions.

data. Basic elements of information—facts, numbers, letters, symbols—that can be processed by a computer.

data communication. The transmission of data from one point to another.

data processing. A series of planned actions and operations upon data to achieve a desired result.

execute. To interpret a machine instruction and perform the specified operation(s).

external memory. A storage facility or device, such as magnetic tape, that is not an integral part of a computer.

field. A combination of one or more characters that are treated as a unit of data; for example, a group of card columns used to represent an account number.

file. A collection of related records; for example, a complete set of invoices is an invoice file.

flowchart. A graphic representation of the major steps of work in process.

hard copy. A printed copy of machine output; for example, reports, listings, documents, and other business forms.

hardware. The physical equipment or devices that together comprise a computer and associated data-processing machines.

information retrieval. The study of methods and procedures for recovering specific information from stored data.

input. Intelligence representing data to be processed and instructions to control processing, which is moved into the internal storage of a data processing system.

input-output (I/O). A general term for the equipment used to communicate with a computer and the data involved in such communication.

instruction. A coded statement or command that causes a data processing system to carry out an operation.

internal storage. Memory devices, such as magnetic cores, forming an integral physical part of a computer and directly controlled by the computer.

interpret. To print on a punched card the information punched on that card.

keypunch. A keyboard-operated device that punches holes in a card to represent data.

label. One or more characters used to identify an instruction.

language. A system for representing and communicating information between people and/or machines.

loop. A sequence of instructions that is repeated a fixed number of times.

machine language. A language designed for interpretation and use by a machine without translation.

magnetic disk. A flat, circular plate with a surface that can be magnetized to store data.

magnetic drum. A rotating cylinder with a surface that can be magnetized to store data.

magnetic tape. A plastic or mylar strip coated with a metallic oxide upon which data can be recorded in magnetized spots.

main frame. A computer that costs at least $100,000 having 10 and more megabytes storage capacity and needing a staff to operate.

main storage. Usually the fastest storage device of a computer and the one from which instructions are executed.

microcomputer. A computer that costs between $500 and $20,000, having storage of 1 to 256 kilobytes. It can be operated by an individual and has a slower processing time than the main frame and minicomputers.

microsecond. One millionth of a second, it is a time measurement used to indicate the operating speed of a computer.

minicomputer. A computer that costs between $20,000 and $100,000 having between 256 kilobytes and 10 megabytes of storage. It is operated by a staff and has processing speed between that of the microcomputer and the main frame.

millisecond. One thousandth of a second, it is a time measurement used to indicate the operating speed of a computer.

nanosecond. One billionth of a second, it is a time measurement used to indicate the operating speed of a computer.

on-line. Pertains to equipment or devices directly connected to the central processing unit.

operations research. The application of scientific principles to business management. This may involve setting up mathematical equations to depict various business problems.

output. Information transferred from internal storage to output devices to produce cards, tapes, business forms, etc.

overflow. The result of an arithmetic operation that exceeds the capacity of the storage space allotted in a digital computer.

peripheral equipment. The auxiliary machines that may be placed under the control of the central computer. Examples of these are card readers, punches, and high-speed printers. Peripheral equipment may be used on-line or off-line depending upon the job requirements.

program. A series of instructions that tell the computer in minute detail how to process data.

programmer. A person who prepares problem-solving procedures and flowcharts and who may also write and debug programs.

random access memory (RAM). A storage technique in which the computer can find one bit of data quickly, regardless of its specific location in storage.

read-only-memory (ROM). A part of the central processing unit that is supplied by the manufacturer. It contains the program that edits the written program or performs other specified functions.

real-time. A method processing data so fast that there is virtually no passage of time between inquiry and result.

record. A group of related facts or fields of information treated as a unit. For example, one invoice is a record in a file containing many invoices.

reset. To return a storage device to zero or to another selected condition.

simulation exercise. An exercise that generally uses a computer as a scorekeeper while people make decisions concerning a mathematical model of the business world.

software. All programs and routines used to extend the capabilities of computers, such as assemblers, compilers, subroutines, etc.

solid state. Refers to electronic components in computers, such as transistors and magnetic cores.

special character. A character other than a number or letter; for example, $ # /.

storage. Pertains to a device capable of retaining data.

tabulating equipment. A term generally referring to data-processing machines using punched cards.

test routine. A short program designed to show whether or not a computer is functioning properly.

time-sharing. Using a computer to process multiple requests by independent users, and providing responses rapidly so that each user feels that the computer is entirely at his or her disposal.

transistors. Tiny elements in an electronic circuit that do much the same job as a vacuum tube. They are highly reliable and generate little heat.

APPENDIX E-1: MICROCOMPUTER EVALUATION FORM

System Name _____ System Cost _____

Manufactured by _____

Evaluated by _____ Date _____

1. Is local maintenance service available?

   _____ yes   _____ no

2. Is an additional maintenance warranty available (beyond the usual 90 days)?

   _____ yes   _____ no

3. What software is available?

   _____ word processing
   _____ business applications
   _____ games
   _____ scientific/engineering
   _____ educational

4. What languages are available?

   _____ BASIC
   _____ PASCAL
   _____ ASSEMBLER
   _____ COBOL
   _____ RPG
   _____ other _____

5. What is the RAM size?

   _____ K bytes.

6. Is memory expandable?

   _____ yes   _____ no   If yes, cost is _____

7. Are modem capabilities available?

_____ yes   _____ no

8. What are the interfacing capabilities with other input/output devices?

_____

_____

_____

9. Is disk drive available?

_____ yes   _____ no   If yes, cost is _____

10. Is cassette storage available?

_____ yes   _____ no   If yes, cost is _____

11. Is color monitor available?

_____ yes   _____ no   If yes, cost is _____

12. Are graphics available?

_____ yes   _____ no

13. Is printer available? _____ yes   _____ no

If yes, type is _____

_____ thermal, cost _____

_____ daisy-wheel, cost _____

14. Is the equipment easy to operate?

_____ yes   _____ no

15. What is the keyboard type?

_____ touch panel   _____ key

16. What is the output quality of:
    a) text   ＿＿＿ excellent ＿＿＿ good ＿＿＿ poor
    b) graphics ＿＿＿ excellent ＿＿＿ good ＿＿＿ poor

COMMENTS:

APPENDIX E-2: SOFTWARE EVALUATION FORM

Software Name _____ Cost _____

Manufactured by _____

Evaluated by _____ Date _____

Rate the software on each of the following criteria using a scale of 1 to 5. The highest rating should receive a 5, with the lowest rating receiving a 1. A piece of software should have a total rating of at least 38 to be seriously considered for purchase.

TECHNICAL

1. Utilizes the capabilities of my microcomputer.   1 2 3 4 5
2. Is "bomb proof."   1 2 3 4 5
3. Has pleasing graphics and/or sound reproduction.   1 2 3 4 5

EDUCATIONAL

1. Is technically correct.   1 2 3 4 5
2. Provides assistance in understanding incorrect responses.   1 2 3 4 5
3. Specifies necessary prerequisite skills needed by the user.   1 2 3 4 5
4. Has clear and appropriate objective(s).   1 2 3 4 5
5. Encourages learning through feedback.   1 2 3 4 5

MANAGEMENT

1. Has directions that are easy to understand and follow.   1 2 3 4 5
2. Assists in tracking student progress.   1 2 3 4 5
3. Is flexible to meet different student needs.   1 2 3 4 5

TOTAL POINTS _____

COMMENTS:

I recommend purchase of this software. _____ yes   _____ no

ANSWER KEYS TO QUICK REVIEWS

Chapter 1

1. a. C   d. S
   b. A   e. A
   c. C   f. S

2. a. AA   d. KS
   b. VS   e. VA
   c. KC

3. In process-oriented learning, the process the learner uses is as important as the end product. The student will learn the necessary prerequisites as they are needed, that is, discovery learning. In product-oriented learning, the end product (capability or skill) is most important. Learning proceeds through a series of small, structured steps, that is, programmed instruction.

4. The classroom teacher must provide learning activities that are appropriate for the student's learning level (concrete, semiconcrete, or abstract) and learning style (visual, auditory, or kinesthetic). At the same time, the teacher must provide a classroom atmosphere that is conducive to the positive development of the learning self-concept and attitude towards mathematics.

Chapter 2

1.a. Before the school year starts:

    a. Review your textbook and make a rough topical outline for the year.
    b. Formulate your general goals for the year.
    c. Decide on the rules for student behavior in your classroom.
    d. Prepare an inventory test that you can give your students during the first week.
    e. Inspect your classroom to view its physical arrangement.
    f. Determine the need for any special instructional aids.
    g. Meet with your department chairperson and principal to discuss your plans for the coming year.
    h. Review the school's rules for student conduct.

1.b. During the first day of school:

    a. Let your students know you mean business.

     b. Make a seating chart and get to know your students.

     c. Have an activity ready for your students.

1.c. During the first week of school:

     a. Check your class roll daily by calling names so you can associate names with faces.

     b. Administer your inventory test.

2.   See answers for 1.a-1.c.

4.   In presenting the daily lesson:

     a. Review before the presentation what you plan to accomplish and how you are going to do it.

     b. Review examples to be used in the presentation beforehand.

     c. Use a variety of techniques and media in your presentation.

     d. Move about the room during your presentation.

     e. Tell your students before the presentation what you want to accomplish.

     f. Summarize your presentation upon completion.

Chapter 3

1. Diagnosis is a process you can use to determine what learners are and are not able to do mathematically. Correction is what you do to help learners progress towards mathematical levels which are appropriate for their chronological and mathematical ages. The diagnostic-corrective process may be summarized by finding the (a) exact nature of the error, (b) cause of the error, (c) student work level (concrete, semiconcrete, or abstract), and (d) appropriate instructional strategy to correct the error.

2. a. whole number addition
     renaming of fractions with like denominators
     renaming of fractions with unlike denominators
   b. multiplication of whole numbers
     renaming a mixed number as an improper fraction
     algorithm for fraction multiplication
   c. whole number division
     procedure for renaming division as a whole number with appropriate renaming of the dividend
     algorithm for decimal division
     rounding off decimal numbers
   d. renaming fractions to have a denominator that is a power of 10
     decimal division (see part c)

   e. meaning of percent
      skills and concepts listed in part d
   f. whole number multiplication
      algorithm for fraction multiplication

4. a. Mary used cancellation in the addition algorithm. Numerators and denominators were then added together to obtain the final answer.
   b. Frank renamed both fractions to have a common denominator. The divisor numerator was then divided into the dividend numerator to obtain the numerator of the answer.
   c. Billy multiplied exponents instead of adding them.
   d. Judy took the square roots of each number under the radical sign. The operation indicated was then performed.
   e. Wilson multiplied base number and exponent to obtain the final answer.
   f. Instead of regrouping, Meredith subtracted the lesser fraction from the greater one regardless of placement in the problem.
   g. Tony did not put a zero in the quotient when necessary.
   h. Beth did not place the third partial product (multiplication by the hundreds digit in the multiplier) in its proper position.
   i. Albert multiplied the ones digits together and the tens digits together. The rest of the algorithm was apparently ignored.
   j. Alice performed the division required, but recorded only the remainders under the dividend with no adjustments to the dividend. These remainders were then added to obtain the final remainder.

7. A student who is able to determine his or her own errors is likely to be more receptive to the corrective process. Hopefully, the student will be less likely to repeat the error at a later time.

Chapter 4

1. Observation, oral interviews, homework, and anecdotal records are useful informal techniques of evaluation.

2. Commercial tests usually have high validity and reliability. They have several possible disadvantages:

   a. Your curriculum content may not be covered by the test.
   b. The reading level of the test may not be appropriate for your students.
   c. The test items are usually of only one variety.
   d. The test is usually timed.
   e. Test results are often misused by teachers and administrators.

3. Teacher-made tests have the advantage of being prepared by the person

who has done the instruction, but the disadvantage is that the person may not be a competent test writer.

4. In planning a teacher-made test, review the objectives and determine the layout of the test. Test items are written at the knowledge (fact), understanding (application of facts), or problem-solving (application of knowledge and understanding) levels. In taking a test, students should be given 8 to 10 times the amount of time it takes you, as the teacher, to completely answer the test. General guidelines for writing test items are:

   a. Give clear, concise, and simple directions.
   b. Group different types of items together.
   c. Arrange test items from easiest to most difficult.
   d. Indicate items' weights or point values relative to the entire test (number of points, percentage, etc.).
   e. Avoid using test items that utilize answers from other items on the test.
   f. Test items should be similar in format to the way material was presented during instruction.
   g. Test items should reflect main ideas rather than trivial details.
   h. Avoid ambiguous questions.
   i. Time alloted to complete the test should allow slower students to finish.
   j. Avoid patterns of correct responses to item; students may answer questions based on a pattern.
   k. Be sure that the test is legible.
   l. All drawings should be neat and clearly labeled.
   m. Prepare a test key *prior* to the time of test.
   n. Number items consecutively from first to last.
   o. Avoid having part of a test item on one page and part on another.
   p. Plenty of work space should be left on test items that ask students to show their work.
   q. Make the first items on the test easy.
   r. Be sure to designate places for answers on the test or provide a separate answer sheet.
   Before giving the test,
   a. Announce the test *a week* ahead of time. Don't depend solely on oral instructions. Write it on the chalkboard.
   b. Tell the students what to study, what "kinds" of questions will be asked, and the points.

8. a. Which of the following fractions (in lowest terms) is the same as 40%? Answers will vary.

   a. $\dfrac{40}{100}$ d. $\dfrac{1}{2}$

    b. $\dfrac{1}{25}$ e. none of these

    c. $\dfrac{2}{5}$

b. $34 \div 13 =$ _____ (to the nearest tenth)

c. The product of (-3) and $(+4)$ is
    a. $+12$ c. 12
    b. -12 d. none of these

Chapter 6

1. General guidelines for presenting algorithms in your classroom include:

    a. Review the algorithm before presenting it to the class.
    b. Prepare your examples prior to class.
    c. Go through the algorithm slowly step by step.
    d. Get the students actively involved in the presentation.
    e. Go through the algorithm more than once.
    f. Follow the presentation with immediate practice.

2. a. addition of whole numbers
        renaming of fractions with unlike denominators
        algorithm for fraction addition
    b. multiplication of whole numbers
        rules for sign adjustment in multiplication
    c. division of whole numbers
        rules for adjustment of decimal point in divisior and dividend
        rounding of decimal numbers to a specific place
    d. definition of square root
        use of a given table to find a square root

5. Have the student represent each fraction as a part of the same rectangle.

Chapter 7

3. A good way to introduce perimeter and area would be to use geometric figures on graph paper. Wooden cubes, in the form of various solids, are useful in introducing volume.

4. The metric system should be introduced as a separate system of measurement from the English System. Do not introduce metrics through conversions from one system to another.

6. 25 squares   1 inch = _____ cm

   9 squares   16 squares

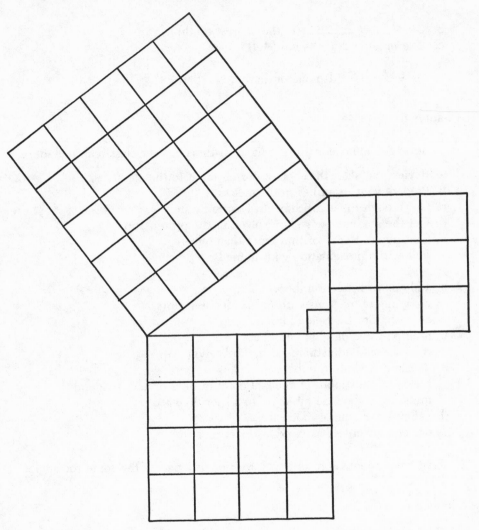

        9 squares
      +16 squares
        25 squares

7. geometric shapes
   perimeter
   area
   multiplication

division
Pythogorean Theorem and triples
...among others

Chapter 8

1. A partial but not exhaustive list of needed problem-solving skills includes abilities to:

   a. Understand the meaning of vocabulary and symbols.
   b. Do basic mathematical computation.
   c. Estimate.
   d. Organize and interpret data.
   e. Test the results of the problem-solving exercise.
   f. Ask questions which yield maximum information.
   g. Design and use different problem solving strategies.

2. Your role in developing your students' problem-solving skills means that you must be a good problem solver yourself and you must effectively manage problem-solving activities in your classroom.

3. In presenting problem situations, present:

   a. problems that are realistic and interesting to your students
   b. problems in an environment where students feel free to explore
   c. problems in more than one way
   d. a summary of the problem after initial presentation

   To help your students develop good problem-solving skills:

   a. Help them develop a basic problem solving strategy.
   b. Practice each skill separately.
   c. Give them problems that differ in format and request solutions from other problems.

   Students need the additional abilities to read and to write and solve mathematical sentences in order to solve word problems. To improve students' skills in reading:

   a. Consult the language arts teacher and reading specialist.
   b. Point out textbook features to your students.
   c. Diagnose reading difficulties.
   d. Spend class time on the meaning of vocabulary and symbols.
   e. Remind students that reading in mathematics is much slower than reading in other content areas.
   f. Choose word problems carefully.
   g. Use some word problems that have too little or too much information.

h. Give students a chance to practice reading word problems.

i. Present word problems in different ways to students with reading difficulties.

j. Don't make it too easy for students *not* to read.

Chapter 9

1. The laboratory approach is one in which students are actively involved and learn by doing. It may be used with individual or small groups of students or with the entire class. Probably no more than one or two class periods a week should be devoted to the laboratory approach. The laboratory approach often, but not exclusively, makes use of manipulatives.

2. Planning and handling small groups is one of the biggest problems faced by teachers using a lab approach.

5. Some guidelines to keep in mind when selecting lab activities are:

   a. The materials required for the activity should be readily available.

   b. Your students must have the necessary prerequisite concepts.

   c. Be sure the activity is appropriate for your classroom management system.

   d. Whenever possible, the activity should have all participants actively involved at all times.

   e. Your students should have a good chance of completing the activity successfully.

   f. The activity's purpose must be appropriate for your instructional needs.

6. In managing the laboratory approach:

   a. Have materials needed for lab activities readily accessible.

   b. Be sure that instructions for each lab activity are clearly understood by students *before* they begin work.

   c. Have activity participants turn in a record of their work.

   d. Be sure that the activity is appropriate for the ability level of the participants.

   e. Go through the activity yourself before using it in class.

   f. Be aware of social factors as well as ability in forming groups to work on a lab activity.

   g. Change group composition periodically.

   h. Appoint a group leader for each group.

8. Observation, study of written work, or a performance test are good techniques for evaluating the laboratory approach.

11. See page 188 of this chapter.

Chapter 10

2. Some potential dangers in using games are:

a. Games can encourage meaningless play.
b. Some games may take too much time to play.
c. Games can be too expensive.
d. Games can cause discipline problems.
e. Games can promote too much competition among your students.
f. Games can encourage cheating on the part of some students.

3. Games may be classified by:

a. style of play
b. number of players
c. medium
d. areas of concepts or skills
e. level of concept or skill development

4. Criteria for selecting games include:

a. The game is appropriate for your instructional objective.
b. Your students have the necessary prerequisite skills to play the game.
c. Little time is needed to make the game.
d. The game is inexpensive.
e. The game is easy to supervise.
f. Your students enjoy playing the game.
g. The instructions for the game are clear and easily understood by your students.
h. Your students are actively involved in each play of the game.
i. The game enables you to maintain good classroom control.
j. The game is self-checking if played by a single player or a small group of players.
k. The game can be completed in a reasonable amount of time.
l. The game has a variety of uses or variations.
m. The game promotes good sportsmanship and does not overemphasize competition.
n. The game can be easily stored.
o. There should be an element of chance involved in the winning of the game.

5 Guidelines for managing games in your classroom include the following:

   a. Have games stored in an easily accessible area.

   b. Be sure that game instructions are clearly understood by each player *before* the game is begun.

   c. Appoint one of the players to see that all pieces (if appropriate) are returned to the game box and the game put in its proper storage area.

   d. Have game players turn in a record (if appropriate) to you of the results of their play.

   e. Make the playing of a game accessible to all students in the class.

   f. Be sure that each player knows the purpose of playing the game.

   g. Be sure the game is appropriate for the ability of the players.

   h. Play the game yourself before using it in class.

   i. If the game involves the choosing of teams, choose the teams yourself or use some random method of choosing teams.

   j. Settle ahead of time with your class how you will handle situations of cheating.

   k. Do everything possible to reduce over-competition.

   l. Give encouragement to the player who is the perpetual loser.

   m. Watch for ideas for new games.

Chapter 11

1. Calculators may be used to: (a) check work done by paper and pencil, (b) debug problems with wrong answers, (c) do problems calling for application of a formula, and (d) possibly develop student motivation.

7. Computer literacy means being aware of the computer, its operation and use, and what it can and cannot do. A unit on computer literacy should contain these areas:

   a. basic parts and operation of a computer

   b. computer uses and misuses

   c. simple programming techniques

   d. computer occupations

   e. history and development of the computer industry

8. Input—device for entering data and instructions into the computer Central Processing Unit (CPU)—"guts" of the computer which includes

   a. Memory—area where computer stores data and instructions for use in processing

   b. Control—area of the computer that controls the processing process (how, where and when)

   c. Arithmetic—area where mathematical calculations take place

   d. Output—device for giving the results of the computer's efforts.

14. START

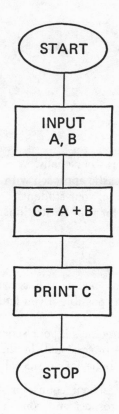

15. Y = 22, Z = 12, W = 8

16. a. LET Y = 2 * A + 3 * B
    b. LET A = Y / (X + 2)
    c. LET R = 8 + / 2 − Z
    d. LET A = 3.14 * R↑2
       or LET A = 3.14 * R * R
    e. LET K = (3 * X − 7) 2 − 2 * Y
       or LET K = (3 * X − 7) * (3 * X − 7) − 2 * Y

17. a. LET Y = 6 * X
    b. LET A = 3 * B↑2
       or LET A = 3 * B * B
    c. LET C = A + B
    d. LET C = 4 + 5 + 7
       or LET C = 16
    e. LET Y = 3 * (A + B)
       or LET Y = 3 * A + 3 * B

18. 10 LET Y = 5
    20 LET Y = 3 * Y + 2 * X↑2
    30 PRINT Y
    40 END

Chapter 12

1. In coping with student stress:

   a. Don't over-react.
   b. Don't take student remarks personally.
   c. Avoid the use of the sarcastic approach with your students.
   d. Work to gain the respect of your students.
   e. Find an outside release for your frustrations.

2. In working with parents:

   a. Be accessible.
   b. Keep parents informed of good as well as bad student progress.
   c. Inform parents as soon as possible if you feel that their youngster is in danger of failing a term.
   d. Attend parent-teacher meetings if your school has such a group.
   e. Treat your parents like a professional should.
   f. Be accountable for your behavior outside of school hours.

Treat fellow teachers, the school counselor, the school secretary and custodians with the same respect and consideration that you desire for yourself.

In dealing with your principal and other school administrators, (a) remember the chain of command, and (b) keep your principal informed.

Index